POPULATION AGEING
AND AUSTRALIA'S FUTURE

POPULATION AGEING
AND AUSTRALIA'S FUTURE

EDITED BY HAL KENDIG, PETER MCDONALD AND JOHN PIGGOTT

Australian
National
University

PRESS

ANU PRESS

Published by ANU Press
The Australian National University
Acton ACT 2601, Australia
Email: anupress@anu.edu.au
This title is also available online at press.anu.edu.au

National Library of Australia Cataloguing-in-Publication entry

Title:	Population ageing and Australia's future / editors: Hal Kendig, Peter McDonald, John Piggott.
ISBN:	9781760460662 (paperback) 9781760460679 (ebook)
Subjects:	Population aging--Australia. Population forecasting--Australia. Older people--Australia.
Other Creators/Contributors:	Kendig, Hal, 1948- editor. McDonald, Peter F., 1946- editor. Piggott, John, 1947- editor.
Dewey Number:	304.610994

Cover design and layout by ANU Press.

Contents

Part 1. Perspectives on ageing

Part 2. Population ageing: Global, regional and Australian perspectives

Part 3. Improving health and wellbeing

Part 4. Responses by government and families/individuals

Foreword

The Academy of the Social Sciences in Australia (ASSA) is one of Australia's four government-recognised Learned Academies and consists of an elected fellowship of more than 550 of Australia's leading social science researchers. Disciplines represented by the Academy's Fellows imclude Accounting, Anthropology, Demography, Economic History, Economics, Education, Geography, History, Law, Linguistics, Management, Marketing, Philosophy, Political Science, Psychology, Social Medicine, Sociology and Statistics.

ASSA promotes high-quality research and scholarly cooperation across the social science disciplines in Australia and our region. ASSA strongly supports cross-sectoral collaboration with the other three Learned Academies (The Australian Academy of the Humanities, The Australian Academy of Science, and The Australian Academy of Technological Sciences and Engineering).

ASSA is particularly concerned with providing social science knowledge and advice to government on issues of national importance. Social scientists have much to contribute to the evidence base for the development of sound public policy, and as a peak body ASSA is well-placed to make independent, expert recommendations to government.

Every November ASSA convenes its feature event, the ASSA Annual Symposium. In 2014, the Annual Symposium took up the questions and opportunities of 'Population Ageing and Australia's Future'. The symposium was convened in partnership with the ARC Centre of Excellence in Population Ageing Research (CEPAR). CEPAR's strength lies in its integrated approach, and its high-level expertise drawn from social science disciplines. CEPAR brings together researchers, government and industry to address one of the major social challenges of the 21st century: an ageing population. CEPAR's mission is to produce research of the highest quality that informs product and service development, and enlighten the public policy debate. The result is dedicated to improving people's wellbeing throughout the full course of their lives. CEPAR recognises the need to build a new generation of researchers in tune with the best of global standards through an appreciation of the multidisciplinary nature of the issue. The Centre is an Australian collaboration between the University of New South Wales, the University of Sydney and The Australian National University and receives important support from government, industry and international university partners.

This volume reflects the contributions to the 2014 ASSA Annual Symposium, updated through 2015 and 2016, which aimed to highlight the latest research and its implications for the long-term challenges and opportunities of an ageing Australia. Leading scholars were invited to present their multidisciplinary expertise and evidence bases for broader public scrutiny and debate on population ageing and the implications for public affairs and policy development. It summarised recent Australian and international research on demographic trends and their likely impact. The research was not just an update of earlier work, but presented new perspectives on the change that is occurring to life-spans and how individuals and societies may adjust to that change. The symposium emphasised the positive aspects involved in expanding life-spans, and the potential for enhancing individual and societal wellbeing. This volume brings together the symposium presentations with updates to 2016, and provides a coherent, scholarly analysis of the significant policy issues facing Australia.

Participation in the symposium extended beyond the ASSA to include policymakers, national peak bodies, and community representatives who added to the diversity of informed views. A subsequent invited Policy Roundtable reflected on the symposium papers and discussions in order to deepen policy engagement between the Academy and government practitioners. The roundtable focused on strategies and policy approaches to improve individual and societal wellbeing in the light of population ageing. The presentations and papers explored the scale and impact of societal ageing; global, regional and Australian perspectives; health and social wellbeing; and the responses required of government, families and individuals. Chapter authors were encouraged to consider the symposium and roundtable discussions when finalising their contributions in order to communicate with wider public and policy audiences as well as academic researchers.

Contributors draw on research evidence and policy directions across the full range of the dimensions of individual and societal ageing including opportunities for enhancing capacities over the life-span and the wellbeing of future generations. Participants at the symposium and roundtable considered responses to the diversity and social inequalities that arise in terms of gender, socioeconomic resources, ethnicity and geographical location. They also considered national directions for action by individuals and families, governments, businesses and not-for-profit organisations. This includes strategies for increasing social engagement and health and wellbeing as well as achieving secure incomes, organising and financing health care, gaining suitable housing and managing intergenerational relations. Australian governments have a further focus on the fiscal implications of population ageing. The overall aim of the symposium and this volume is to stimulate and inform a deeper consideration of the impact of an ageing population and options for positive responses in the medium- to long-term for Australia's economy, social cohesion and security.

The primary contributors to this volume are, of course, the chapter authors. Each brought their own particular expertise to the symposium and the breadth of their combined contributions provide an impressive account of the current status and future prospects for our ageing population.

This volume would not have been possible without the redoubtable contributions of its three editors—ASSA Fellows Hal Kendig, John Piggott and Peter McDonald—with assistance from Murray Radcliffe. They convened the symposium, participated strongly in the roundtable, contributed chapters to the volume and, of course, edited it.

Through the efforts of the editors and their colleagues we see quite clearly how social science research can help to shape this nation. It draws together research from many disciplines—including Sociology, Demography, Economics and Psychology—to produce a rich assessment of the impact of population ageing in Australia and provide sound, practical evidence for future policy development.

I would particularly like to thank the Hon Susan Ryan for her keynote address to the symposium about older peoples views, attitudes and age rights.

In addition to the presenters and their teams, whose members are represented through the authorship of the individual chapters in this volume, the Chair of the Public Forums and Communications Committee of ASSA, Peter Spearritt, with support from the ASSA secretariat including the Executive Director Dr John Beaton and Ms Sunita Kumar, provided sage advice and oversight to the organisation of the symposium.

I would also like to thank the Social Sciences Editorial Board, in particular, Marian Sawer and Francis Bongiorno, as well as copyeditor Freya Job for her invaluable assistance in bringing this manuscript to publication. The valuable intellectual input of all of these people to the symposium is gratefully acknowledged.

Professor Glenn Withers AO FASSA
President
The Academy of the Social Sciences in Australia

Acknowledgements

This paper uses unit record data from the Household Income and Labour Dynamics in Australia (HILDA) Survey. The HILDA Project was initiated and is funded by the Australian Government Department of Families, Housing, Community Services and Indigenous Affairs (FaHCSIA) and is managed by the Melbourne Institute of Applied Economic and Social Research (Melbourne Institute). The findings and views reported in these papers, however, are those of the authors and should not be attributed to either FaHCSIA or the Melbourne Institute.

This research was completed using data collected through the 45 and Up Study (www.saxinstitute.org.au). The 45 and Up Study is managed by the Sax Institute in collaboration with major partner Cancer Council NSW; and partners: the National Heart Foundation of Australia (NSW Division); NSW Ministry of Health; NSW Government Family & Community Services – Carers, Ageing and Disability Inclusion; and the Australian Red Cross Blood Service. We thank the many thousands of people participating in the 45 and Up study.

Contributors

Professor Kaarin Anstey FASSA is Director of the Centre for Research on Ageing, Health and Wellbeing (CRAHW), and Director of the Dementia Collaborative Research Centre at ANU. Her research interests include cognitive and brain ageing, chronic disease and mental health, prevention of cognitive decline and dementia, life-span approaches to mental wellbeing, the impact of cognitive decline on productive ageing, and older drivers. Kaarin leads the PATH Through Life Project, an epidemiological study focusing on identifying risk and protective factors that influence mental health, cognitive decline and brain ageing from early to late adulthood. She is an ANU Public Policy Fellow, Director of the Alzheimer's Australia Dementia Research Foundation, a member of the National Health and Medical Research Council (NHMRC) Knowledge Translation Faculty and a member of the NHMRC Guidelines Adaptation Committee for Dealing with Cognitive and Related Functional Decline in Older People.

Professor Hazel Bateman is Head of the School of Actuarial Studies at the University of New South Wales. Her research interests in public and private provision for retirement includes current studies on retirement saving, investment and benefit decisions; the structure, governance and performance of pension and superannuation funds; and effective public policy for an ageing society. Prior to joining the University of New South Wales, she worked as an economist in the Australian Treasury. She has been a consultant on retirement income issues to a range of Australian and international organisations including the Organisation for Economic Co-operation and Development (OECD), the World Bank, the Social Insurance Administration (China), Asia-Pacific Economic Cooperation and the Korean Institute for Health and Social Affairs. She is a member of UniSuper's Consultative Committee and in 2012–13 was a member of the Australian Government's Superannuation Roundtable.

Professor Colette Browning is Director of the Royal District Nursing Service Research Institute and Adjunct Professor in the School of Primary Health Care at Monash University. She is recognised as a national and international leader in psychology and health. Her research focuses on healthy ageing and improving quality of life for older people, chronic disease self-management and consumer involvement in health care decision-making. Professor Browning is co-Director of the Melbourne Longitudinal Studies on Healthy Ageing program and the convener of the Healthy Ageing theme and Management Committee member of the Australian ARC/NHMRC Research Network in Ageing Well. She is a member of the International Research Centre for Healthy Ageing and Longevity International Scientific Advisory Committee.

Dr Richard A Burns serves as Fellow in the ANU CRAHW in the Research School of Population Health. He completed his PhD thesis examining the impact of organisational climate on subjective and psychological wellbeing in a multinational study of high school teachers. Since 2007, he has been working with CRAHW on a range of studies: between 2009 and 2015 he has been funded on various ARC and NHMRC project grants and as an Early Career Researcher at CEPAR. He has a diverse research program that focuses on issues related to psychiatric epidemiology, flourishing and wellbeing, psychological capital, self-concept, organisational climate, and longitudinal research methodologies.

Lisa Cannon is a Research Assistant at CRAHW in the ANU Research School of Population Health. With a background in psychology and population health, her research interests include attitudes, ageism, mental health, gender and age differences, and life-span approaches to wellbeing.

Rachel G Curtis is a PhD candidate in the Department of Psychology at Flinders University. Her research interests include aspects of adult development and ageing, such as cognitive ability, subjective wellbeing, and activity engagement.

Dr Cathy Gong is a Research Fellow at ANU CRAHW and CEPAR. She is an economist who contributes primarily to the CEPAR Research program in Healthy and Productive Ageing and collaborates in other CRAHW research on China. Her research has focused on income inequality, income mobility, employment, social exclusion and disadvantage across the life-course. She works closely with policymakers and the community sector to provide an evidence base to inform the development of effective social policy. She has published on intergenerational mobility, income inequality, spatial disparity, disadvantage and social exclusion in both international and domestic journals.

Professor Jane Hall FASSA is Professor of Health Economics in the Business School at the University of Technology Sydney, after having served as the founding Director of the Centre for Health Economics Research and Evaluation (CHERE) for over 20 years. Her work spans many areas of health economics, including health technology assessment, measurement of quality of life, health workforce and comparative policy analysis. Her work has always been concerned with improving resource allocation and improving outcomes in health services delivery, including a major research program currently in the Finance and Economics of Primary Health Care. She is a board member of the NSW Bureau of Health Information, and a member of the Independent Hospital Pricing Authority. She is involved in health policy issues internationally through her involvement with the Commonwealth Fund International program in Health Policy and Practice.

Professor Hal Kendig FASSA is a gerontologist and sociologist who serves as Professor of Ageing and Public Policy at CRAHW in the ANU Research School of Population Health. He is a Chief Investigator at CEPAR, leading research on healthy and productive ageing, social inequalities over the life-course, and attitudes to ageing as well as a new ARC Discovery project on China. He has previously served as the National Convenor of the ARC/NHMRC Research Network in Ageing Well (Sydney University), Director of the ARC Key Centre in Gerontology (La Trobe), and Coordinator of the multidisciplinary Ageing and the Family project (ANU). He is actively engaged in international, national and state policy developments on ageing including the Living Longer, Living Better reforms.

Professor Sang-Hyop Lee is Professor of Economics at the University of Hawai'i. He is also Managing Director of the East-West Center and Korea Development Institute and East-West Center annual collaborative project. His primary research objective is to find key measures of the human resources and their relationship with economic development. His recent studies focus on how population ageing affects labour markets, individuals' decisions to work, and other aspects of the economy. He is co-editor of four recent books on Korea, and has been investigator of numerous projects related to ageing issues.

Professor Mary A Luszcz FASSA is Emerita Professor at Flinders University after having served as Director of the Centre for Ageing Studies and Matthew Flinders Distinguished Professor in the School of Psychology. She leads the Australian Longitudinal Study of Ageing, which provides the basis for much of her current research efforts. Her areas of research interest are cognitive ageing, longevity, and psychosocial wellbeing. Understanding how these can be maintained or enhanced through behavioural means, to culminate in successful ageing at an individual and societal level, is the overriding goal. Within the Cognitive Ageing Laboratory, research focuses on normal age-related memory changes. She has used time sampling techniques to understand how very old adults spend their days, and the interdependencies of health, cognition, interpersonal relationships and affect.

Rikiya Matsukura is a researcher at the Nihon University Population Research Institute. He has also been working as a guest researcher and lecturer of demographic analysis at the Statistical Research and Training Institute of the Japanese Ministry of Internal Affairs and Communications since 2002. As a UN consultant, he has also contributed to the formulation of the most recent five-year economic plan of the Laotian government. He has more than 20 years experience in demographic research, focusing on the development of statistical methods for complicated models and the application of these methodologies to socioeconomics and population. In the field of population and economy, in recent years he has been contributing to the development of the economic indices, the National Transfer Accounts.

Professor Peter McDonald OA FASSA is Professor of Demography in the Crawford School of Public Policy at The Australian National University. He was President of the International Union for the Scientific Study of Population 2010–13 and is a member of the Council of Advisers of Population Europe. He frequently consults on the issue of population futures (causes, consequences and policies) for governments around the world, especially in Australia, Europe and East Asia. He is Deputy Director of the ARC Centre of Excellence in Population Ageing Research. He was a member of the Australian Ministerial Advisory Council on Skilled Migration in 2012–13 and of the panel of the Australian Government's 2014 Independent Review of Integrity in the Subclass 457 Programme. He has worked previously at the Australian Institute of Family Studies, the World Fertility Survey and the University of Indonesia. In 2008, he was appointed a Member in the Order of Australia and, in 2012, as an inaugural ANU Public Policy Fellow.

Professor Naohiro Ogawa is Professor of Population Economics at the Nihon University College of Economics and Director of the Nihon University Population Research Institute. Over the past 30 years he has written extensively on population and development in Japan and other Asian countries. More specifically, his research has focused on issues such as socioeconomic impacts of low fertility and rapid ageing, modelling demographic and social security–related variables, as well as policies related to fertility, employment, marriage, child care, retirement and care for the elderly. His recent work includes measuring intergenerational transfers. He has published numerous academic papers in journals such as *American Economic Review*, *Journal of Labor Economics, Demography, Population Studies* and *Population and Development Review*. In collaboration with other scholars he has also edited several journals and books, the most recent being *Low Fertility and Reproductive Health in East Asia*, published in 2015 by Springer.

Associate Professor Rachel Ong is a Principal Research Fellow at the Bankwest Curtin Economics Centre, Curtin University. She has conducted investigations into the housing pathways of older Australians, the tax-transfer treatment of the family home, the uses and risks of housing equity withdrawal in mid-to-late life, intergenerational issues that influence decisions surrounding the use of housing assets to fund needs in old age, and factors influencing self-provision in retirement. Her research has been supported by sources such as the Australian Housing and Urban Research Institute and Australian Research Council. She has also completed projects for policy and industry organisations, including the Commonwealth Treasury, WA Council of Social Service and WA Department of Housing. She is currently a member of the Steering Committee for the Asia Pacific Network for Housing Research (APNHR), the Commonwealth Treasury's Housing Research Panel and AusAID's Research Advisory Panel.

Professor Jan Pakulski FASSA is Emeritus Professor at the University of Tasmania. He is a well-published author on social inequality, elites, social movements, postcommunism in Central and Eastern Europe, and social change. His two main areas of current sociological research are political elites, democratisation and social inequality. He also maintains interest in mass social movements, including the environmental movement in Australia. He is a Fellow of the Stanford Center for Poverty and Inequality and a member of editorial/advisory boards of *Polish Sociological Review*, *Citizenship Studies*, *Australian Journal of Social Issues*, and the *Australian Social Monitor*.

Professor John Piggott FASSA is Director of the ARC Centre of Excellence in Population Ageing Research, and of the Australian Institute for Population Ageing Research at the University of New South Wales, where he is Scientia Professor of Economics and also holds an ARC Australian Professorial Fellowship. His Australian policy experience includes membership of both the Henry Tax Review Panel and the Ministerial Superannuation Advisory Committee. Internationally, he worked for nearly a decade with the Japanese Government on pension and ageing issues, and in 2004 was tasked with evaluating World Bank assistance on pension reform in the Asian region for the Bank's Operations Evaluation Department. He has been a consultant on pension issues to several foreign governments, including Russia and Indonesia. In 2007 he was appointed Visiting Professor, Zhejiang University, China, and from 2008 to 2010 was Visiting Scholar with the Department of Insurance and Risk Management, Wharton School of Business, University of Pennsylvania.

Professor Andrew Podger AO FASSA FIPAA is Professor of Public Policy at The Australian National University. He was previously a career public servant having started as a cadet with the Australian Bureau of Statistics and become Secretary of various Commonwealth departments and the Public Service Commissioner. His research interests include public management and social policy. Before leaving the Australian Public Service in 2005, he chaired a review of the delivery of health and aged-care services.

Associate Professor Kees van Gool is a health economist at the Centre for Health Economics at the University of Technology, Sydney. His extensive experience in international, national and regional health policy research includes a leading team working on the financing and economics of primary care. His projects include work conducted for the Commonwealth Department of Health, MBF and the Australian Senate. Kees has previously worked at the Department of Health, NSW Health and the OECD. He has been a chief investigator on a number of competitive grants, including a current NHMRC capacity building grant. He has worked extensively on cancer care, screening, cystic fibrosis and policy evaluation. He has quantitative skills in micro-economic modelling and has established a track record in using linked data. In 2011 he completed his PhD at the University of Technology, Sydney, looking at the out-of-pocket costs faced by Medicare patients.

Dr Tim D Windsor is Director of the Centre for Ageing Studies at Flinders University. He spent 10 years conducting research concerned with psychosocial aspects of adult development and ageing at The Australian National University, after completing his postgraduate studies in psychology at the University of New England. His research focuses on changes in the nature of social relationships that occur with ageing, and their implications for wellbeing. Additional interests are concerned with how personality characteristics, self-regulation (e.g. the ways in which people engage with, and disengage from different goals), and emotion regulation relate to mental health and wellbeing over the life-course.

Part 1. Perspectives on ageing

1

Introduction: A multidisciplinary approach to ageing

Hal Kendig, Peter McDonald and John Piggott

Increasing longevity is an historic triumph and population ageing is emerging as one of the major global issues of the 21st century. Australia's future will be deeply affected by the ageing of the baby boom cohort, with large numbers expected to reach advanced ages during a time of economic uncertainty, pressures on health budgets, and the likely need for ongoing fiscal restraint. A new policy era is emerging, illustrated by the redesign of superannuation over the last 20 years, ongoing debate about retirement incomes policy, the establishment of a Commissioner on Age Discrimination and the 'rights' approach, and consumer-led directions in the Living Longer Living Better reforms of aged care. The government's *2015 Intergenerational Report* is the latest in a series of Intergenerational Reports (IGR) that serve as barometers of the sustainability of national government spending programs and raise wider questions about public policy priorities (Commonwealth of Australia 2015). These initiatives are bringing additional evidence and critical arguments to the public debates, extending consideration of ageing well beyond health and welfare concerns to a consideration of its pervasive influences on national priorities including productivity, incomes, taxation, federal relations, and population policy.

Multidisciplinary concepts on ageing: New directions

Before reviewing social science conceptions of ageing, it is essential to recognise the social purposes of knowledge and the deep personal meanings of ageing. In an earlier statement for the Academy of Social Sciences in Australia (ASSA), we argued that 'the quest for ageing well is arguably as old as humanity itself and it is deeply embedded in individuals' consciousness and collective ideas of social advancement' (Kendig and Browning 2011). Qualitative sociology has revealed how older people strive to maintain their identities, independence, and continuity as they grow older and face opportunities as well as constraints in their lives. Among the most enduring psychological models of successful ageing is the process of selective optimisation with compensation, in which older people are understood to 'orchestrate' their lives to adjust their aspirations and make other adaptations in line with changing orientations and declining capacity (Baltes and Baltes 1990).

A constructive approach to ageing aims to understand what is 'improvable' in later life by identifying the resources and social factors that can enable positive experiences. As this volume demonstrates, there is accumulating evidence that ageing processes, previously thought to be immutable and based on biological facts, in fact have been changing and can remain changeable in the light of social forces. As Anstey demonstrates in her chapter on cognition, the phenomenon of 'plasticity' recognises that brain function is influenced by social exposures. A powerful use of social research is to understand the structural forces that accompany decline in people as they grow older, and to inform the public case for action and advocacy on their behalf.

The complexity of ageing from a social science viewpoint is apparent in the distinctions that need to be made between individual, population, and societal dimensions of ageing. *Individual ageing* involves complex bio-psychosocial developments embedded in the family, community, work, and social institutions in which individuals negotiate changing social relationships as they move through the life-course. *Population ageing* is fundamentally about the forces behind demographic change and the consequences for changing age structures. *Societal ageing* extends beyond individual and demographic ageing to encompass the social constructions of ageing and the 'treatment' of older people in wider social, cultural, economic, and political life.

It is important to appreciate the ways in which depictions of individual and societal ageing are shaped by the viewpoints of commentators. Personal views on ageing are, of course, important but they provide a very limited basis on which to assess the variation and complexity in societal ageing. The Intergenerational Reports provide reasonably objective projections on ageing populations but their interpretations, being couched in the interests of government, require careful scrutiny (Woods and Kendig 2015). The interplay between demographic imperatives and associated fiscal implications, and the social influences on individual ageing, provide the potential for a greater span of intervention than has been traditionally appreciated.

Notable advances are underway in the multidisciplinary understanding of population ageing. Among the most important is recognition that many of the age differences assumed to be inherent in ageing are, in fact, cohort phenomena grounded in the different periods of history that people have experienced during their lifetimes. We therefore need to question the relevance of studies and depictions of ageing that are based on the Depression cohort of older people now in advanced old age. Understanding the future of ageing requires an understanding of the large post-war baby boom cohort that has had strikingly different life opportunities and now faces the profound challenges of increased longevity in later life.

Cross-sequential cohort analysis is a powerful demographic method for unravelling the confounding effects of ageing and cohort progression. An important direction here is McDonald's analyses of workforce participation, which show that relatively recent entrants to later life have in fact been working longer than their predecessors during this recent period of economic uncertainty. Collaboration between ASSA and the Bureau of Statistics has brought new understandings to longevity and emergent policy and social issues (Gibson and ASSA 2010).

Our knowledge of the economic and fiscal consequences of ageing populations is being advanced in several important ways. Understanding age and intergenerational transfers in Australia—long a vexed topic of debate—is improving with new work on National Transfer Accounts. These accounts now span many countries, and provide powerful new bases for understanding the public and private consequences of population ageing in Australia as contrasted with comparable populations and economies. Further, a range of economy-wide modelling initiatives aim to inform policy formulation on the impacts of an ageing demographic on retirement incomes and pension reform (for example, Kudrna, Tran and Woodland 2015). The interplay between pension accumulations, tax treatment, public transfers and aggregate fiscal balance is complex, because both labour supply and saving behaviour (and further human capital accumulation) are affected by policy change. While these models do not capture the policy detail of micro-simulation models, they allow for the fundamental movements of relative prices and behavioural change that accompany large-scale economic policy reforms.

In sociological thinking on ageing, the life-span framework provides a powerful way to understand social processes behind age differences and ageing experiences. From a developmental perspective, the most deeply seated psychosocial orientations, values, and attitudes are largely inculcated from early childhood and these understandings are fundamental in shaping subsequent life actions and experiences. Applications of the Cumulative Advantage/Disadvantage (CAD) theory (Dannefer 2003; Dannefer and Phillipson 2010) examine the consequences of divergent life pathways as people move through social structures during their lives. The life-span approach thus enables us to better understand variation in social inequalities and other outcomes through to later life. The life-span approach also enables us to consider how investments earlier in life can yield longer-term benefits as younger people grow older and become the next generations of middle-aged and older people in the future.

A relatively new approach in life-span research builds on life history concepts and methods in order to examine the effects of earlier life experiences in later age (Kendig and Nazroo 2016). Retrospective data collection techniques are improving but consideration needs to be given to the process of selective survival, which sees many disadvantaged people dying or dropping out of studies before reaching later life. Our Australian life-course research is showing that socioeconomic circumstances, health, and education in childhood have persistent consequences for subsequent life trajectories and for wellbeing among the baby boom cohort on entry to later life (Kendig et al. 2015). This ongoing comparative study with England is also providing insights into the ways in which the differing post-war development experiences and policies of the two countries are influencing their ageing populations.[1]

The mainstay of Australian psychosocial research on ageing, as per Part 3 of this volume, is longitudinal surveys of people from mid-life through advanced old age. Over the past 15 years these studies have yielded new knowledge and been used in various research programs with a variety of special foci, for example, on particular cities, women, health, income and work. But what is really needed as a national priority is a comprehensive Australian survey focused on older cohorts that is multidisciplinary, nationally representative, and can be linked to administrative data sets. The gold standard for such surveys is represented by the US Health and Retirement Survey (HRS), the English Longitudinal Survey of the Aged (ELSA), and the Survey of Health, Ageing and Retirement in Europe (SHARE). These studies cover multiple dimensions including family circumstances, health status—both self-assessed and through biomarkers—work and retirement, financial conditions, and cognitive ability, and service use. Questions, while not identical, are harmonised across countries, and this family of surveys now covers two-thirds of the world's population.

Our ageing population means that it is increasingly urgent that Australian researchers be given access to survey information of this kind. Using a format that harmonises with existing international studies, while taking careful account of the Australian context, would immeasurably strengthen the value of the data. Australia would be included in international studies using this 'state of the art' method, and cross-national studies by Australian researchers would be facilitated. The data bank could be made available widely on a public access basis with appropriate privacy protections.

---

1   They include the Australian Longitudinal Survey on Ageing (ALSA) (with innovative couples research) (Luszcz et al. 2014); the Personality and Total Health (PATH) cross-sequential study through the life-span (Anstey et al. 2011); the Melbourne Longitudinal Surveys of Ageing (MELSHA) (now completed so experiences through to the end of life can be examined) (Browning and Kendig 2010). The large-scale 45 and Up study (45 and Up Study Collaborators 2008) and the Australian Longitudinal Survey of Women's Health (Byles et al. 2015) have large samples and they are also notable for data linkages to administrative records. The DYNOPTA study (Anstey et al. 2010) has attempted to coordinate these various surveys.

Studies of ageing also need to take account of younger people and generational differences and relationships. Indeed, as Jean Martin demonstrated in her classic study, *The Migrant Presence* (1978), some of the best insights into a subgroup of a society and the social challenges they face can be revealed by observing mainstream views about them[2] (see also Shaver et al. 2015). As emphasised in the Symposium Opening Address by the Age Discrimination Commissioner Susan Ryan, attitudes and related practices towards older people in the community and in workplaces are powerful influences on older people's self-respect and their opportunities for economic independence. A CEPAR-supported national *Attitudes to Ageing* study (Kendig et al. 2015) has examined the views of different age groups on intergenerational equity. It is also examining perceptions of the respect accorded to older people in everyday life and their 'social treatment' in other spheres of life including the workplace and health care. A follow-up survey now in the field will examine ways in which attitudes have changed over the 2010–17 period of significant policy and socioeconomic change.

The broader, social determinants' literature reminds us that health and wellbeing are influenced not only by our absolute access to economic and social resources but also by our 'social positions' relative to those of others in work, local communities, and other spheres of life. Wilkinson and Pickett (2011) make a UK-based case that social inequalities not only disadvantage individuals but also erode societal capacities for achieving health, wellbeing, and productivity. However, inclusion of ageing in these broader, social and political debates on public health, in Australia as well as overseas, has been surprisingly limited (Schofield 2015). For example, while the English Marmott Review took a life-span approach in its landmark *Fair Society Healthy Lives* report, the emphasis was on opportunities in early and mid-life; the recommendations for later life were largely restricted to concerns for comfort or care (Kendig and Phillipson 2014).

---

2   Martin's impeccable scholarship, as an empirical anthropologist informed by social theory, was brought to full public engagement through her 1978 report commissioned by the demographer Mick Borrie when he led the National Population Inquiry. Shaver and colleagues' recent intellectual biography *The Martin Presence: Jean Martin and the Making of the Social Sciences in Australia,* has documented how she established a continuing 'social science for public knowledge' that has made deep contributions to understanding and building multiculturalism and public responses to social inequalities.

International perspectives

Understanding global priorities on ageing and Australia's comparative position in the region and internationally provides an important context for addressing ageing in Australia. Australia is a significant contributor to international work on ageing and gerontology (Kendig, Lucas and Anstey 2013) and in turn benefits from knowledge and collaboration in regional and global initiatives. We are increasingly connected with other countries through trade and political engagement with ageing emerging as an area of national opportunity, for example, in the development of pensions and health and aged care in China. At the same time, Australia faces increasing global competition for skilled workers and investment.

An international perspective is also helpful in benchmarking how well Australia is faring in addressing ageing issues. Appendix 1 outlines the notable societal variations in the dimensions of population ageing and ageing well outcomes for Australia in comparison to other countries reviewed in Part 2 of this volume as well as New Zealand, the UK, and the US. As reviewed in Kendig and Browning's chapter, positive directions on ageing are being determined by the United Nations, World Health Organization, World Bank, and other international organisations.

International scholarship is moving beyond conceptual development and empirical research to challenge established thinking and is seeking to 're-image' societal directions on ageing. In their aptly titled 'Rethinking Age and Ageing', the demographers Sanderson and Scherbov (2008) observe that, with increasing life expectancy, public policy will need to take more account of life expectancy beyond a given age (e.g. 65 years as a traditional age of retirement) relative to expectancy at birth. Several decades ago, Riley, Kahn and Foner (1994) provided a sociological analysis of what even today are still 'lost opportunities' as a result of 'age and structural lag: society's failure to provide meaningful opportunities in work, family, and leisure'. Their argument is that rigid social institutions, outdated attitudes, and entrenched interests have yet to adapt to the increasing capacities and potential of older people. The emergent idea of a third age, where increasing numbers of capable people are in a new life stage—between a second age of paid work and a fourth age of dependence—raises important questions as to the uses of these additional years of later life. The English historian Peter Laslett (1989) observed that the relatively recent emergence of 'this third age' can be approached as 'a fresh map of life'.

In summary, this brief review has aimed to illustrate concepts and research directions in the social sciences that are contributing to policy-relevant thinking about population ageing in Australia. It has drawn principally on work in the disciplines of demography, economics, public health, psychology, and sociology as well as the field of social gerontology. It is important to note the range of contributions from across the social sciences—including anthropology, history and political science—to a broader understanding of ageing and its social and policy applications. There also is a large international literature in each of these areas as can be seen in the *Handbook of Aging and the Social Sciences* (George and Ferraro 2016), the *Handbook of the Psychology of Aging* (Schaie and Willis 2015), and the *SAGE Handbook of Social Gerontology* (Dannefer and Phillipson 2010). While each of the disciplines has their specialised contributions, the case advanced in this volume is that a comprehensive multidisciplinary approach has the greatest potential to address the complex, multidimensional challenges of an ageing Australia.

Volume overview

This volume aims to bring a scholarly and policy-relevant approach to critically assess the outlook for Australia of the population ageing changes that arguably are among the most significant in human history. The chapters draw on multiple social science disciplines to marshall ideas and evidence to inform constructive actions to address the public and policy challenges ahead.

Part 1 presents perspectives on ageing that underpin the social science approach taken in later chapters on specific topics. This first chapter outlines our multidisciplinary directions in advancing ageing research and policy.

Gong and Kendig, an economist and a sociologist, then examine historical developments that have shaped Australia's emerging response to ageing over the post-war era and directions for the future.

They demonstrate how the post-war baby boom cohort has been at the centre of profound socioeconomic and policy changes that have shaped their life trajectories towards later life and consequences for quality of life, social inequalities, and intergenerational equity.

In his chapter, Piggott, an economist, reviews emerging policy challenges in the areas of retirement and retirement incomes, health and aged care, infrastructure and housing, and regionalisation. He recognises that issues of intergenerational relationships, taxation and international interactions present considerable challenges and he points towards ways of addressing them.

Part 2 considers demographic change and diversity in Australia with the perspective of related international developments. McDonald assesses the demographic scenarios that underlie the four Intergenerational Reports that present evolving government views on Australia's ageing future. He shows that, with each successive report, the newer demographic projections have placed Australia in a much more favourable position in relation to population ageing than almost all other developed countries on the basis of current policy settings. The implication for Australia is that population ageing requires long-term sensible planning not hasty short-term fixes.

Can the effects of population ageing be mitigated through pronatalist policy approaches? Ogawa, Matsukura and Lee investigate comprehensive National Transfer Accounts for eight Asian countries with rapidly ageing populations to examine health and education costs of children as key influences on fertility rates and the 'quality' of children. They argue that higher wages for younger workers would lower the age at which young people become self-supporting and thus contribute to somewhat earlier childbearing.

Pakulski reviews European experiences with socioeconomic and policy issues in population ageing. These include changing health profiles, reduced dynamism in the workforce and requirements for developing health, housing, and retirement income systems that are fair and adequate but also efficient and affordable. He compares policy options for Australia and Poland in terms of the fundamental '4Ps': *Population growth* through immigration; *Participation* rates that increase the labour force; *Productivity* by promoting innovation and investment; and *Pensions*, or, more broadly, effective income-support programs. He suggests that similar policy approaches can be applied to mitigate or adapt to population ageing by countries with different economic and political contexts.

Part 3 moves beyond negative images of ageing, with their emphases on decline and dependency, to consider social and societal options for improving health and wellbeing. Kendig and Browning examine research and action on 'ageing well' as a constructive approach to investing in health capacities over the life-course, and maintaining and recovering health and wellbeing in later life through self-care and health promotion. In her chapter on enhancing cognitive capacities, Anstey presents ground-breaking research on how psychological and social actions over the life-span can improve cognitive capacities as resources for independence, contributions and wellbeing in an increasingly complex Australia.

Windsor, Curtis and Luszcz consider social engagement as a hallmark of ageing well. Their chapter shows how social networks provide resources for navigating transitions through retirement, managing the challenges of advanced old age, and making contributions to families and communities. They present evidence-based approaches to combating social isolation and other interventions for promoting social engagement in later life.

Burns and Browning critically assess the emerging science of wellbeing for individuals and its importance for population-level policy. They recognise the importance of including social as well as economic indicators of a nation's 'wealth'. They reflect on the way forward in terms of incorporating wellbeing outcomes in Australian national policy, and the measurement and data collection issues that need to be addressed.

The final part of this volume concentrates on policy challenges and responses by governments and by families and individuals, with an emphasis on retirement income strategies, health and financing aged-care services.

Bateman analyses Australia's relatively new and highly regarded retirement income strategies that include the age pension, the superannuation guarantee and voluntary superannuation and other savings. She concludes that the Australian retirement income system relies on engaged, highly skilled, knowledgeable individuals to make good financial decisions throughout their life. However, problems remain with poor financial literacy and poor understanding of retirement income products as well as substandard financial advice. She asserts that while the accumulation phase of retirement income saving has a high policy focus, the same cannot be said for the deaccumulation phase that leaves Australian retirees vulnerable to investment risk, inflation risk and longevity risk.

Hall and van Gool focus on the impact of an ageing population on the costs to health care. Contrary to much of the conventional assumptions, their chapter concludes that ageing per se is not necessarily a threat to the sustainability of the Australian health-care system. They make the case that redesigning incentives and services and making better use of the options provided by modern technology are essential to meet the challenges of chronic and continuing illnesses.

Ong considers options for financing aged-care services in the context of a projected doubling of costs to government by 2050. Financial pressure over the life-span is increasing for individuals as government is requiring more user contributions to education (usually earlier in life) as well as to care costs in later life. She proposes a housing asset–based system of paying for care given that people now approaching retirement are likely to have more savings, high home ownership rates and high home values. The trend towards more private and public co-funding of services does, however, raise concerns about inequalities experienced by the increasing numbers of people who have not attained home ownership as they grow older.

Podger concludes the volume with his interpretation of the chapters and notes that the historic triumph of ageing nonetheless presents 'big' policy challenges. He reviews the substantial scope for individuals' own actions as well as comprehensive policy development to improve prospects for an ageing Australia:

- Social and economic participation of older people could be enhanced through reconsidering the concept of retirement in the light of increasing longevity and capacities in later life.
- Health and wellbeing could be enhanced by improved retirement income systems, better public health programs and health services inclusive of ageing people, and improved community engagement.

Overall, while Australia fares well with population ageing and the wellbeing of older people, international comparisons show that it has a way to go before reaching the world's best standards for ageing societies (Appendix 1).

Concluding remark

New social science thinking and evidence point the way towards social, economic, and political changes that can improve individual and population ageing but many areas remain unexplored. More critical thinking and research investment is required in priority areas for personal wellbeing and policy action:

- healthy and productive ageing
- fertility and migration
- labour force participation and retirement
- longevity risk and risk management
- changing family structures and intergenerational relations
- the organisation of care and support.

We need to be aware of the variable ways in which population ageing impacts on successive cohorts of men and women, advantaged and disadvantaged social groups, and the overall wellbeing of Australian society. Attitudinal and political factors set a changing social context that can facilitate or impede constructive responses. The implications of the staged timing of different societal ageing impacts and changes in the life-course also need to be explored further.

In conclusion, this volume is a testament to the range of research and thinking being conducted on population ageing. At the same time, it is a call for new research, policy and public affairs initiatives addressing what is one of the most important social phenomena of the 21st century.

References

45 and Up Study Collaborators (2008). Cohort profile: The 45 and Up Study. *International Journal of Epidemiology,* 37(5): 941–947. doi:10.1093/ije/dym184.

Anstey Kaarin, Byles Julie, Luszcz Mary, Mitchell Paul, Steel David, Booth Heather, Browning Colette, Butterworth Peter, Cumming Robert, Healy Judith, Windsor Tim, Ross Lesley, Bartsch Lauren, Burns Richard, Kiely Kim, Birrell Carole, Broe Tony, Shaw Jonathan, and Kendig Hal (2010). Cohort profile: The Dynamic Analyses to Optimize Ageing (DYNOPTA) project. *International Journal of Epidemiology,* 39(1): 44–51.

Anstey Kaarin, Christensen Helen, Butterworth Peter, Easteal Simon, Mackinnon Andrew, Jacomb Trish, Maxwell Karen, Rodgers Bryan, Windsor Tim, Cherbuin Nicolas and Jorm Anthony (2011). Cohort Profile: The PATH through life project. *International Journal of Epidemiology,* 41(4): 1–10. doi:10.1093/ije/dyr025.

Baltes Paul and Baltes Margret (1990). Psychological perspectives on successful aging: The model of selective optimization with compensation. In PB Baltes and MM Baltes (Eds), *Successful Aging: Perspectives from the Behavioral Sciences.* Cambridge: Cambridge University Press, pp. 1–34.

Browning Colette and Kendig Hal (2010). Cohort profile: The Melbourne Longitudinal Studies on Healthy Ageing Program. *International Journal of Epidemiology,* 39(5): e1–e7.

Byles Julie, Hockey Richard, McLaughlin Dierdre, Dobson Annette, Brown Wendy, Loxton Deborah, Mishra Gita (2015). *Chronic conditions, physical function and health care use: Findings from the Australian Longitudinal Study on Women's Health,* Report prepared for the Australian Government Department of Health, June 2015. www.alswh.org.au.

Commonwealth of Australia (2015). *2015 Intergenerational Report: Australia in 2055.* Canberra: Department of Treasury. www.treasury.gov.au/PublicationsAndMedia/Publications/2015/2015-Intergenerational-Report.

Dannefer Dale (2003). Cumulative advantage/disadvantage and the life course: Cross-fertilizing age and social science theory. *Journals of Gerontology Series B: Psychological Sciences and Social Sciences,* 58(6): S327–S337.

Dannefer Dale and Phillipson Chris (Eds) (2010). *The SAGE Handbook of Social Gerontology*. London: Sage Publications, pp. 459–471.

George Linda and Ferraro Kenneth (Eds) (2016). *Handbook of Aging and the Social Sciences* (8th edition). San Diego, USA: Elsevier Science Publishing Co. Inc.

Gibson, Diane and The Academy of the Social Sciences in Australia (ASSA). (2010). Beyond life expectancy, Occasional Paper 2010: C5#5, Canberra: The Academy of the Social Sciences in Australia. www.assa.edu.au/publications/occasional/111.

Kendig Hal and Browning Colette (2011). Directions for ageing well in a healthy Australia. *Dialogue,* Canberra: Academy of the Social Sciences in Australia, 31(2): 22–30.

Kendig Hal and Nazroo James (Eds) (2016). Life Course Influences on Inequalities in Later Life: Comparative Perspectives. Special Issue, *Journal of Population Ageing*, 9(1): 1–7.

Kendig Hal and Phillipson Chris (2014). Building Age-Friendly Communities: New Approaches to Challenging Health and Social Inequalities. In N Denison and L Newby (Eds) *'If you could do one thing…' Nine local actions to reduce health inequalities*. British Academy Policy Centre, pp. 102–111. www.britac.ac.uk/policy/Health_Inequalities.cfm.

Kendig Hal, Loh Vanessa, O'Loughlin Kate, Byles Julie and Nazroo James (2016). Pathways to Well-Being in Later Life: Socioeconomic and Health Determinants across the Life Course of Australian Baby Boomers. *Journal of Population Ageing*, 9(1): 49–67. doi: 10.1007/s12062-015-9132-0.

Kendig Hal, Lucas Nina and Anstey Kaarin (2013). Thirty years of the United Nations and Global ageing: An Australian perspective. *Australasian Journal on Ageing,* 32(s2): 28–34. doi: 10.1111/ajag.12101.

Kendig Hal, O'Loughlin Kate, Hussain Rafat, Heese Karla and Cannon Lisa (2015). Attitudes to Intergenerational Equity: Baseline Findings from the Attitudes to Ageing in Australia (AAA) Study. *CEPAR Working Paper*, 2015/33. Sydney: ARC Centre of Excellence in Population Ageing Research.

Kim Sarang, Sargent-Cox Kerry, French Davina, Kendig Hal and Anstey Kaarin (2012). Cross-national insights into the relationship between wealth and wellbeing: A comparison between Australia, the United States of America and South Korea. *Ageing & Society*, 32: 41–59. doi: 10.1017/S0144686x11000080.

Kudrna George, Tran Chang and Woodland Alan (2015). The dynamic fiscal effects of demographic shift: The case of Australia. *Economic Modelling*, 50(C): 105–122. doi:10.1016/j.econmod.2015.05.010.

Laslett Peter (1989). *A Fresh Map of Life: The emergence of the third age*. London: Weidenfeld and Nicolson.

Luszcz Mary, Giles Lynne, Anstey Kaarin, Browne-Yung Kathryn, Walker Ruth and Windsor Tim (2014). Cohort Profile: The Australian Longitudinal Study of Ageing (ALSA). *International Journal of Epidemiology* 1–10. doi: 10.1093/ije/dyu196.

Martin, Jean (1978). *The Migrant Presence, Australian Responses 1947–1977*, Research Report for the National Population Inquiry. Sydney: George Allen & Unwin.

Productivity Commission (2013). *An Ageing Australia: Preparing for the Future*. Research Report, Canberra: Productivity Commission.

Riley Matilda, Kahn Robert and Foner Anne (1994). *Age and Structural Lag: Society's failure to provide meaningful opportunities in work, family, and leisure*. New York: Wiley.

Sanderson Warren and Scherbov Sergei (2008). Rethinking Age and Ageing, *Population Bulletin*, 63(4): 1–16.

Schaie Warner and Willis Sherry (Eds) (2015). *Handbook of the Psychology of Aging* (8th edition). San Diego, United States: Elsevier Science Publishing Co. Inc.

Schofield Tom (2015). *A Sociological Approach to Health Determinants*. Cambridge: Cambridge University Press.

Shaver Sheila, Beilharz Peter and Hogan Trevor (2015). *The Martin Presence: Jean Martin and the Making of Social Sciences in Australia.* Sydney: UNSW Press.

Wilkinson Richard and Pickett Kate (2011). *The Spirit Level: Why Greater Equality Makes Societies Stronger.* New York: Bloomsbury Press.

Woods Mike and Kendig Hal (2015). The Intergenerational Report 2015: A limited and political view of our future. *Australasian Journal on Ageing,* 34(4): 217–219. doi: 10.1111/ajag.12293.

2

Ageing and social change in Australia

Cathy Gong and Hal Kendig

This chapter aims to provide a constructive understanding of social change and ageing in Australia. It presents a history of ideas and evidence on ageing in order to reveal the societal context that has shaped successive cohorts reaching later life. Contemporary commentators are reviewed to show evolving ways in which ageing has been conceptualised and 'problematised', thus shaping as well as reflecting expectations and interests concerning ageing and older people. The history provides a backdrop to the policy and social context for issues considered in later chapters and influences the scope for constructive change.

Central to this chapter and indeed to Australia's future, is the experience of the large post-war baby boom cohort that has been centre stage throughout the post-war era and is now entering later life. Baby boomers, along with overseas migrants, have led the 'younging' of Australia in earlier decades and now the 'ageing' of the population; both groups bring to later life varied life experiences that are fundamentally different from those of the Depression cohort now in advanced later life. The longevity revolution over recent decades, in which people are living many years beyond their 60s, is further reshaping the course of later life. Population ageing may be entering a new era in which lifelong economic prospects could be more limited for ascendant cohorts. Divergence of 'life chances' within cohorts, notably in terms of gender and socioeconomic resources, draws attention to social processes generating inequalities over the life-span and the implications for intergenerational relations, social justice and policy actions (Dannefer 2003).

This chapter begins with a brief history of ageing in Australia from colonial days to the present. It then considers the increasing longevity, capacities, and resources of ageing people while living longer. The discussion turns next to the remarkable changes in stages in life-span experiences over the past few decades and recent shifts in people's expectations as to how they will fund their retirement. Outcomes for individuals and cohorts are considered in terms of economic resources and quality of life for age groups and generations. In the conclusion, critical issues of intergenerational equity are considered in the light of recent evidence on attitudes towards ageing and the socioeconomic prospects for cohorts into the future.

Changing views on ageing

Australia has long thought of itself as a 'young' country as we are reminded by the phrase 'for we are young and free' whenever the national anthem is sung. We have been slow in coming to think of ourselves as an ageing country and this has arguably restricted our capacities to respond constructively to ageing individuals and an ageing society. Although debatable, the significance of ageing for Australia, as a major social change, was largely invisible until the 1980s. Nevertheless, it is important to appreciate that the seeds of many negative responses to ageing, particularly in times of economic stress, have been sown and perpetuated for more than 100 years.

A penetrating analysis of Australia's early experiences in ageing was provided in Davison's (1995) 'Our Youth is Spent and our Backs are Bent: The Origins of Australian Ageism'. The conflation of the young age of the new colonies and the youthful European migrant population had some truth at the time (notwithstanding the now painful recognition that no account was taken of Aboriginal people and their ancient culture). In the 1850s, only 1 per cent of the population was aged 65 years or older, as a result of limited life expectancy and the youth of migrants who had left their older relatives in the 'old country'. Concern for intergenerational conflict through the 1880s centred on newly affluent parents (notably in Victoria during the gold rush era) who were said to have invested heavily in children but who did not receive reciprocal support in turn as the parents reached old age.

Davison cites evidence that by the turn of the 20th century 'old age' was considered to begin at 55 years for women and 60 for men. The life-span at that time typically involved men entering the workforce at age 14 and remaining in work as long as health and opportunity allowed—often only into the 40s for manual workers. Compared to today, women had children early and continued through middle age; seldom was there an 'empty nest' before one or both parents had died. The Depression of the 1890s saw the numbers of the poor-old increasing with homeless older people turning to charities and private asylums (and even prisons). At the time of Federation, state governments began to provide modest old age pensions to 'deserving persons of good moral character' (p 48), with the state thus defining retirement and old age.

The roots of Australian ageism arguably were located in the powerlessness of older people who were termed at the time as having a 'lack of vital energy in old age' (attributed in part to moral failure and poor health habits in middle age). Contemporary literature by middle-aged writers largely echoed these negative views, with disparaging depictions of 'old women'. Some early feminist writers, however, noted that preparation in mid-life could slow the 'inevitable' effects of ageing, and a release from domestic duty could potentially allow 'emancipation' for older women (p 55). 'Granny' remaining as a working member of the household was 'part of the natural order of things' (p 56). Davison concludes: 'The value of an historical approach is that it provides us with benchmarks against which we may measure current attitudes, and poses models of past change that might sensitise us to the forces transforming attitudes and structures to the present' (p 59).

A more recent account by Jalland (2015) covers the history of old age in Australia from 1880 to 1980, including policy-focused issues. She demonstrates the ongoing nature of many historical issues in ageing policies—including questions of user pays, means testing, and the balance of older peoples' autonomy, perceived worthiness, and the inevitable matter of constrained state resources and difficult choices for governments. Topic coverage includes state and federal government and department perspectives, retirement villages and aged care, and the failure of geriatric medicine from 1954–72. Drawing on family case studies, she establishes a sharp contrast between the lives of most older women and older men; and recounts improvements over the past 100 years, while cautioning that 'parsimonious' approaches continued into the post war era. As with Davison, she argues for the contemporary value of historical understandings of the early precedents of ageing policy; and raises concerns about the prospective inadequacy of government responses in the decades ahead.

After the watershed World War II years, Australia as with other countries was preoccupied by nation building and investment in economic and social development particularly for younger people. An early post-war advocate on ageing, Hutchinson (1954) argued that older people were being abandoned and isolated by 'modernisation' and that urgent housing and welfare measures were required on their behalf. The post-war era saw massive social change attributable to migration, increasing longevity, marriage and baby booms, increasing marital dissolution, rising home ownership and, perhaps most notable of all for economic wellbeing, the rising workforce participation among women and rising housing costs. Overall, the generations have remained close in emotional and mutual aid terms while they were increasingly living in separate households, by choice, as incomes rose and housing shortages eased (Kendig and Lucas 2014). The more recent rise of households with no workers and single parents, however, is accelerating income inequalities as housing markets and standards of living are increasingly set by two-income households.

Over the post-war era, older people have been increasingly recognised as a major disadvantaged group (National Commission of Inquiry into Poverty 1975) and included in universal health and welfare initiatives since the Whitlam Government. Recognition of population ageing as a major social change, however, was belated as is noted in McDonald's chapter. The National Population Inquiry (1975) made scant mention of ageing as one of the major social changes underway at the time. Not until a decade later did the National Population Council commission *Greying Australia: Future Impacts of Population Ageing* (Kendig and McCallum 1986), which anticipated future changes such as rising needs for care services, and increases in retirees relative to workers.

Families, home ownership and rising education were identified as important resources for ascendant cohorts of older people. The report did not anticipate very well subsequent increases in longevity, and the rapid development of occupational superannuation and community care. Thirty years ago this report concluded that 'the view of old age as a defeated stage of life, so rampant today, is unlikely to last long when the baby boom joins the ranks of the aged' (p 59).

Over subsequent decades a series of academic books, including those with a social science and policy focus noted below, have charted changes in thinking about ageing along with evolving social and policy developments in the field:

- Howe's pioneering *Towards an Older Australia* (1981) set an early foundation for the study of ageing and gerontology. Its chapters describe and raise issues concerning older populations, their needs, and services (written by the few researchers who were working in the field at the time).

- *Grey Policy: Australian Policies for an Ageing Society* (Kendig and McCallum 1990) brought together growing national expertise in interpreting the ageing policy reforms by the Hawke/Keating Government of the 1980s.

- *Ageing and Public Policy in Australia* (Sax 1993),[1] which began with the chapter 'Perceptions and Attitudes' and concluded with 'A Good Old Age', provided a comprehensive account of health and aged-care developments in a societal context.

- *Ageing and Social Policy in Australia* (Borowski et al. 1997), building on further research investments such as the Commonwealth-funded UNSW Social Policy Research Centre, provided more comprehensive accounts of what was to become the current policy framework of aged and health care, income support, superannuation and related policies.

---

1   This was the first of three books that Sidney Sax wrote after his 'retirement' from a distinguished career, which included practising in geriatric medicine, being head of the Commonwealth Social Welfare Policy Secetariat, and principal advisor on health and welfare to Prime Minister Malcolm Fraser. Sax served as the first President of the Australian Association of Geronontology.

- Gibson's *Aged Care: Old policies, new problems* (1998) brought critical feminist and political economy perspectives to understanding ageing and dependency and key policy developments. For example, the book provides insights into complex topics such as 'Regulating Quality of Care' and 'The Problem of Older Women Redefined'.

- *Contemporary Issues in Gerontology: Promoting positive ageing* (Minichiello and Coulsen 2005), argues for a 'new gerontology' challenging the disease and decline approach to ageing, and included chapters on ageism, mental health, sexuality, and 'vehicles to promote positive ageing'.

- *Longevity and Social Change in Australia* (Borowski et al. 2007) reviewed developments primarily during the Howard/Costello era, widening the scope of ageing studies with chapters on lifelong learning, law, politics, advocacy, state governments, and the 'ageing without longevity' experienced by Indigenous Australians (Cotter et al. 2007).

Most recently, *Challenges and Opportunities for an Ageing Australia* (O'Loughlin et al. 2016) brings together CEPAR and health sciences researchers to present a constructive approach to population and policy issues in ageing (see also publications on www.cepar.edu. au). The book includes a chapter on Indigenous health and ageing (Clapham and Duncan 2016) that brings the perspectives of Indigenous researchers to a better understanding of the lifelong disadvantage of their diverse peoples as well as appropriate support and care in their own communities. Another chapter (Radermacher and Feldman 2016) examines the complexity of 'addressing difference' in service systems inclusive of culturally and linguistically diverse communities.

Overall, these books show growing emphases on the positive contributions by older people, their wellbeing, and more effective and equitable policy responses, for example, in superannuation and health services. As indicated by the government's Intergenerational Reports, debates on population ageing are increasingly focused on rising costs to government, fiscal sustainability, and questions of intergenerational equity for younger people and their futures. Some themes are recurrent (and remain unresolved), for example, the vulnerability of groups experiencing lifelong disadvantages such as those of private tenants. There has been increasing attention to gender issues while important matters such as social class and politics (for the latter see Butler 2015) remain relatively less examined. The literature is enriched by increasing accounts from the viewpoints of older people and authors having experience across university research and education, public policy in government, and public advocacy.

Increasing longevity

The contours of later life in Australia have been changing, with life expectancy rising steadily since well before Federation (Figure 1). The usual life span has risen from the 50s age range in the 1890s to the 80s age range in recent years. During the lifetimes of people alive today, social and economic life has had to adapt to the increasing proportions of older people in families and communities. The social meanings and consequences of death and the patterns of intergenerational relationships have changed dramatically as dying moved increasingly from babies and young mothers to men and women in advanced later life. Overall, the expectation for living into advanced older ages has become a 'normal' and relatively predictable part of contemporary life rather than the preserve of a small number of privileged survivors among past generations.

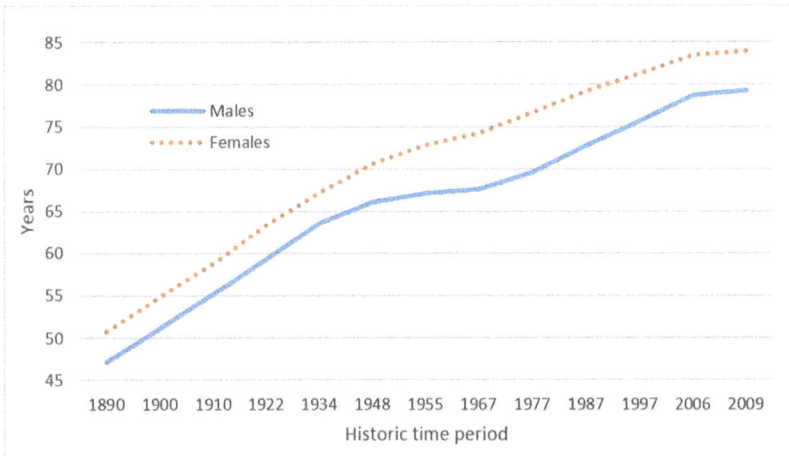

Figure 1. Life expectancy at birth in Australia by gender, 1884–2009
Source: Australian Bureau of Statistics (2011).

The increases of life expectancy have included more years after reaching what traditionally have been the markers for entering later life. The trend has been continuing: from 1998 to 2012, life expectancy at 65 years increased from 16.1 to 19.1 years for men and from 19.8 to 22.0 years for women (Figure 2). Moreover, the additional years of later life included relatively more years free of disability; years of disability were increasingly being concentrated in the final years of life.

Expected life years with and without disabilities

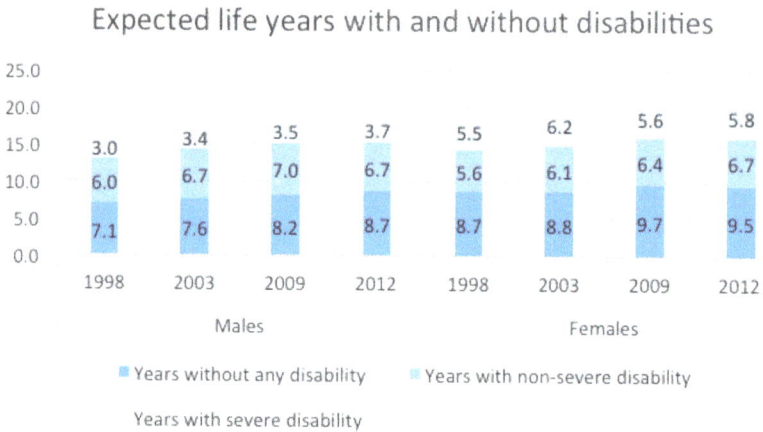

Figure 2. Expected life years with and without disabilities at age 65 in Australia, 1998–2012
Source: Australian Institute of Health and Welfare (2014).

Socioeconomic status is a key influence on inequalities of life expectancy. There is a life expectancy gap (at age 20) of six years between Australians in the top income quintile and those at the bottom income quintile; and a gap of five years between the highest and lowest quintiles for education (Clarke and Leigh 2011). An even greater socioeconomic disparity is seen in the 10-year life expectancy gap between Aboriginal and Torres Street Islanders and other Australians (AIHW 2011).

Change in the life-span

A life-span and social change framework provides a powerful way in which to understand age differences and ageing experiences over time. Lasslet's (1989) thinking on the 'new life course', enables us to consider the impacts of increasing longevity and social change on the 'second', 'third' and 'fourth' stages of life for successive cohorts and intergenerational relationships.

As shown in Figure 3, a life-span could be roughly defined in terms of four indicative ages according to capacities for productivity and independence: 1) a first age of dependency and education indicated by the average age of leaving parent's home (around age 21); 2) a second age of independence and work to the average age of retirement (around age 59); 3) a third age of independence and contribution until commencing care services (around age 80); and 4) a fourth age of significant dependency until death.

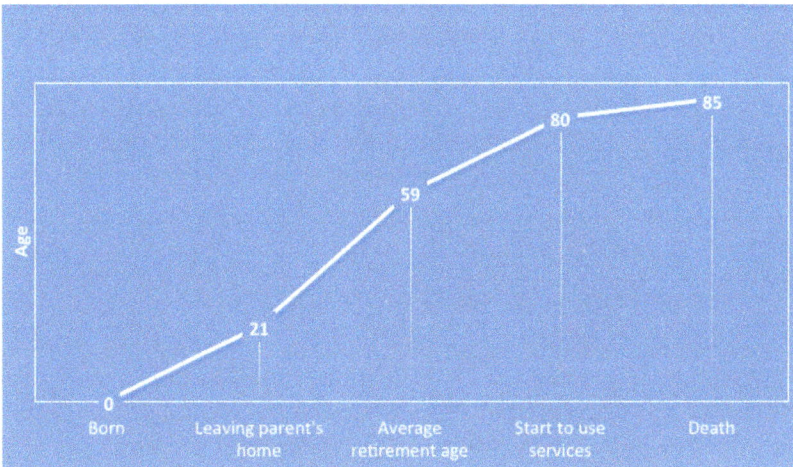

Figure 3. Indicative ages of four life stages across the life-span
Source: Gong's own work based on the data on social trends from Australian Bureau of Statistics (2012).

With increasing years of formal education and training, as required for a knowledge economy, and additional healthy years in late life, the first three stages have been lengthening, while the last stage continues to be concentrated in the final years of life. Since the 1970s, young people have tended to reach many of the major life milestones later, and this will have an impact on how many years they can work in total to support themselves.

In broad terms, there has been increasing scope for the emergence of the 'third age'—that is an extended period of relatively active life—prior to a 'fourth age' characterised typically by a few years in states of frailty and dependency. These trends have shifted Australian and global perspectives on ageing populations from an historical focus on 'welfare and health' to more emphases on the 'inclusion and participation' of older adults. This shift is reflected by more emphases over time in research and policy on 'active ageing' and 'healthy and productive ageing', focusing more on health promotion, employment and social engagement.

Work and the 'second age'

The 'second age' is the period of adult years characterised primarily by labour force participation and productivity. In the context of population ageing and possible workforce shortages, working longer can not only increase productivity and tax revenue, but also assist individuals to build up their own retirement income, thereby reducing the government's potential liability (Commonwealth of Australia 2015; McDonald 2011). With longer and relatively healthier life expectancies, working longer is becoming necessary and more feasible: a significant challenge is how to enable people to continue to work as mild chronic diseases or disabilities arise in their 50s and 60s (Richardson 2014).

Workforce participation has recently been increasing for women at working ages as well as for both men and women at mature age (Figure 4). Although participation in paid work for Australian women aged 55–64 has increased dramatically, much of this growth represents part-time rather than full-time work (ABS 2005). There are two factors contributing to these increases. One is that gender roles have changed significantly as more women have remained in the workforce through mid-life while also maintaining responsibilities as primary carers; by comparison men have been contributing only slightly more to family responsibilities (Richardson 2014). The other change is that more people have been planning later retirement. For instance, in 2007, the average age at which employed people intended to retire was 64 years for men and 62 for women. This was about five years later than the average age of 59 of reported retirement for those who were already retired at the time (60 years for men, 57 years for women) (ABS 2012).

Labour force participation rate by age and gender

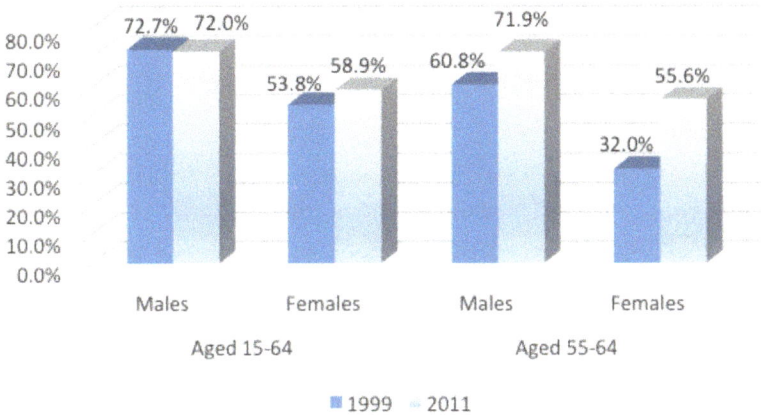

Figure 4. Labour force participation rate by age and gender in Australia, 1999–2011

Source: Australian Bureau of Statistics (2012).

Ongoing contributions and the 'third age'

The third age is the period after retirement, but prior to the onset of disability, in which individuals have the capacity to remain actively engaged (Laslett 1989). With recent increases in living standards and healthy life years after retirement, people in the third age have been able to expect to enjoy a life with self-fulfilling leisure and community participation after completing their responsibilities for paid work and dependent children (Chatzitheochari and Arber 2011). Realising these opportunities may require significant individual and societal adaptations by people at all ages in their family and social life as well as among employers and community organisations.

The emergence of a longer third age and the additional years of good health in later life provide a critical focus for considering social opportunities, risks and action possibilities for an ageing society (Biggs 2014). In Australia, older people already make substantial contributions beyond paid work to their families and the wider community through volunteering and other forms of unpaid work

(Loh and Kendig 2013). For example, their child care and caregiving to family members was valued conservatively at $7 billion in 2009 (National Seniors Australia 2009).

A shift is underway in how people expect to fund their retirement

The Australian retirement income system consists of three major components: the age pension, superannuation and other private savings. The age pension has developed as a social welfare safety net, providing a modest income for those who are not able to support themselves during retirement and a supplement for those with some private resources. Currently, government pensions and allowances are by far the most common source of personal retirement income for both men and women, with around two-thirds of both sexes relying on these as their main source of income.

With the introduction of the superannuation guarantee in 1992, coverage increased substantially and the gender gap has narrowed. In 1974, only 32 per cent of employees (41 per cent of men and 17 per cent of women) were covered by superannuation and they were generally higher paid professionals, managers and administrators in large corporations and the financial sector, as well as public servants and members of the defence force. By 1991, nearly one-third of private sector employees still had no superannuation (Warren 2008). In 1993, just after the introduction of the superannuation guarantee, 81 per cent of employed persons (86 per cent of full-time workers and 61 per cent of part-time workers, 82 per cent of employed men and 78 per cent of employed women) were covered by superannuation (Warren 2008).

The government age pension is still expected to be the main source of retirement income for the next two or three decades until the occupational superannuation system is fully mature (Warren 2008). In 2007, only 25 per cent of adult men and 10 per cent of adult women listed superannuation as their primary source of expected retirement income. The expectations of younger workers suggests that it will be decades before superannuation becomes the main source of retirement income as it is likely to rise moderately and slowly. This change reflects the impact of compulsory superannuation initiatives that were introduced in the late 1980s and early 1990s.

There has been a lengthy debate that the age pension replacement rate (the pension compared to earlier earnings) in Australia is low among OECD countries, although it has been compensated to some extent by the low housing outlays afforded by a higher home ownership rate among older Australians (see Appendix 1 and Chapter 13). However, difficulties meeting the high entry costs of buying present major challenges for younger generations.

The gender gap in retirement incomes requires emphasis. First, women's labour force participation has been limited (notably due to childbearing and child rearing) and marked by more interruptions, more part-time work, and lower rates of pay, hence less superannuation and wealth accumulation. Second, women are likely to live significantly longer than men, including more years requiring what can be expensive aged care. Third, marital breakdown and widowhood present particularly severe financial risks for women.

Outcomes for individuals and cohorts

Economic resources

Historically, Australia has been regarded as a country of egalitarian values with relatively equal distribution of wealth, a lack of visible poverty and generally comfortable incomes. In the 1960s, Prime Minister Harold Holt stated that he knew of no other free country where 'what is produced by the community is more fairly and evenly distributed among the community' (Whiteford 2014). However, this view of Australia came under scrutiny from the 1980s onwards as inequality increased rapidly: from around 2010, Australia became the 11th 'most unequal' of the 34 OECD members. At that time, the richest 20 per cent had 61 per cent of the wealth, while the poorest 20 per cent accounted for a mere 1 per cent of total household net worth (Whiteford 2014).

Over recent decades, poverty in Australia has encompassed more vulnerable groups beyond older pensioners, including more single parents, unemployed youth and other groups, especially those who rent privately. The Productivity Commission reported that people aged 65 years and over (especially singles) nonetheless remain at high risk of experiencing deeper or multiple forms of disadvantage (McLachlan et al. 2013; see also Gong et al. 2014). Among elderly singles in 2010, the vast majority of whom were women, 24 per cent experienced relative income poverty. People aged 65 years and over are far more likely to experience persistent poverty than average households (6.3 per cent compared to 4.4 per cent) (Table 1).

Table 1. Prevalence of forms of disadvantage among older Australians, 2010 (%)

	Relative income poverty 2010	Multiple deprivation 2010	Deep social exclusion 2010	Deep and persistent social exclusion 2001 and 2010
Single adults over 65 years	23.6	3.3	11.9	6.3
Total adults over 65 years	13.2	7.9	7.6	6.3
Total	12.8	13.2	4.8	4.4

Source: McLachlan, Gilfillan and Gordon (2013), Table 1.

Notes: (1) Relative income poverty is defined as the household equivalised income being less than 50 per cent of the median household equivalised income.

(2) Multiple deprivation indicates a combination of low income, low consumption and low net wealth.

(3) Deep social exclusion was defined by 29 indicators across seven key life domains (including material resources, employment, education and skills, health and disability, social connection, community and personal safety).

(4) Deep and persistent social exclusion is defined as the household was having deep social exclusion in both years of 2001 and 2010.

A recent report on the wealth of generations by the GRATTAN Institute indicates that property and savings have driven wealth accumulation differently across age groups from 2003–04 to 2011–12 (Daley and Wood 2014). As a result of increases in housing prices, accumulated superannuation and other invested savings, the net wealth of people aged 45 and over increased substantially: people aged 65 to 74 have benefited most with an annual growth of net wealth of 2.9 per cent, followed by 2.6 per cent for people aged 75 and over. At the same time, households headed by those under 35 have had less wealth in their homes than did the same group eight years ago. They have to borrow more relative to income in order to adapt to the declining housing affordability, although compulsory superannuation could boost their lifetime savings to some extent.

Age and cohort changes

Longitudinal research is beginning to shed light on how ageing and social change are related to inequalities over the life-span and the implications for social justice and policy actions. As indicated in Figure 5, successive birth cohorts have experienced different social, economic and policy circumstances during their childhood, education, work and retirement. For instance, the Depression generation born in the 1930s entered into late life in 1990 and the large baby boom cohort born in the 1950s is now gradually arriving in what has traditionally been regarded as later life.

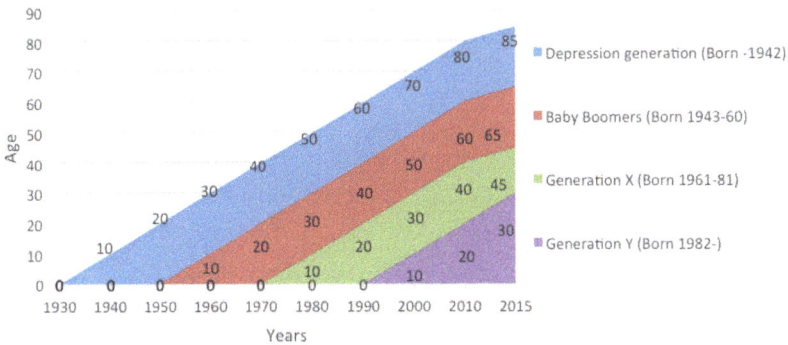

Figure 5. Indicative age, cohort and time period
Source: Gong's own work based on the definitions of generational cohorts.

Figure 6 presents the major global economic events that occurred from the 1930s to 2015, helping to provide historical context for the experiences of different generational cohorts. The post–World War II era has provided the fundamental historical context for understanding the changing face of ageing in Australia, and set legacies that are still influencing future directions. The shock of the 2007 global financial crisis (GFC), after 25 years of strong economic growth, changed perceptions of the adequacy of expected retirement incomes, although in contrast to the recession of the early 1990s it did not result in large-scale unemployment for older workers. It also increased policy and public concern for the costs of population ageing, and led to increased access to partial age pensions and other changes in the direction of government policies (Kendig et al. 2013).

33

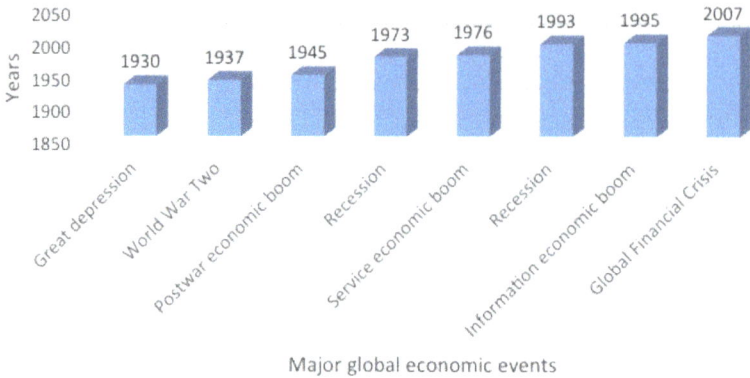

Major global economic events

Figure 6. Indicative historic major global economic events, 1930–2015
Source: Gong's own work based on the well-known major historical events.

Four generational cohorts can be defined by their periods of birth and their subsequent exposures to global economic environments over recent decades (Figure 6). These generations can be characterised in terms of related social values, attitudes and behaviours:

- *The Depression generation*, the current cohort of older people who were born in 1944 or before, grew up in the Great Depression and World War II during the 1930s and 1940s with low education but access to full-time and relatively less-skilled employment when they were young (Carson and Kerr 2001). They subsequently experienced tremendous changes in work patterns, such as the rapid decline of the manufacturing sector, and restructuring that had particularly severe consequences for low-skilled workers, including precarious employment prospects and increasing risks of long-term unemployment in mid- and late life.

- *Baby boomers*, who were born between 1945 and 1960, grew up in the post-war economic boom era, characterised by rising educational and employment opportunities, with *relatively* less gender inequality on entering adulthood (Carson and Kerr 2001; Biggs 2014). Their expanding opportunities and resources contrast sharply with the limited expectations and economic opportunities of the Depression generation who have, thus far, shaped images of ageing.

- *The Younger generation* (Generation X born 1961–1981 and Generation Y born 1982 or later), who grew up or entered adulthood during the slow and/or variable economic growth of the early 1970s, the early 1990s and then the GFC in the early 21st century, with the expanding tertiary sector. They have faced a more uncertain economy with less job security and higher income inequality, with more demand for adaptability to changes (Tetrick and LaRocco 1987; McDaniel et al. 2013). We have included only Generation X in this study by restricting individuals to those aged 35 and over in the data analysed from the Household, Income and Labour Dynamics in Australia (HILDA) surveys of 2001 to 2011.

Cohort succession is significantly increasing diversity in later life and generating new perspectives on ageing. The GFC of 2007 and diminishing public programs over recent years have further changed perspectives. Younger generations will be particularly affected by rising income inequality and reduced expectations for job security, income growth, health care and other public benefits (for Canada see also McDaniel et al. 2013). Among the Australian generational cohorts, the baby boomers are commonly thought to be the most advantaged on the basis of their rising educational and employment opportunities and the booming residential housing market through the 1980s and 1990s.

Recent changes in life satisfaction

This section examines the ways in which ageing and social change are related to quality of life as indicated by life satisfaction through adult life from the turn of the century. The opportunity to examine these issues arose with the longitudinal HILDA study that has surveyed Australians annually since 2001 (Summerfield et al. 2012).

Figure 7 (top three lines) shows that over the first decade of this century (from 2001 to 2011), overall life satisfaction increased slightly for the ageing baby boomers while they were moving towards later life. For the older Depression cohort, life satisfaction was higher than for the boomers, notwithstanding their advanced age, and it remained largely steady as they moved through to advanced old age. For the young cohort, however, life satisfaction on average was relatively lower when compared to the two older generations and declined slightly as they moved towards middle age.

In terms of satisfaction with health (bottom three lines), there was an understandable but only modest decline for all the three generations with increasing age. Overall, the findings suggest considerable stability of satisfaction with life and health as the birth cohorts have been moving through middle to later life. However, in interpreting these findings it is important to keep in mind that people who were very old and/or in poor health in 2001 were more likely to have died before 2011.

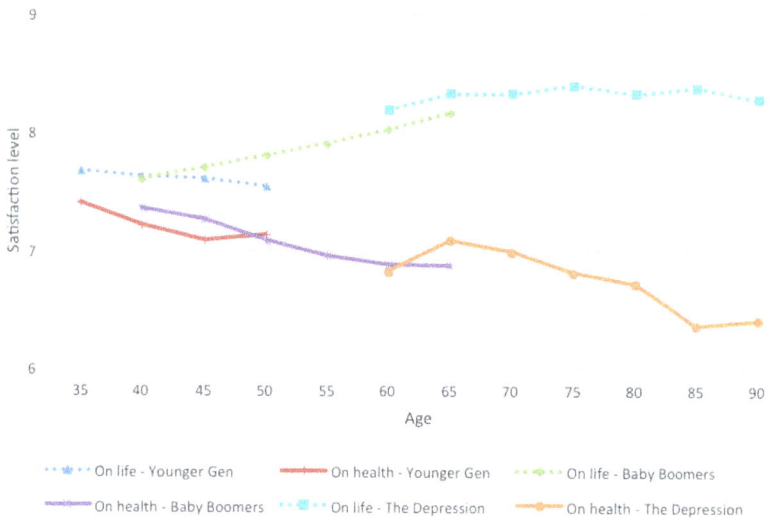

Figure 7. Satisfaction levels with life overall and health by age and cohort
Source: HILDA 2001–2011, Gong's own calculation.

More detailed findings (not shown on the figure) show that overall education and health confer relatively higher levels of health and life satisfaction across the cohorts:

- The *Depression birth cohort had a relatively higher level of satisfaction* in specific areas of life—free time, home, neighbourhood, local community and relationships with partner, children and parents, *with very little decline in these areas with ageing even for those at advanced ages.*

- The *youngest cohort had the highest satisfaction with financial situation and employment opportunities* (but this declined slightly as mid-life approached).

- The *baby boomers cohort had the least satisfaction in relationships with their children*, although this was rising over the 10 years.
- The *younger generation cohort had achieved the highest education levels* followed by the baby boomers and then by the Depression cohort.
- For all birth cohorts, *higher education is associated with better self-reported health as well as higher satisfaction with life overall*, financial situation, employment opportunity and living environment (but lower satisfaction with free time and relationships).
- Again for all cohorts, *women have relatively slightly higher life satisfaction levels than men*; life satisfaction is the highest for those reporting excellent health (and it decreases significantly for those in poor health).
- The *better-educated in the young generation were slightly more satisfied with their life overall than their peers at other ages*. Education beyond high school conferred relatively less advantage for baby boomers; and it conferred more advantage for those in the Depression cohort who had certificates or more education. The findings suggest that requirements for education and skill sets have increased over time for successive cohorts.

Other studies indicate significant overall impacts of the GFC on satisfaction with health and life. A national survey of baby boomers showed that the GFC was a significant 'shock' for their financial expectations, especially for those who were still employed compared to those who were retired at the time (Kendig et al. 2013). A longitudinal study in Canberra concluded that the GFC had a delayed effect in increasing depression and anxiety, particularly among baby boomers whose expectations for high standards of living in retirement apparently were threatened (Sargent-Cox et al. 2011).

The future and intergenerational equity

Anticipating directions for the future is important to inform and guide constructive action, notwithstanding the difficulty of unforeseen developments such as the GFC. It is heartening that there has been notable progress for older people over recent generations along with rising standards of living in Australia. Understanding the past is important for appreciating social progress and also the cultural and institutional inertia in social organisation, including the relative positions and power of various interests that can shape and resist change.

The expectation for a longer and healthier 'third age', with more scope for productivity in paid and unpaid work, is now being realised for the majority of ageing people. Their socioeconomic standing, notably with wealth in owner-occupied housing, has risen appreciably. Their psychological wellbeing overall is high relative to those in middle age and it appears to improve as people approach later life. There remain, however, pockets of intense deprivation among older people as there are among younger age groups. Notable disadvantage continues among older Aboriginals, women without partners, non–home owners, and those in poor health, including rises in the prevalence of chronic disease.

Some aspects of the future are relatively easy to anticipate. Baby boomers now in late-middle age have been advantaged by their educational and career opportunities from the 1960s and 1970s; they are now bringing these resources, life skills and expectations to their later life. Family relations are evolving in complex and varied ways but intergenerational bonds are deeply seated and generally remain strong. Housing assets for this cohort are generally high as a result of increased access to home ownership and appreciating real values from the 1980s onward. Superannuation accumulating since the 1990s, with substantial employer contributions and tax subsidies, will be maturing.

The cohort momentum behind these promising directions for older people is in some ways reversing earlier patterns in which people had been disadvantaged by their cohort of birth as well as ageing. The major proviso here, of course, is that the 'accumulation' of advantage has not been available to all groups of older (and younger) people and socioeconomic disparities appear to have been increasing. Current directions are for older single women to continue to be at a substantial disadvantage relative to men in terms of their vulnerability to poverty, poor health, and housing insecurity.

Attitudes to ageing and older people have also evolved since the 'ageism' in the colonial era of 'a society without grandmothers' (Davison 1995). A CEPAR-supported national Attitudes to Ageing in Australia

(AAA) study (Kendig et al. 2015) in 2010 found that the majority of younger people at the time were sympathetic to policies beneficial to older people as most believed that they were getting 'less than their fair share of government benefits'. O'Loughlin and Kendig (2016), drawing on this same data base, report that attitudes on the capacities of older people, however, were less favourable: the findings indicate considerable ambivalence and negativity towards older people in the workplace. Across all age groups only a small proportion of people perceived strong intergenerational conflict. There were divided views on the lifelong opportunities of the baby boom cohort as compared to those who are following them.

There are uncertain prospects for directions in real incomes, wealth, and the future of work. An optimistic note is struck in the otherwise pessimistic Intergenerational Report (Commonwealth of Australia 2015), which, in its technical document, assumes growth of real income into the future. Home ownership, which has proved so important to mitigate the effects of reduced income in later life, is projected to decline for future cohorts of older and younger people (Stebbing and Spies-Butcher 2015). Employment is central to accumulating resources for one's own later life and also for taxation supporting public transfer programs. While workforce participation has been increasing at older ages, ageing workers are likely to be in industries and occupations where jobs are under major threat from technological change and reorganisation of workplaces (CEDA 2015). Economic modeling has shown that the recent direction of government budgets has been to widen inequalities between the rich and poor and between the younger and older generations (Phillips 2015).

Notwithstanding the significant concerns and uncertainties ahead, the chapters in this volume indicate that Australia is relatively well placed in terms of its demography, economy, and policies to respond constructively to population ageing. We may, however, be at a turning point in which future generations may well have lower lifelong economic prospects than the baby boom cohort now entering later life. Further, experiences over the life course are becoming more precarious for many in terms of family and work life. While some older people will continue to be disadvantaged by poor health and limited financial resources, the overall pattern is for older people to have an increasing share of national wealth. This growing trend for at least a decade ahead raises the capacities of advantaged older people to pay for services and to contribute more to their families and to government revenue.

The future can be influenced positively by governments, employers, and individuals that take action on the considerable potential for 'improvability' for an ageing Australia. Big ideas that can assist in achieving better wellbeing outcomes include building human capital over the entire life span; 'ageing well' approaches in health and social policy; and employment and care practises that reinforce independence (Kendig 2016). Positive outcomes for all age groups and generations can be facilitated by further social change that recognises diversity over the life span and fosters positive attitudes and opportunities for older people.

References

Australian Bureau of Statistics (ABS) (2005). *Australia Labour Market Statistics*, January 2005. ABS Cat. no. 6105.0. Canberra: Australian Bureau of Statistics.

Australian Bureau of Statistics (ABS) (2011). *Australian Social Trends: Life Expectancy Trends*, March 2011. ABS Cat. no. 4102.0. Canberra: Australian Bureau of Statistics.

Australian Bureau of Statistics (ABS) (2012). *Australian Social Trends*, December 2012. ABS Cat. no. 4102.0. Canberra: Australian Bureau of Statistics.

Australian Institute of Health and Welfare (AIHW) (2011). The health and welfare of Australia's Aboriginal and Torres Strait Islander people, an overview 2011. Cat. no. IHW 42. Canberra: AIHW.

Australian Institute of Health and Welfare (AIHW) (2014). Healthy Life Expectancy in Australia: Patterns and trends 1998 to 2012. Australian Institute of Health and Welfare. Bulletin no. 126. Cat. no. AUS187. Canberra: AIHW.

Biggs Simon (2014). Adapting to an ageing society: The need for cultural change. *Policy Quarterly*, 10(3): 12–16.

Borowski Allan, Encel Sol and Ozanne Elizabeth (Eds) (1997). *Ageing and Social Policy in Australia*. Cambridge: Cambridge University Press.

Borowski Allan, Encel Sol and Ozanne Elizabeth (Eds) (2007). *Longevity and Social Change in Australia*. Sydney: University of New South Wales Press.

Butler Mark (2015). *Advanced Australia: The Politics of Ageing*. Melbourne: Melbourne University Press.

Carson Ed and Kerr Lorraine (2001). Bust for the 'baby-boomers': The real mid-life crisis. *Journal of Economic and Social Policy*, 6(1): art.5.

Chatzitheochari Stella and Arber Sara (2011). Identifying the Third Agers: An Analysis of British Retirees' Leisure Pursuits. University of Surrey. *Sociological Research Online*, 16(4): 3.

Clapham Kathleen and Duncan Cathy (2016). Indigenous Australians and Ageing: Responding to Diversity in Policy and Practice. In Kate O'Loughlin, Colette Browning and Hal Kendig (Eds). *Ageing in Australia: Challenges and Opportunities*. New York: Springer.

Clarke Phillip and Leigh Andrew (2011). Death, Dollars, and Degrees: Socioeconomic Status and Longevity in Australia. *Economic Papers*, 30(3): 348–355.

Committee for Economic Development of Australia (CEDA) (2015). *Australia's future workforce?* Committee for Economic Development of Australia, June 2015. dx.doi.org/10.4225/50/557FA860CD297.

Commonwealth of Australia (2015). *2015 Intergenerational Report: Australia in 2055*. Canberra: Department of Treasury, March 2015. www.treasury.gov.au/PublicationsAndMedia/Publications/2015/2015-Intergenerational-Report.

Cotter Philippa, Anderson Ian and Smith Len (2007). Indigenous Australians: Ageing Without Longevity. In Allan Borowski, Sol Encel and Elizabeth Ozanne (Eds) *Longevity and Social Change in Australia*. Sydney: University of New South Wales Press, pp. 65–98.

Daley John and Wood Danielle (2014). *The Wealth of Generations*. Melbourne: GRATTAN Institute. grattan.edu.au/report/the-wealth-of-generations/.

Dannefer Dale (2003). Cumulative advantage/disadvantage and the life course: Cross-fertilizing age and social science theory. *Journals of Gerontology Series B: Psychological Sciences and Social Sciences*, 58(6): S327–337.

Davison Graeme (1995). Our Youth is Spent and our Backs are Bent: The Origins of Australian Ageism. *Australian Cultural History*, 14: 40–62.

Gibson Diane (1998). *Aged Care: Old policies, new problems*. Cambridge: Cambridge University Press.

Gong Cathy, Kendig Hal, Harding Ann, Miranti Royara and McNamara Justine (2014). Economic Advantage and Disadvantage among Older Australians: Producing National and Small Area Profiles. *Australasian Journal of Regional Studies*, 20(3): 513–539.

Howe Anna L (Ed) (1981). *Towards an Older Australia*. St Lucia, Queensland: University of Queensland Press.

Hutchinson Bertram (1954). *Older People in a Modern Australian Community: A Social Science Survey*. Melbourne: Melbourne University Press.

Jalland Patricia (2015). *Old age in Australia: A History*. Carlton, Victoria: Melbourne University Press.

Kendig Hal (2016). Directions and Choices for the Future. In Kate O'Loughlin, Colette Browning and Hal Kendig (Eds), *Ageing in Australia: Challenges and Opportunities*. New York: Springer.

Kendig Hal and Lucas Nina (2014). Individuals, Families and the State: Changing responsibilities in an aging Australia. In Amaryllis T Torres and Laura L Samson (Eds), *Aging in Asia-Pacific: Balancing the State and the Family*. Diliman, Philippines: Philippine Social Science Council.

Kendig Hal and McCallum John (1986). *Greying Australia: Future Impacts of Population Ageing*. Canberra: Australian Government Publishing Service.

Kendig Hal and McCallum John (1990). *Grey Policy: Australian Policies for an Ageing Society*. Sydney: Allen & Unwin.

Kendig Hal, O'Loughlin Kate, Hussain Rafat, Heese Karla and Cannon Lisa (2015). Attitudes to Intergenerational Equity: Baseline Findings from the Attitudes to Ageing in Australia (AAA) Study. *CEPAR Working Paper,* 2015/33. Sydney: ARC Centre of Excellence in Population Ageing Research.

Kendig Hal, Wells Yvonne, O'Loughlin Kate and Heese Karla (2013). Australian baby boomers face retirement during the Global Financial Crisis. *Journal of Aging and Social Policy,* 25(3): 264–280.

Laslett Peter (1989). *A Fresh Map of Life: The emergence of a third age.* London: Weidenfeld and Nicolson.

Loh Vanessa and Kendig Hal (2013). Productive engagement across the life course: Paid work and beyond. *Australian Journal of Social Issues,* 48(1): 111–137.

McDaniel Susan A, Gazso Amber and Um Seonggee (2013). Generationing relations in challenging times: Americans and Canadians in mid-life in the Great Recession. *Current Sociology,* 61(7): 931–948.

McDonald Peter (2011). Employment at Older Ages in Australia: Determinants and Trends. In Tabatha Griffin and Francesca Beddie (Eds) *Older Workers: Research Readings.* Adelaide: NCVER.

McLachlan Rosalie, Gilfillan Geoff and Gordon Jenny (2013). Deep and Persistent Disadvantage in Australia, Canberra: Productivity Commission, Staff Working Paper.

Minichiello Victor and Coulsen Irene (2005). *Contemporary Issues in Gerontology: Promoting positive ageing.* Sydney: Allen & Unwin.

National Commission of Inquiry into Poverty (1975). *Poverty in Australia.* Canberra: Australian Government Publishing Service.

National Population Inquiry (1975). *Population and Australia: A demographic Analysis and Projection,* 2 volumes. Canberra: Australian Government Publishing Service.

National Seniors Australia (2009). *Still Putting In: Measuring the Economic and Social Contributions of Older Australians,* Research Report, National Seniors Australia Productive Ageing Centre. Canberra: Department of Health and Ageing.

O'Loughlin Kate and Kendig Hal (2016). Attitudes to Ageing. In Kate O'Loughlin, Colette Browning and Hal Kendig (Eds), *Ageing in Australia: Challenges and Opportunities*. New York: Springer.

O'Loughlin Kate, Colette Browning and Hal Kendig (Eds), *Ageing in Australia: Challenges and Opportunities*. New York: Springer.

Phillips Ben (2015). *Living Standard Trends in Australia: Report for Anglicare Australia*. NATSEM, University of Canberra, September 2015. www.natsem.canberra.edu.au/storage/Living%20Standard %20Trends%20Final.pdf.

Radermacher Harriet and Feldman Susan (2016). Cultural Diversity, Health and Ageing. In Kate O'Loughlin, Colette Browning and Hal Kendig (Eds), *Ageing in Australia: Challenges and Opportunities*. New York: Springer.

Richardson Susan (2014). Do We All Want Permanent Full-time Jobs? *Insights*, 15(April).

Sargent-Cox Kerry, Butterworth Peter and Anstey Kaarin (2011). The global financial crisis and psychological health in a sample of Australian older adults: A longitudinal study. *Social Science and Medicine*, 73(7): 1105–1112.

Sax Sidney (1993) *Ageing and Public Policy in Australia*. Sydney: Allen & Unwin.

Stebbing Adam and Spies-Butcher Ben (2015). The decline of a homeowning society? Asset-based welfare, retirement and intergenerational equity in Australia. *Housing Studies* 31(2). doi: 10.1080/02673037.2015.1070797.

Summerfield Michelle, Freidin Simon, Hahn Markus, Ittak Peter, Li Ning, Macalalad Ninette, Watson Nicole, Wilkins Roger and Wooden Mark (2012). *HILDA User Manual—Release 11*, Melbourne Institute of Applied Economic and Social Research, University of Melbourne.

Tetrick Lois E and LaRocco James (1987). Understanding, prediction and control as moderators of the relationships between perceived stress, satisfaction, and psychological well-being. *Journal of Applied Psychology*, 72(4): 538–543.

Warren Diana (2008). Australia's Retirement Income System: Historical Development and Effects of Recent Reforms. *Melbourne Institute Working Paper Series*, Working Paper No. 23/08.

Whiteford Peter (2014). Income and wealth inequality: How is Australia faring? *The Conversation*. 5 March 2014.

3

Population ageing in Australia— National policy challenges and future directions

John Piggott

Population ageing comprises two related but distinct forces: the ageing of the baby boomer generation, and related policy challenges around retirement support, health care, aged care, and the management of intergenerational relationships; and the impacts of population dynamics and evolving changes in demographic structure, nationally, regionally and globally. The first is generally given more attention, for understandable reasons—the policy challenges are very direct and relatively near-term. In particular, retirement and retirement financing, health and ageing, and aged care are all important national priorities, requiring evidence-based changes in policy formulation, business practice, and family behaviour.

But the longer-term influences of shifting population dynamics may eventually have the more profound impact on Australians. I have in mind here the impact of generational imbalance on intergenerational solidarity, on taxation policy, on the structure of our labour force, and the impact of changing population structures within our major trading partners on demand for our trade, our investment, and migration.

These two aspects of population ageing are related not just because demographic change will evolve steadily and inexorably for at least the next generation. They are also linked through national response: what we do about an ageing demographic will profoundly impact the longer-term outcomes of population dynamics. The issue becomes even more complex because population dynamics internationally, but especially in Asia, will likely impact the Australian demographic transition and its economic and social correlates, through migration, sources of international investment, trade patterns, and ultimately the global level of economic activity.

While Australia, in common with most of the world's nations, is ageing by most agreed measures, such as dependency ratio or median age, average remaining life expectancy is also increasing. Intergenerational dynamics are much more complex than the simple arithmetic used in measuring the traditional dependency ratio, the population over some arbitrary age, often 65, divided by the population aged between 15 and 64. For policymakers, dependency lies at the heart of the issue, because, unless self-provision has been mandated, and/or family support is forthcoming, providing adequate services for those whose human capital has been mostly depleted requires taking resources from elsewhere, which in most cases means younger workers. Higher taxes and more informal resource commitment are the inevitable consequences of an ageing demographic, although alternative measures of dependency project differing impressions of the nature, timing and extent of this process. For example, a calculation of dependency ratios that holds constant remaining life expectancy as the cut-off for switching to 'dependant' status, rather than chronological age, generates dependency ratios that decline for some significant period before rising again (Spijker and MacInnes 2013). On the other hand, using National Transfer Accounts (NTA), of the type generated by Peter McDonald and his team for Australia (Rice et al. 2014), gives the opposite result (Prskawetz and Sambt 2014).

In what follows, much is speculative. I will first make some remarks about the challenges and opportunities generated by the ageing of the baby boomers, focusing especially on retirement incomes, and health and aged care, but also touching on housing and risk. I then take up the question of demographic dynamics, both domestic and international, and their impact on Australia's future.

The challenges of an ageing demographic

There seems little doubt that an ageing population will lead to greater public sector support, simply because government, in its role as insurer of last resort, will be called upon more and more to cover the risks to which older people with depleted earning capacity are exposed. In an OECD background paper prepared by Ed Whitehouse and myself for a meeting of Ministers of Social Security in 2011 (Piggott and Whitehouse 2011), we reported projections for a range of countries of outlays on pensions, health and long-term care, comparing 2010 and 2050. I reproduce Figure 1 from that paper here. In all these countries, outlays are projected to rise significantly, with the proportionate increase greatest for those countries, such as Korea, with the most rapidly ageing projections. Australia, along with demographically and economically similar countries such as Canada, registered about a 30 per cent increase, from 10 per cent to about 13 per cent of GDP. While these calculations are now a few years old, their import remains clear.

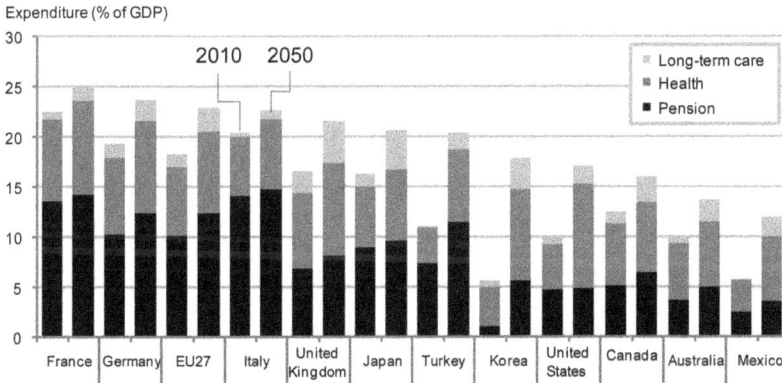

Figure 1. Fiscal costs of ageing populations (projected pension, health and long-term care expenditures, 2010 and 2050, per cent of GDP)

Source: OECD (2011), *Pensions at a Glance: Retirement-Income Systems in OECD and G-20 Countries*; OECD (2011), *Help Wanted? Providing and Paying for Long-Term Care*; European Commission (2009), 'The 2009 Ageing Report: Economic and Budgetary Projections for the EU 27 Member States (2008–2060)', European Economy, No. 2/2009, Brussels; International Monetary Fund (2009), 'Fiscal Implications of the Global Economic and Financial Crisis', Staff Position Note No. 09/13, Washington, DC; Standard & Poor's (2010), 'Global Aging 2010: An Irreversible Truth'.

Retirement and retirement incomes[1]

Australia is, on the whole, well served by the existing framework of retirement policy. While many questions remain unanswered, and there is much room for improvement, the current system is sustainable, has a high degree of integrity, and will, once the superannuation guarantee becomes mature, provide adequate resources in retirement.

It is useful to think of our retirement income structure in terms of the three-pillar framework adopted by the OECD. The first pillar operates as a non-contributory transfer, which means it is potentially available to all.[2] This is represented in Australia by the Age Pension. The second pillar offers payments related to pre-retirement labour income, on some mandatory basis (in Australia, the Superannuation Guarantee). Typically, this is based on contributions computed as some proportion of wages or salary, paid either by employer, employee, or both. The third pillar comprises voluntary retirement saving, typically tax-preferred.

Focusing on the first two pillars allows us to loosely link the instruments of policy to targets. The first pillar is designed to alleviate poverty, while the second pillar aims to encourage consumption smoothing between working and retirement life. Because the Age Pension is non-contributory, and the value of the maximum single benefit has recently been increased from 25 per cent to 27.8 per cent of average earnings, it does a remarkably good job of ameliorating poverty among the elderly. If, like the US, we set the poverty line at 40 per cent of median income, then the elderly poverty rate is only 5 per cent (Chomik and Piggott 2014). Further, even when poverty is set at the OECD level, taking account of housing reduces elderly poverty to 13.5 per cent (Yates and Bradbury 2010). The calculation of high poverty rates reported by, for example, the OECD misses two important points. First, most households with a head aged 65 or more

---

1   This material draws in part on my 2013 ASSA Hancock Lecture, www.youtube.com/watch?v=lb6Uv4kIGfU. My views have also benefited from many discussions with my colleague Cagri Kumru.

2   It may only be available subject to a means test, since its function is to ensure the elderly are adequately provided for.

own a home outright.[3] Second, the gap between the poverty line (set at 50 per cent of median household equivalised income) and the value of the full Age Pension is quite small.

When we turn to incentives, conventional economic wisdom emphasises the disincentive impacts of high effective marginal tax rates (EMTRs). But the overall economic impact of means testing is poorly understood, and is an important topic for further research. Here, we simply note three caveats to the presumption that means testing a social pension induces net perverse disincentives. First, like any other tax-financed financial transfer, retirement income transfers impact on incentives at two points in economic transactions: when the tax is levied, and when the transfer is received. These two points of price distortion need to be considered together in assessing the overall incentive impact of means testing. As the taper rate (and the associated EMTR) is reduced, the overall revenue requirement of the program will increase, and this will require higher tax rates to be applied to others in the economy, probably workers. If they already pay high taxes, as in developed countries, then the same argument about disproportionate efficiency costs of high marginal tax rates will apply, offsetting the EMTR reduction among pension recipients.

Second, while a means-tested pension will impose high EMTRs on those at the margin of eligibility, where withdrawal of the pension is operative, many individuals potentially impacted by a universal pension will be unaffected by a targeted pension, whereas their behaviour would be impacted by a demogrant. For a given full pension value, steeper tapers will reduce the number of consumers affected by the social pension overall. It seems plausible that the group excluded by a steeper taper is likely on average to have more possibilities of behaviour modification than less well-off groups in the community.

Third, recent analysis (for example, Conesa et al. 2009) suggests that a tax on capital income may have efficiency-enhancing properties in an economy where there are restrictions on age-based taxes, and where liquidity constraints prevail. A means test is an age-based tax on capital income, and more precisely, a tax on retirement capital (Kumru

---

3   Those Age Pension recipients who rent receive rental assistance, which goes some way to making up the shortfall from the absence of principal residence.

and Piggott 2010). In more recent research with economy-wide models capturing these points, it is frequently found that steeper tapers may be efficiency-preferred.

The current Australian discussion around steeper tapers is therefore one that the recent economics literature supports, if at this stage only in a preliminary way (Sefton et al. 2008; Kumru and Piggott 2009). There is a major research agenda around means testing just getting underway.

A final point on means-testing structures relates to the inclusion of earned income in the means test. Many countries with conventional social security have an 'earnings test', which effectively operates as a means test on earned income, while ignoring capital resources. Recent analysis (Hernaes et al. 2016) suggests that relaxing the 'earnings test' on social security, which in the context of a social pension such as Australia's can be interpreted as relaxing the means test on earned income, may lead to improved mature labour force participation. As we will see below, this is perhaps the most important family and market adjustment available to respond to the pressures of an ageing demographic, and a major policy challenge is to ensure as far as possible that policy structures and settings encourage rather than impede working longer.

When it comes to income replacement or consumption smoothing, however, the picture is less sanguine. The Superannuation Guarantee (SG) provides resources for retirement, on a pre-funded basis, which makes it sustainable. But especially for workers whose pre-retirement income sits in the upper third of the earnings distribution, the SG falls well short of a well-designed retirement income. This is a major challenge for retirement design in Australia. Of the small group of countries relying on pre-funded mechanisms for income-replacement policies, Australia is alone in specifying no drawdown structure. Recent policy discussion concerning retirement income policy suggests that policymakers are aware of this. While much more research is required before we have a comprehensive understanding of this policy area, enough is known to give us a direction for policy reform. Much of the available and relevant evidence is summarised in three requested CEPAR submissions to the Financial Systems Inquiry (CEPAR 2014a, 2014b, 2014c).

Overall, while many unanswered research questions remain, and there is much policy reform to be undertaken, the directions for retirement income policy reform are becoming clear. My assessment is that, in policy terms, we're ahead of the game compared with most comparable economies. This may be cold comfort—many existing systems are clearly unsustainable, and will likely be subject to arbitrary reductions in benefits into the future, implemented at a time when households are least able to adapt—after their earnings capacity has been depleted. Perhaps the least settled aspect relates to the tax treatment of superannuation, although the blueprint laid out in the 2009 Henry Review (Commonwealth of Australia 2009) provides an excellent starting point.

Health and aged care

Health and aged care provision is a major challenge even without the additional pressures associated with an ageing demographic. This is not my area of expertise, so I will be briefer. The Intergenerational Report (IGR) (Commonwealth of Australia 2009) suggests that the major source of increases in government health outlays to 2050 will not be population ageing, but technology improvement. Other reports suggest that the most important source of outlay increase will be demographic change. In a way, it doesn't matter. To deliver up-to-date health care to Australians 30 years from now will cost a lot more than it does today, unless something changes.

One possible cost reduction measure is the promotion of e-health. A high proportion of public health outlays is devoted to hospital stays for chronically ill patients, whose acute episodes occasioning hospitalisation may have been avoided with closer monitoring. International evidence on the benefits of remote monitoring (I have in mind monitoring through home-based devices to a central hub that flags indications of acute attacks) is clear. One would think Australia, with its unique challenges around remote communities, would be at the forefront of these initiatives, but this does not appear to be the case. This is an example of infrastructure development for an ageing demographic, which I allude to briefly below, but there is a culture issue as well. Scalable adoption of e-health monitoring requires cultural acceptance by both the health professions and their clients, and this may be as formidable a barrier to implementation as the installation of the required technology.

A second aspect of health and aged care worthy of note relates to cognitive decline. With increasingly longevity, the incidence of debilitating cognitive decline, either dementia or simply major dysfunction, will grow, by rates that vary by source, but that are alarming. As Hurd et al. (2013) have demonstrated for the US, the potential costs of Alzheimer's disease into the future are very high. But the costs of generalised cognitive decline may be even higher. To the extent that cognitive capital, to use Kaarin Anstey's term, can be maintained, these costs may be avoided. There is mounting evidence that maintaining workforce attachment is associated with lower rates of cognitive decline, even after self-selection is controlled for. For example, Rohwedder and Willis (2010), using data across countries with substantially different policies regarding retirement age, find that early retirement has a significant negative impact on the cognitive ability of people in their early 60s that is both quantitatively important and causal. This has implications for policies towards mature labour force participation, discussed later.

In a way, the issue of cognitive decline provides a convenient bridge between health and aged care. Aged care presents enormous challenges: the strain on carers and family relationships, both intra- and intergenerational; the work-care dilemma; and the fiscal cost of care.

On a framework for aged care, Australia has made a good start, with a policy stance articulating clear guidelines about the future shaping of policy. Missing is any clear account of funding sources. But for those owning one, it will probably be the owner-occupied home. The high owner-occupier rate among the elderly, combined with high home prices, certainly constitutes serious resources to purchase residential aged care when that becomes necessary, and the home and community emphasis of the new policy should ensure that happens less, and for shorter durations, than is currently the case. Work needs to be done, by academe, both government and business, to develop home equity drawdown instruments that elderly Australians feel comfortable and safe with. But that is doable, and there is some time in which to do it.

Mature labour force participation

This is perhaps the greatest challenge, and greatest opportunity in economic, social and familial adjustment to population ageing, and in particular increased longevity. Working for longer is an inevitable consequence of living for longer, yet is resisted by many whose expectations of chronological age of retirement are challenged by this surprising shift in mature life expectancy. Yet many people, even the majority, of those now in their 50s, can expect to live to their 90s. And their healthy lives will extend also. Policies have to be adjusted to reflect this—superannuation access age, worker compensation insurance, and most importantly, attitudes have to change. Age discrimination is increasingly under challenge by regulators and policymakers. Susan Ryan has suggested 'career checks' to see whether a job is conducive to working longer. Relatedly, continuing education should be directed to guiding workers into occupations in later years that they can pursue into their late 60s.

A number of workforce issues will likely arise as demographic change sets in. Diversity in the workplace needs to embrace age diversity as well as gender and ethnic diversity. Little research has been conducted into the impacts of age diversity in the workplace. An improved understanding of the implications of an age-diversified workforce would assist firms in establishing workplace practices to induce an accepting culture. Superannuation entitlements that are linked to final salary need to be changed so that a worker can stay in the workforce at a reduced wage without having his or her benefits reduced. Generally, workers will have to adjust to working longer, in response to longer and healthier lives.

Housing and infrastructure

If a senior government official had been asked, 50 years ago, to predict the path of future urbanisation in Australia, he would very likely have indicated that the then major centres of Sydney, Melbourne, Brisbane and Perth would be joined by major regional centres. Population growth and urbanisation would take place without extreme agglomeration. Nothing like that has eventuated. Instead, site rents in these four major centres have increased more than wages, and housing affordability has become a major social issue.

It is unclear why Australia's population has become so concentrated in capital cities. One possibility is that technological innovation has allowed certain cities to become knowledge-intensive, creating new jobs, and that has meant that the best career opportunities are available in those cities (Glaeser and Resseger 2010). But the result is that housing affordability is currently strained, in spite of historically low interest rates.

This is a challenge in political economy. Local interests, represented by political groupings across Australia's fiscal federal structure, severely constrains affordable housing development, and lack of complementary infrastructure exacerbates the problem. It is relevant to the ageing of the population because of its link with intergenerational equity (the baby boomers hold the bulk of housing wealth), and because of its implications for the intragenerational distribution of wealth in future generations. I return to this point below.

Risk and risk management

Overwhelmingly, our financial services sector is geared to wealth management rather than insurance. At least two major social issues—the ageing demographic and climate—mean that this will change over the next two decades. This change may not yet be fully appreciated, either by government or private insurers. The impact of climate risk on the financial sector has been explored by Whalley and Yuan (2009). Here we focus on the risks of being older, and the appropriate policy stance to maximise private coverage of the associated risks.

The central point here is that to induce the private sector to accept more retirement risk, government has to develop financial instruments, and design policies and regulations such that these risks can be managed by private institutions. It is often observed that government already bears much longevity risk, for example, and does not wish to extend its exposure. But it should be recognised that the insurer of last resort is always the government—disaster and drought relief is just one example. So by carefully designing the nature of the additional risk it takes on, it can make it attractive for the private sector to insure where no products would be offered in the absence of government covering, for example, tail risk.

The challenges of population dynamics

Intergenerational relationships

Unbalanced demographies can place intergenerational relationships under strain. Because of the nature of intergenerational transfers, and the impossibility of enforcing contracts necessary for the commercial provision of many intergenerational goods, most intergenerational exchange is mediated through family or government. There are enormous benefits to these exchanges, but in the case of governments, they require political will, and in the case of family, they require trust.

Most aged care is still provided by family; much child care is provided by grandparents. Depending on your starting point, existing generations provide environmental protection for future generations, or deplete the environment for future generations. R&D investment, often subsidised by government, will predominantly benefit future generations, a forward intergenerational good, with benefits flowing to younger generations. Government-funded retirement transfers, such as the Age Pension, are a backwards intergenerational good.

To maintain the institutional basis for these exchanges under demographic shift is challenging. Again, Australia is in a relatively favourable position. Its demographic change is slow and its policies are geared toward considerable self-sufficiency among the older generation.

Nevertheless, caution is required. The current older generations are resource-rich as a whole, but the wealth is unevenly spread. If policies, driven by the fiscal strains of demographic change, are adopted that disadvantage members of the younger generation who do not have access to parental resources, then this could well precipitate an intergenerational tendency toward increased intragenerational inequality. If home purchase cannot be achieved without parental aid, or university education becomes so expensive that only those with family resources will risk the debt, then we have the beginnings of a process where major conduits to wealth and human capital accumulation are denied to a segment of the next generation. This will happen only in the long term, but is all the more invidious for that. And once it has happened, it will be difficult to reverse.

Along with higher education, housing will likely continue to be a major channel for wealth accumulation for successive generations of Australians. But where in the past access to these conduits to affluence has been available to most, it is possible that in the future it will be accessible only to those with the liquidity to accumulate a substantial deposit. In many cases, these will be the same people as those with family resources behind them.

Tax revenues

Whatever we do, tax revenue will increase with an ageing demographic, and tax structure will need to be modified to meet the increased revenue requirement as tax bases change with changing population structure. We have a tax system where capital income tax is separated from the labour income tax. Major sources of capital income, the home and superannuation, are effectively taxed under an expenditure tax regime. To me, this is intuitively appealing. While there may be arguments for taxing the returns to both capital and labour income, there is no argument that the tax rates should be the same. Although some capital income taxation may be efficiency-improving, low capital income tax rates make economic sense. I find myself disagreeing with many tax analysts, that the way to increase tax revenue is to close the 'gaps' in the capital income tax base, whether it be the taxation of superannuation, negative gearing, or other capital income targets. This is not to say those tax structures could not be improved. But this is not the way to raise the revenue take.

Two avenues for increasing tax revenue present themselves. First, the GST. Through a broader base and an increased rate, for example 12 per cent, significantly more revenue could be raised. Because government benefits are indexed to prices, people who rely heavily on these as a source of income would be largely protected from the impacts of this tax increase. Low-income workers would be affected, however, as would self-funded retirees. To maintain overall progressivity, the two highest marginal rates in our personal income tax could be increased by two percentage points. This would impact in only a minor way on saving, because the major saving channels are protected from the capital income tax. It would of course impact labour incomes. But most people who earn at these levels of income are motivated by considerations other than disposable income per hour. The labour supply impact would be small. Overall, our taxation system, while it could be greatly improved, functions well. It would function just as well, and raise more revenue, with these two adjustments.

International interactions

At the moment, these are largely unmapped, another research program to be done. Some idea of the range of stage of demographic transition, and speed of adjustment, of our regional neighbours, is given in Figure 2. To see how these might matter, consider the following. China is currently still a young economy, but is ageing rapidly. The demographic dividend is still positive—it is a highly productive country, with relatively few dependants, old or young. In the next 15 to 20 years that will flip. The workforce will decline, and an ever larger cohort of older people will come to rely on what will be largely government pensions. This will likely change expenditure priorities in China. Instead of government spending on infrastructure, it will be spending on transfers that will flow to households. And direct foreign investment from China may decline as well. This will generate changes in the pattern of import demand, impacting Australia's terms of trade and overall welfare, and the shape and scale of our evolving infrastructure.

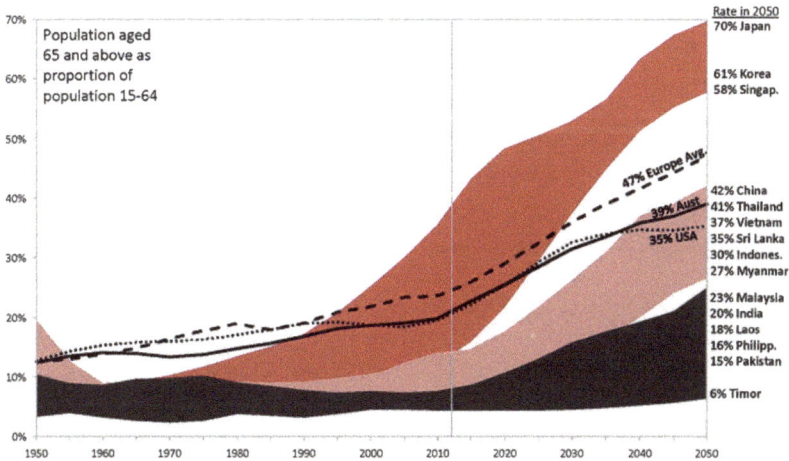

Figure 2. Population ageing: Dependency ratio
Source: Chomik and Piggott (2012).

Migration patterns will also change. There will likely be fewer migrants from China, more from Indonesia and India. Specific workforce requirements, such as for aged care, may be sourced from other countries, such as the Philippines.

Of course, this is just one scenario, and an oversimplified one at that. But Australia, as a small developed country with strong trade ties to the rapidly ageing and ever larger economies of Asia, will doubtless be affected by the unfolding demographic transition underway there. Surely a national policy challenge.

Acknowledgements

Financial support from the ARC Centre of Excellence in Population Ageing Research (CEPAR) (CE110001029) is gratefully acknowledged.

References

CEPAR (2014a). CEPAR Submission to the Financial System Inquiry, 31 March. ARC Centre of Excellence in Population Ageing Research, UNSW Business School, UNSW Australia.

CEPAR (2014b). CEPAR Supplementary Submission to the Financial System Inquiry, 12 June. ARC Centre of Excellence in Population Ageing Research, UNSW Business School, UNSW Australia.

CEPAR (2014c). CEPAR Submission Number 3 to the Financial System Inquiry: Drawdown defaults, 23 August. ARC Centre of Excellence in Population Ageing Research, UNSW Business School, UNSW Australia.

Chomik Rafal and Piggott John (2014). The Australian and United States Retirement Income System: Comparisons with and Lessons for the United States. In Olivia Mitchell and Richard Shea (Eds) *Re-imagining Pensions: The next 40 years*. Oxford: Oxford University Press, pp. 274–297.

Commonwealth of Australia (2009). *Australia's Future Tax System, Report to the Treasurer, December 2009, Part One: Overview*. Canberra: Department of Treasury.

Commonwealth of Australia (2015). *2015 Intergenerational Report: Australia in 2055*. Canberra: Department of Treasury, March 2015.

Conesa Juan Carlos, Kitao Sagiri and Krueger Dirk (2009). Taxing Capital? Not a Bad Idea after All! *American Economic Review*, 99(1): 25–48.

Glaeser Edward and Resseger Matthew (2010). The Complementarity Between Cities and Skills. *Journal of Regional Science*, 50(1): 221–244.

Hernaes Erik, Markussen Simen, Piggott John and Roed Knut (2016). Pension Reform and Labour Supply, *Journal of Economics*, 142: 39–55.

Hurd, Michael, Martorell Paco, Delavande Adeline, Mullen Kathleen and Langa Kenneth (2013). Monetary Costs of Dementia in the United States. *The New England Journal of Medicine*, 368: 1326–1334.

Kumru Cagri and Piggott John (2010). Social Resilience, Means-testing, and Capital Taxation—Reflections on Economic Paradigms in *Towards a More Resilient Society: Lessons from Economic Crises*. Report of the Social Resilience Project, October. Japan: The Japan Institute of International Affairs, pp. 45–56.

Piggott John and Whitehouse Edward (2011). Session 3: Paying for the Past, Providing for the Future: Intergenerational Solidarity. Issues Paper, OECD Ministerial Meeting on Social Policy, OECD Conference, Paris, 2–3 May.

Prskawetz Alexia and Sambt Joze (2014). Economic support and the demographic dividend in Europe. *Demographic Research*, 30(34): 963–1010.

Rice James, Temple Jeromey and McDonald Peter (2014). *National Transfer Accounts for Australia: 2003–04 and 2009–10 Detailed Results*. ARC Centre of Excellence in Population Ageing Research and Crawford School of Public Policy, The Australian National University. www.cepar.edu.au/media/134354/nta_report_2014.pdf.

Rohwedder Susann and Willis Robert (2010). Mental Retirement. *Journal of Economic Perspectives*, 24(1): 119–138.

Sefton James, van de Ven Justin and Weale Martin (2008). Means testing retirement benefits: Fostering equity or discouraging savings? *Economic Journal*, 188(528): 556–590.

Spijker Joroen and MacInnes John (2013). Population ageing: The timebomb that isn't? *BMJ*, 347. doi: 10.1136/bmj.f6598.

Whalley John and Yuan Yufei (2009). Global Financial Structure and Climate Change. *Journal of Financial Transformation*, 25: 161–168.

Yates Judith and Bradbury Bruce (2010). Home ownership as a (crumbling) fourth pillar of social insurance in Australia. *Journal of Housing and the Built Environment*, (25)2: 193–211.

Part 2. Population ageing: Global, regional and Australian perspectives

4

Ageing in Australia: Population changes and responses

Peter McDonald

Population ageing is the historical outcome of falling rates of fertility and mortality with fertility having the larger effect. While population ageing has only occupied the minds of policymakers since the 1980s, Australia's population has been ageing continuously for over a century. Figure 1 shows that ageing accelerated in the late 1920s and the 1930s. This was because of the substantial fall in fertility that occurred during the 1920s and the sustained low levels of fertility during the 1930s as a result of the economic depression (Figure 2). Counter to the long-term trend, the population stopped ageing in the 1950s and 1960s, this time as a result of the higher fertility that occurred during the 'baby boom' years. The number of births in Australia from 1946 to 1965 exceeded the number in the previous 20-year period by 1.63 million births. Today, those born in the 1946–65 period are beginning to enter the retirement ages and are replacing the much smaller generation that was born from 1926 to 1945. This is why the rate of population ageing accelerates from 2010 through to 2040 (Figure 1) but this acceleration was not inevitable. It became so only because of falls in fertility and mortality rates from the mid-1970s onwards.

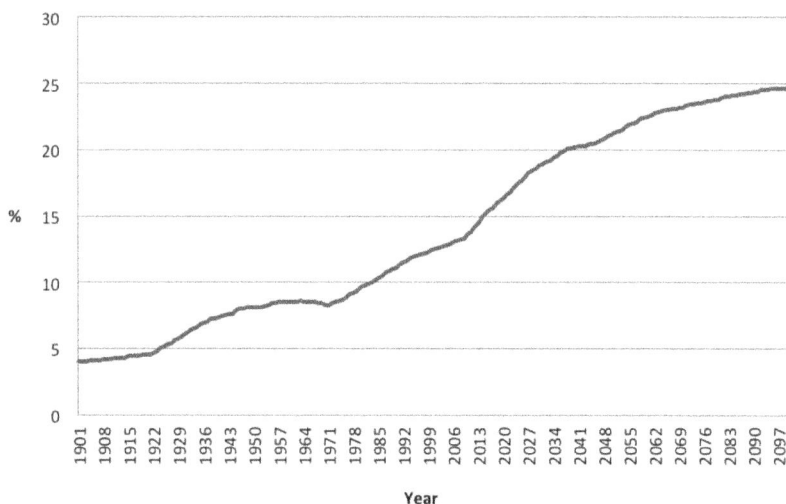

Figure 1. The percentage of the Australian population aged 65 years and over, 1901–2097

Sources: Produced by the author from Australian Bureau of Statistics. *Australian Historical Population Statistics 2014*. ABS Catalogue No. 3105.0.65.001. www. abs.gov.au/AUSSTATS/abs@.nsf/ProductsbyCatalogue/632CDC28637CF57ECA 256F1F0080EBCC?OpenDocument and Australian Bureau of Statistics (2013).

That the extent of population ageing today was not inevitable is illustrated by examination of the report of the National Population Inquiry (NPI) (1975). In the early 1970s, the Australian Government instigated a national population inquiry led by WD Borrie. In the Inquiry's report, the most comprehensive report on Australia's population ever undertaken, population ageing received only passing reference and no mention at all in relation to policy. Indicative population projections from 1970 to 2070 forecast that the proportion of the population aged 65 years and over would peak at between 9 and 15 per cent, with this peak being reached by 2030 (NPI 1975, 1: 294). In only two of the Inquiry's six indicative projections did the proportion aged 65 years and over peak at 12 per cent or more, a level that was in fact reached in 1996. The reason the Inquiry failed to predict the future level of population ageing is that the demography of Australia changed dramatically soon after the report was completed.

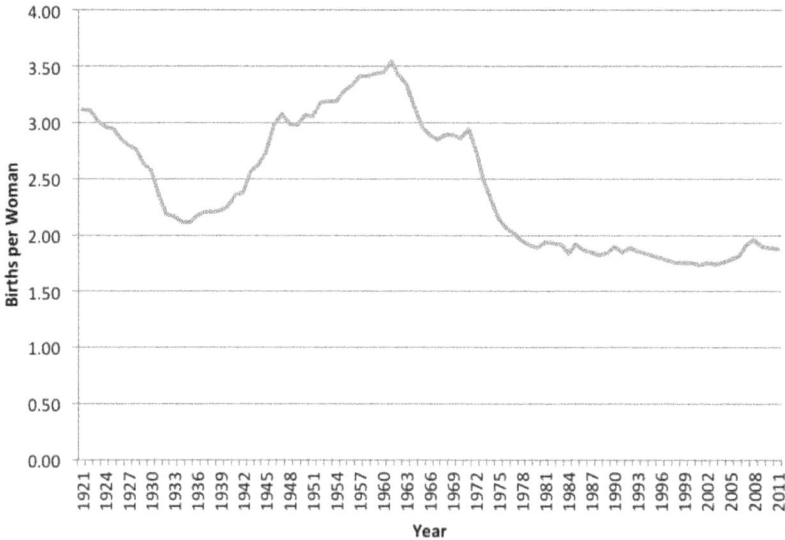

Figure 2. Total fertility rates, Australia, 1921–2011

Source: Produced by the author from Australian Bureau of Statistics. *Australian Historical Population Statistics 2014*. ABS Catalogue No. 3105.0.65.001. www. abs.gov.au/AUSSTATS/abs@.nsf/ProductsbyCatalogue/632CDC28637CF57ECA 256F1F0080EBCC?OpenDocument and Australian Bureau of Statistics (2015).

From around 1975, both fertility and mortality rates in Australia fell much more rapidly than had been assumed in the projections. The fertility rate in Australia in 1972, the last year for which the authors of the report had data, was 2.74 births per woman. By 1980, the rate had fallen to 1.89 births per woman and it has remained around that level ever since (Figure 2). Also from around 1972 onwards, death rates at older ages in Australia fell rapidly after having been almost constant in the previous 50 years (Figure 3). For example, in 1920–22, the expectation of life for Australian men at age 65 was 12 years. This was little changed at 12.2 years in 1970–72. However, by 2010–12, it had increased significantly to 19.1 years. Thus, while it is often said that population ageing today is driven by the baby boom generation reaching the older ages, this is only the case because of the massive reductions in both fertility and mortality that occurred from the early 1970s onwards.

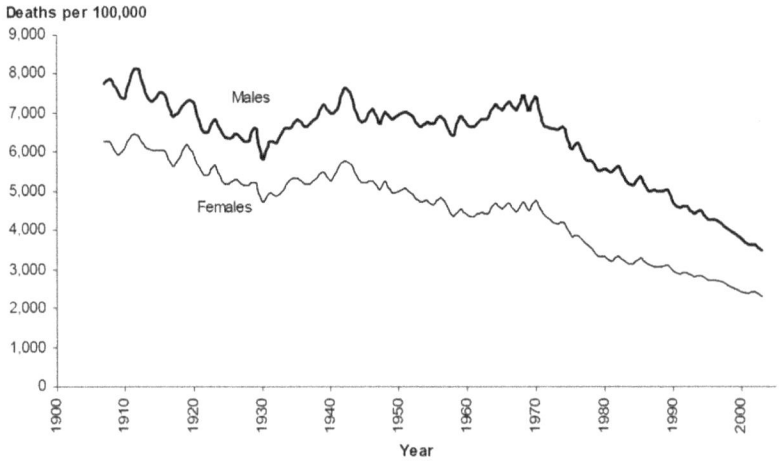

Figure 3. Age-specific death rates, 65–84 years, Australia, 1907–2003
Source. Australian Institute of Health and Welfare (2006), Figure 6.3: 109.

Population ageing in Australia

As shown in Figure 1, in the period 2012–36, ageing in Australia increases at a sharper rate than at any other time in the 200-year history shown in the figure. In numerical terms, the percentage of the population aged 65 years and over increases from 13.8 per cent in 2012 to 19.8 per cent in 2036. Subsequently, the speed of ageing slows. Figure 4 shows the changes in the age structure of the Australian population between 2011 and 2061 as estimated by the Australian Bureau of Statistics (ABS). The two age distributions are 'bee-hive' shaped, a relatively favourable outcome (McDonald and Kippen 1999) as the bulk of the population remains concentrated in the working ages and, by 2061, in the middle working ages rather the older working ages. As discussed below, this is a much more favourable outcome than most OECD countries, providing Australia with a relative advantage. The favourable outcome is the result of a relatively high fertility rate projected into the future in association with a high level of migration, with the migrants being mainly young adults. Table 1 shows the impact of four different levels of migration upon future levels of ageing in Australia. With zero net migration, the percentage of the population aged 65 years and over would increase from 14 per cent in 2013 to 28.4 per cent in 2053. With migration of 300,000 per annum, only 21.2 per cent of the population would be aged 65 years and over in 2053. The ABS projections shown in Figure 4 are based on the assumption that annual net migration will be 240,000 per annum. The percentages in the working ages, 15–64 years, move in the opposite direction, being six points higher with the high level of immigration compared with zero migration.

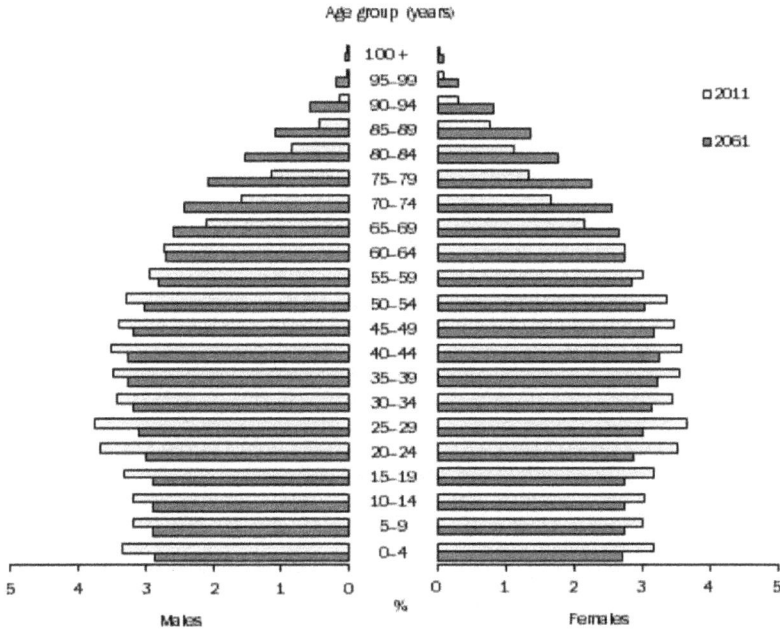

Figure 4. Australia's age distributions in 2011 and 2061
Source: Australian Bureau of Statistics (2013): 40.

Table 1. Long-term demographic assumptions in the 2002 and 2015 Intergenerational Reports and the 2003 and 2013 projections of the Australian Bureau of Statistics

	Total fertility rate (births per woman)	Annual net migration (000's)	Expectation of life at birth in 2051(years)	
			Males	Females
IGR 2002	1.6	90	83.2	88.2
IGR 2015	1.9	215	87.5	90.1
ABS 2003	1.6	100	84.2	87.7
ABS 2013	1.8	240	84.2	87.7

Sources: Commonwealth of Australia (2015); Australian Bureau of Statistics (2003); Australian Bureau of Statistics (2013).

Why population ageing matters

Population ageing matters to governments because of the typical age pattern of consumption and income as shown in Figure 5. Per capita consumption is much lower than per capita income at the older ages and becomes increasingly so as people get older. This deficit must be met from either public or private sources and, to the extent that the deficit is met from public sources, governments are faced with an increasingly more difficult fiscal situation the greater the proportion of the population in the older ages. This is shown more directly in Figure 6 in terms of government revenue and expenditure. Per capita expenditure exceeds per capita taxation from about age 62 onwards and the gap gets increasingly wider as age increases. In net terms, a typical 78-year-old costs all governments in Australia about $24,000 per annum while the typical 43-year-old benefits government revenue by around $15,000 per annum. The more the population consists of 78-year-olds rather than 43-year-olds, the greater the fiscal challenge for governments.

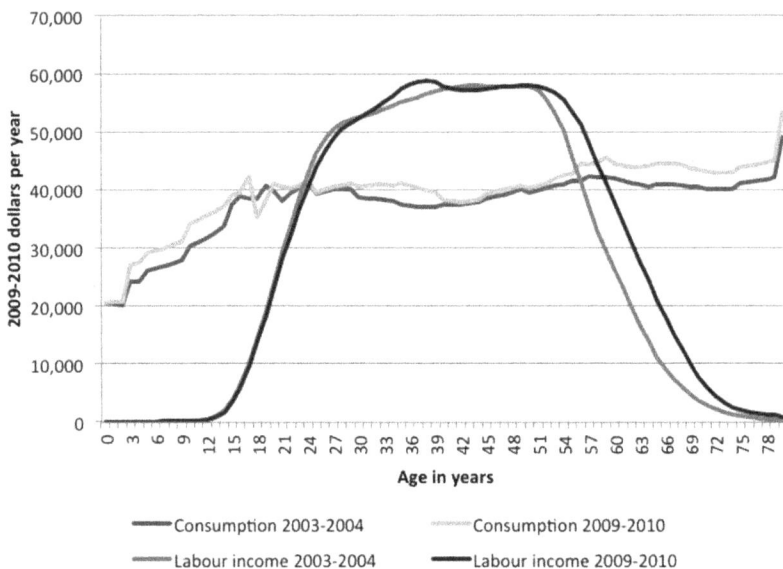

Figure 5. Per capita consumption and income by age, Australia, 2003–04 and 2009–10

Source: Rice, Temple and McDonald (2014): 11.

This fiscal challenge is addressed by the Australian Government once every four years in the series of Intergenerational Reports (IGR) (Commonwealth of Australia 2002, 2007, 2010 and 2015). As required by the government's Charter of Budget Honesty Act 1998:

> An Inter-Generational report is to assess the long term sustainability of current government policies over 40 years by taking account of the financial implications of demographic change (Commonwealth of Australia 2002: iii).

The first Intergenerational Report narrowed this to:

> The report provides a basis for considering the Commonwealth's fiscal outlook over the long term, and identifying emerging issues associated with an ageing population (Commonwealth of Australia 2002: iii).

The models used in the IGRs treat demography as exogenous, that is, demography trends simply to occur without being influenced by the economic or social outcomes of the model. This is despite the fact that international migration is almost certainly endogenous, that is, a product of future social and economic trends, and its level is subject to government policy. The IGRs do not talk about migration as a policy instrument despite the growing body of literature (see below) showing that migration in the long term has substantial impacts on the economy and therefore upon the government's fiscal outcome. Fertility and mortality are 'less endogenous' than migration but expenditure on health interventions reduces mortality and international comparisons show that work-family policy explains why some advanced economies have very low fertility and others do not (McDonald 2006).

The implicit IGR assumption is that demographic trends are slow to change. Accordingly, the demography can be included as an assumed input model without much danger of being wrong. However, if we compare the demographic assumptions of the 2003 IGR with those used in the 2015 IGR (Table 2), they are substantially different, indicating that the demography can change in a relatively short time-frame. An increase in the fertility rate from 1.6 to 1.9 births per woman may not appear to be a large change but the implications are substantial. An increase in annual net migration from 90,000 to 215,000 per annum is obviously considerable and, as demonstrated below, has a large impact on population and economic outcomes. Finally, the increases in the assumed expectation of life at birth in 2050 are 1.9 years higher for women and 4.3 years higher for men.

These changes imply a considerable increase in joint survival of partnered people. In relation to aged care, partners are the leading carers implying fiscal savings for governments as the providers of non-familial care.

Table 2. Impact of varying levels of net annual overseas migration on the age structure of the Australian population in 2053

Level of net annual overseas migration	Per cent of population aged 15–64 in 2053 (%)	Per cent of population aged 65 and over in 2053 (%)
0	56	28.4
100,000	58	25.2
180,000	60	23.4
300,000	62	21.2
Per cent in 2013	67	14.0

Source: McDonald and Temple (2013).

The age structure effects of the changes in the demographic assumptions across the IGR reports is illustrated by considering the effects of similar changes in assumptions made in the ABS population projections published in 2003 and 2013 (Figure 7).[1] The figure shows by how much the 2051 projected population increased in each age group due to the changes in assumptions made in the 2003 ABS projections and in the 2013 ABS projections. The bar for age group 0–9 means that the 0–9 population in 2051 is 78 per cent higher in the 2013 ABS projections than it was in the 2003 projections. This means the future child population in 2051 almost doubles simply because of changes in the assumptions about future demography.

This large increase is due both to assumed fertility moving up from 1.6 to 1.9 births per woman and to the additional births born to net migration being 125,000 per annum higher in the 2013 projections than was assumed for the 2003 projections. It is sometimes said in error that migration does not slow the ageing of the population because migrants also age. The statement is wrong because, besides the fact that migrants with an average age at arrival of 25 years are younger on average than the general population (37.3 years), migrants also have a lot of births before they get old. Indeed, they have grandchildren before they get old.

---

1   The ABS projections are used because the age structure outcomes in the IGR projections are not published.

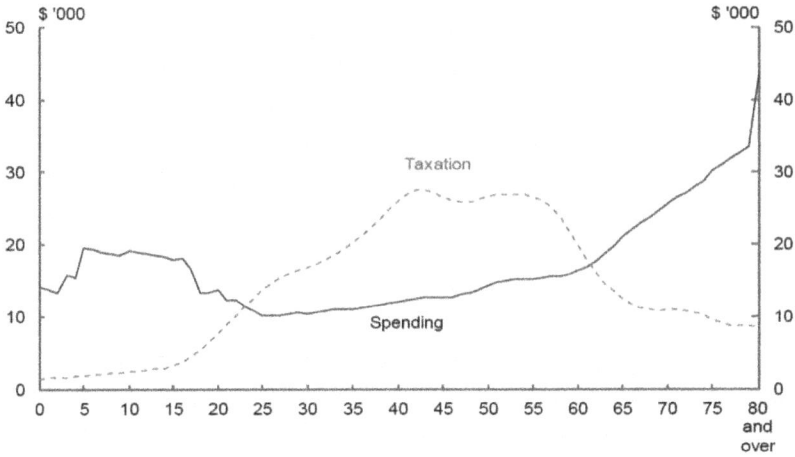

Figure 6. Per capita total government spending and taxes by age (total government means the Australian Government and State and Territory Governments), 2009–10

Source: Commonwealth of Australia (2015): 58, using data from Rice, Temple and McDonald (2014).

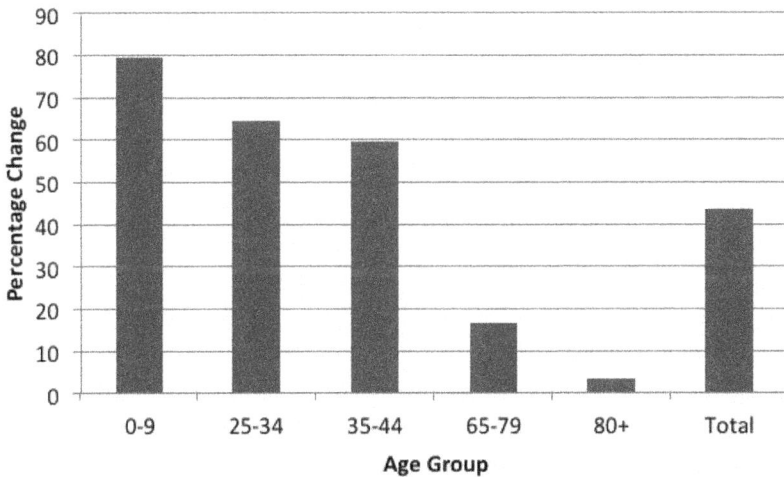

Figure 7. Percentage increase in the population in each age group in 2051 due to changes in the demographic assumptions made between the ABS 2003 and 2013 official population projections

Source: Produced by the author from data published in Australian Bureau of Statistics (2003) and Australian Bureau of Statistics (2013).

The changes in assumptions between the two projections also substantially increase the numbers in the young working ages (25–34 and 35–44) but the numbers at older ages do not increase very much at all, especially for the old-old age group (80+). If there is one demographic certainty, it is that, over 40 years, a projection of the population aged 80 and over will be relatively accurate as it will be affected only by errors in the mortality assumption. So, shifting from the 2003 IGR to the 2015 IGR, the future population of Australia becomes much younger. This has the following implications.

In relation to consumption (public and private), it makes no difference whether the person is age 15 or 79 or any age in between (Figure 5). The profile of age-specific consumption is flat. Consumption is lower for children under 15 and higher for those aged 80 and over. Importantly, this means that consumption expenditure is relatively resilient to changes in age structure. The real issue with ageing of the population is on the income side of the equation. Figure 5 shows that aggregate income is highly susceptible to changes in age structure. It also shows what a huge benefit it was to the aggregate bottom line that employment rates increased for persons aged 55 and over between 2003–04 and 2009–10. In relation to the fiscal bottom line, more children are a problem in the short-term because their income is far less than their consumption. But further out, the additional children already born since the 2003 IGR was published enter the labour force just at the time that the baby boom generation hits the old-old ages. This will have obvious benefits for the fiscal outcome. Furthermore, the additional children have been born to more educated women and to skilled migrants, thus we can expect them to have high levels of human capital when they hit the labour market.

The shape of income and expenditure for governments (Figure 6) is a little different from the aggregate (private and public) income and expenditure shown in Figure 4. Government expenditure is higher for children than for working-age Australians and rises with age from age 25 onwards and sharply from age 60 onwards. Taxation revenue mirrors the aggregate income curve of Figure 4 except for the fact that children and older people are also tax generators. This is particularly the case in relation to the Goods and Services Tax (GST). In 2009–10 dollars, the average 13-year-old generated $1,500 per annum in GST and it would be a lot more if the GST was levied on fresh food and education, both major private expenditures for 13-year-olds. The average 80-year-old also pays about $1,500 in GST and this also would be a lot more if the GST covered fresh food. Income tax, not unexpectedly, is closely related to income-earning and this is the key reason that changes in age structure put governments under fiscal pressure.

In summary, the income side of the government's fiscal situation is much more sensitive to changes in age structure than is the expenditure side. It is important that government expenditure is efficient and equitable and there are many improvements that can be made in this regard, but given the sensitivity of budgets to income rather than to expenditure as the age structure changes and with the successive IGRs consistently showing massive increases in living standards over the 40 years, it seems reasonable to think that much of the solution to population ageing may lie on the income side of the equation. Aside from taxation, the income side of the government's equation is aided by migration and by increases in labour force participation, and government fiscal outcomes swing massively on future growth in labour productivity. All three of the three Ps (productivity, participation and population), therefore, have important impacts in the context of population ageing.

The impact of immigration on future GDP per capita

Per capita gross domestic product, a frequently used measure of living standard, is the product of the employment to population ratio and output per worker. If the employment to population ratio falls because of population ageing, GDP per capita will also fall unless there is a commensurate rise in output per worker (labour productivity). However, the Australian employment to population ratio rises with increases in migration (McDonald and Temple 2013). This means that if labour productivity is at least as high for migrants as it is for non-migrants, migration will increase the growth rate of GDP per capita. The effect of varying migration levels upon the future growth rate of GDP per capita in Australia is shown in Figure 7, under the assumption that labour productivity is the same for migrants as for non-migrants, and its growth rate is constant across the projection period at 1.6 per cent per annum. The ageing of the population (fall in the employment to population ratio) has a large impact on the growth rate of GDP per capita between 2013 and 2023 because of the retirement from the labour force of the baby boom generation. For example, with zero migration, the growth rate of GDP per capita would fall from 1.83 per cent in 2013 to 1.33 per cent in 2023 simply because of the ageing of the population. The figure shows that this impact is mitigated to a meaningful extent by migration both in the short-term and the long-term. The impact of the additional births to migrants has an evident secondary impact on the growth of GDP per capita in the 2030s and 2040s.

Beyond this employment to population ratio effect on the growth of GDP per capita, if migrants are more skilled than non-migrants or if migrants fill pivotal roles in new investment endeavours, migration will also have the effect of increasing labour productivity. There is some evidence that this is the case in that the education levels of migrants are well above the general education level of the population. Furthermore, contrary to the popular perception, two studies have shown that migration in Australia, through its stimulatory effects, increases the wages of low-wage workers (Peri, Docquier and Ozden 2010; Migration Council of Australia 2015). In the international comparative study, this result was only evident for two countries, Australia and Singapore, both of which run large skilled migration programs (Peri, Docquier and Ozden 2010).

There is also an argument that young workers are an important source of economic dynamism and that they are the assimilators of new technology in each era of new technology (McDonald and Temple 2006). The skilled migration program that Australia runs substantially shifts the median age of the labour force to a younger age than would be the case with no migration. Many new skilled immigrants are recent graduates of the Australian university system and therefore can be expected to have skills that are well honed to the needs of the Australian labour market (Migration Council of Australia 2015). Over the next 40 years, largely because of migration, Australia will experience significant increases in the number of its young workers. Many other OECD countries will experience the opposite: rapidly declining numbers in the young working ages.

International comparisons of population ageing

Among OECD countries, there is a bifurcation of countries according to the current level of fertility. One set of countries, that includes all of the Nordic countries, all of the English-speaking countries and all of the French- and Dutch-speaking countries, have fertility rates of 1.7 births per woman and above. The other set of countries, that includes all of the Southern European countries, all of the German-speaking countries and all of the advanced East Asian countries (including China), have fertility rates that are below 1.5 births per woman (McDonald 2006). Population ageing is much more severe in countries with very low fertility.

Across countries, there is considerable variation in the speed and extent of population ageing. Essentially, there are two groups of countries: those where fertility fell to near-replacement level by the 1930s and those where fertility has fallen from the 1950s onwards. For the first group of countries, essentially European countries and the advanced English-speaking countries, the most rapid period of ageing is from 2010 to 2030, mainly because most of these countries experienced post-war baby booms and all have experienced falls in mortality rates at older ages since the 1970s. The baby boom was largest in the United States, Canada, Australia and New Zealand and moderately large in almost all Western and Northern European countries but small in the Southern European countries (van Bavel and Reher 2013). However, as described above for Australia, contemporary ageing is also affected by the levels of fertility and migration since the 1970s. Variations in ageing across these countries from 2010 to 2030 are shown in Figure 8. By 2030, Australia will be the 'youngest' of all of these countries according to the United Nations, followed by the other English-speaking countries and then the Nordic countries. As these were the countries that had the largest baby booms, it is evident that the relatively high levels of fertility in all of these countries, and for some high levels of migration, have offset the ageing effect of the baby boom generation to some extent. Despite relatively low fertility and a sizeable baby boom, Switzerland ages only slowly between 2010 and 2030 because of its expected high levels of migration. The 'oldest' of these countries will be Italy and Germany because of sustained low levels of fertility.

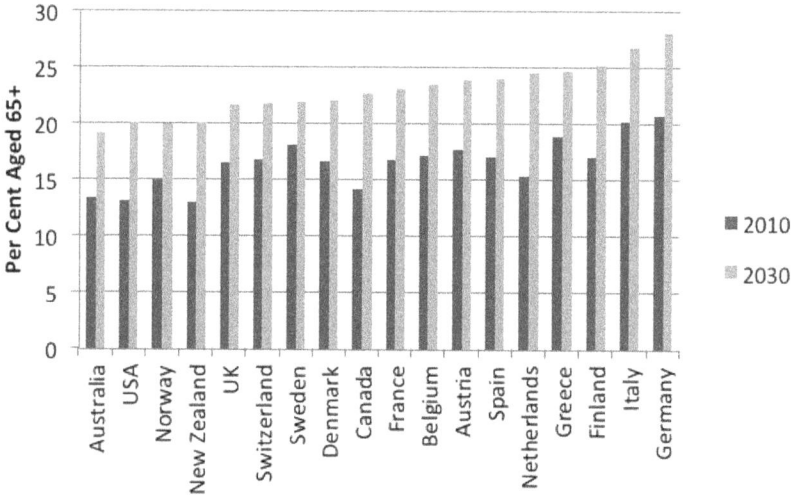

Figure 8. Percentage of population aged 65 years and over, 2010 and 2030

Source: United Nations, Department of Economic and Social Affairs, Population Division: esa. un.org/unpd/wpp/unpp/panel_indicators.htm.

In the countries where fertility has fallen from high levels only since the 1950s, ageing is determined by the speed, recentness and level of the country's fertility decline. When the fertility rate falls rapidly, a large generation is followed fairly closely by a small generation. When the large generation reaches the older ages the subsequent smaller generations are in the working ages, leading to rapid population ageing. The recentness of the fertility decline, of course, determines the time at which the large generation reaches the older ages. Finally, the extent of the fertility decline, the most important of the three factors, determines the difference in the sizes of the successive generations. There seems also to be a relationship between the speed and the level of the decline. Countries that experienced a very rapid fall in fertility tend also to be the countries where fertility has fallen to very low levels (under 1.5 births per woman).

Figure 9 shows the extent of ageing across selected Asian countries from 2010 to 2050. In the countries where ageing is not so prominent in 2050 (the Philippines, India, Indonesia and Malaysia), fertility has fallen slowly over the past 40–50 years and still remains above the replacement level. For the other countries in Figure 9 (except for Japan), the extent of population ageing is very great in the next 40 years. This is because fertility fell very rapidly between 1970 and 2000 in these countries and, in China,[2] Singapore, Thailand and Korea, fertility has fallen to very low levels. Japan was older in 2010 than most of the countries in Figure 8 will be in 2030, and it gets much older over the next 50 years. This is essentially the result of very low fertility sustained over a long period.

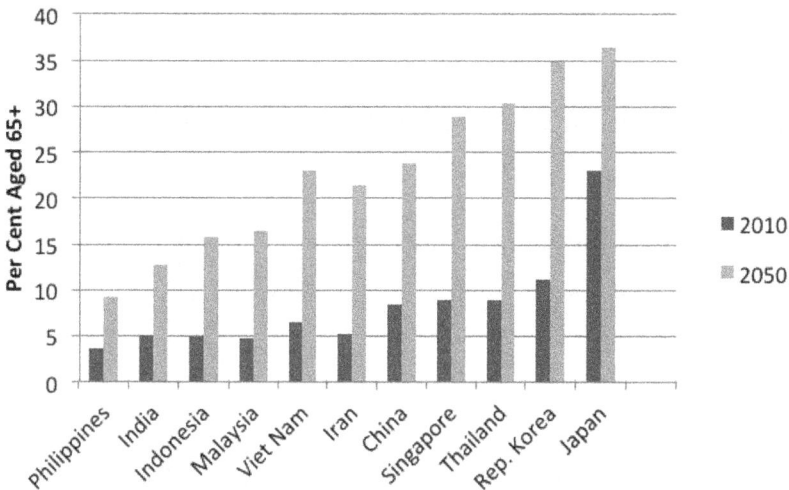

Figure 9. Percentage of population aged 65 years and over, 2010 and 2050

Source: United Nations, Department of Economic and Social Affairs, Population Division. esa. un.org/unpd/wpp/unpp/panel_indicators.htm.

2   The Wittgenstein Centre also produces population projections for all countries of the world. Its projection of the percentage of the population of China aged 65 years and over in 2050 (28 per cent) is much higher than the United Nations level shown in Figure 9 (23 per cent) (Lutz, Butz and KC 2014). The two agencies differ on what is the current level of fertility in China. I consider that the Wittgenstein Centre estimate is more reliable. Differences for other countries shown in Figures 8 and 9 are small.

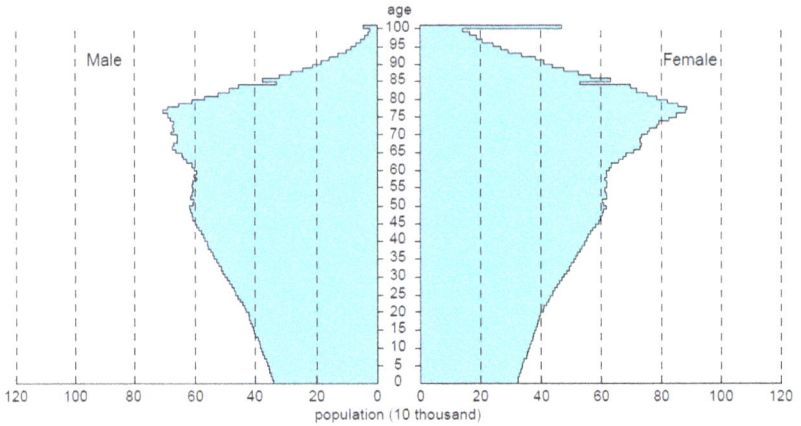

Figure 10. The 2050 age distribution of Japan

Source: National Institute of Population and Social Security Research (2002): 11.

The age distribution of Japan in 2050 (Figure 10) contrasts dramatically with that of Australia (Figure 4). In Japan in 2050, the largest numbers of people are aged between 75 and 80 and the age structure tapers downwards with ever smaller numbers as the age gets younger. The working-age population is comparatively old with a considerable shortage of young workers. This age structure has been referred to as the 'coffin' shape (McDonald and Kippen 1999) and, indeed, if the demography of Japan were to remain unchanged, the population would largely disappear in the 100 years after 2050. For many years, the Government of Japan has been attempting to raise the fertility rate so that the longer-term future is rosier than this, but, to date, fertility has remained below 1.5 births per woman and Japan is still heading on this trajectory. If the fertility rate were to increase in the future, the Japanese economy would still face a major struggle to support its aged population before the new larger generation reached the labour force ages. There are no easy solutions to this dilemma, especially when Japan already has a high debt to GDP ratio.

Concluding remark

The Intergenerational Reports produced by the Department of Treasury have focused on the challenges that Australia faces because of population ageing. These challenges are addressed in other chapters. However, it is important to note that with every successive IGR, the projected population is relatively younger than in the previous one. This is because the Australian fertility rate has risen and is close to the replacement rate and because the level of international migration has increased substantially. It is important that these favourable demographic trends continue. As shown in the analysis above, by 2030, Australia will be the youngest among the English-speaking countries and the countries of Western Europe. It will also be younger than many of the current advanced economies in Asia. Thus, from the demographic perspective, Australia is in a favourable position. This means that accommodating to population ageing becomes a matter of long-term sensible planning not hasty short-term fixes.

References

Australian Bureau of Statistics (2003). *Population Projections Australia, 2002–2101*. Canberra: ABS Australian Bureau of Statistics.

Australian Bureau of Statistics (2013). Population Projections, Australia. ABS Cat. No. 3222.0. Canberra: Australian Bureau of Statistics.

Australian Bureau of Statistics (2015). Australian Demographic Statistics, September 2014. ABS Cat. No. 3101.0. Canberra: Australian Bureau of Statistics.

Australian Institute of Health and Welfare (AIHW) (2006). Mortality over the twentieth century in Australia: Trends and patterns in major causes of death. Cat. no. PHE 73. Canberra: AIHW.

Commonwealth of Australia (2002). *Intergenerational Report: 2002–03*. Canberra: Department of Treasury.

Commonwealth of Australia (2007). *Intergenerational Report: 2007.* Canberra: Department of Treasury.

Commonwealth of Australia (2010). *Australia to 2050: Future Challenges. The 2010 Intergenerational Report.* Canberra: Department of Treasury.

Commonwealth of Australia (2015). *2015 Intergenerational Report: Australia in 2055.* Canberra: Department of Treasury.

Lutz Wolfgang, Butz William and KC Samir (2014). *World Population and Human Capital in the 21st Century.* Oxford: Oxford University Press.

McDonald Peter (2006). Low fertility and the state: The efficacy of policy. *Population and Development Review*, 32(3): 485–510.

McDonald Peter and Kippen Rebecca (1999). *Population futures for Australia: The policy alternatives.* Parliamentary Library Seminar Series, Research Paper No. 5, 1999, Canberra: Australian Parliamentary Library.

McDonald Peter and Temple Jeromy (2006). *Immigration and the Supply of Complex Problem Solvers in the Australian Economy.* Canberra: Department of Immigration and Multicultural Affairs. www.immi.gov.au/media/publications/research/index.htm.

McDonald Peter and Temple Jeromy (2013). *The Long Term Effects of Ageing and Immigration upon Labour Supply and Per Capita Gross Domestic Product: Australia 2012–2062*, Final Report, Canberra, October.

Migration Council of Australia (2015). *The Economic Impact of Migration.* Canberra: Migration Council of Australia.

National Institute of Population and Social Security Research (NIPSSR) (2002). *Population Projections for Japan: 2001–2050.* Tokyo: NIPSSR.

National Population Inquiry (1975). *Population and Australia: A Demographic Analysis and Projection*, 2 volumes. Canberra: Australian Government Publishing Service.

Peri Giovanni, Docquier Frederic and Ozden Cagler (2010). *The Wage Effects of Immigration and Emigration*, NBER Working Paper No. 16646.

Rice James, Temple Jeromy and McDonald Peter (2014). *National Transfer Accounts for Australia: 2003–04 and 2009–10 Detailed Results*. ARC Centre of Excellence in Population Ageing Research and Crawford School of Public Policy, The Australian National University. www.cepar.edu.au/media/134354/nta_report_2014.pdf.

van Bavel Jan and Reher David (2013). The baby boom and its causes: what we know and what we don't know. *Population and Development Review*, 39(2): 257–288.

5

Declining fertility and the rising costs of children and the elderly in Japan and other selected Asian countries: An analysis based upon the NTA approach

Naohiro Ogawa, Rikiya Matsukura and Sang-Hyop Lee

Since the late 1960s, the growth of the world population has been steadily slowing down, primarily owing to an almost worldwide decline of fertility. Because of the reduction in world population growth rates in the second half of the 20th century, the outlook we have today is substantially different from the one we had a few decades ago. It is often mentioned by some demographers that while the 20th century was the century of 'population explosion', the 21st is likely to become the century of 'population ageing' (Lutz et al. 2004).

At present, 60 per cent of the world population resides in Asia, and, of this percentage, almost half live in societies with below-replacement fertility. In particular, East Asia's fertility has been at the lowest level in the world in recent decades. In addition, mortality has been steadily improving over the past several decades, particularly in East and Southeast Asia. As a consequence of these demographic shifts, numerous Asian countries have been experiencing rapid population ageing, which is also being reflected in the increasing number of reports on a host of population ageing–related problems in the popular press in these countries. To address these ageing-related issues, a new analytical methodology called National Transfer Accounts (NTA) has been developed in the past 10 years (Lee and Mason 2011).

By drawing heavily upon the NTA system, Ogawa et al. (2015) have recently attempted to (1) examine, on the basis of a pool of time-series data, primarily from three low-fertility East Asian countries or areas (Japan, South Korea and Taiwan), the nexus between the direct public and private costs of children and the number of children that parents would raise during their reproductive span; and (2) investigate whether or not there exists a competing relationship between the young and the aged as recipients of private and public financial resources in the three East Asian countries. Along a similar line of interest, this chapter will expand the scope of analysis by adding a few more Asian countries (China, India, Thailand, the Philippines, and Vietnam) and by utilising more recent data for Japan and South Korea.

In the next section, we briefly highlight fertility, mortality and age compositional transformations that occurred over the last few decades in Japan and neighbouring East Asian countries (South Korea and Taiwan). In the subsequent section, some of the basic features of the system of NTA, which serves as the basic analytical framework of the present study, are succinctly presented. Following the NTA approach, we then analyse, for illustrative purposes, Japan's changing pattern of intergenerational transfers, both public and familial, over the past 25 years, especially focusing on the cost of children and the elderly. By combining computational results for Japan with those for seven other selected Asian countries (South Korea, Taiwan, China, India, Thailand, the Philippines, and Vietnam), we estimate the relationship between the cost of children and the fertility rate in those economies. In addition, we test, by employing a pooled dataset on the cost of children and the cost of the elderly, the applicability of the 'crowding out' hypothesis to these selected Asian countries. The final section summarises the major findings in the present study.

Declining fertility and population ageing in East Asia

According to the most recent vital statistics available in the three East Asian countries, Taiwan's Total Fertility Rate (TFR) for 2013 was 1.07 children, the lowest among the three nations, followed by South Korea (1.24 children for 2014) and Japan (1.43 children for 2013). In hope of raising fertility, the three East Asian countries have been implementing a wide range of pronatalist policies and programs, but have had only limited success so far (Retherford and Ogawa 2009; Ogawa et al. 2015).

In Asia as a whole, Japan was the first country to experience a steep fertility decline. Furthermore, the magnitude of Japan's TFR decline, which occurred in post-war years, was one of the greatest among all industrialised nations. In fact, following a short baby boom period (1947–49), Japan's TFR declined by more than 50 per cent, from 4.54 to 2.04, during 1947–57. This dramatic reduction of fertility over a single decade is the first such experience in recorded history. Subsequent to this unprecedented fertility reduction in the 1950s, there were only minor fluctuations around the replacement level until the first oil crisis of 1973. Thereafter, the TFR started to fall again, hitting the 1.26 mark in 2005, which was an all-time low in Japan's modern history. It should be noted, however, that, after 2005, the Japanese TFR slowly recovered to 1.43 in 2013. Nonetheless, if fertility were to remain constant at the current level, each new generation would decline by 31 per cent.

East Asia's rapidly declining fertility has been attracting a substantial amount of attention, inside and outside the region in the past few decades. In contrast, however, a relatively limited amount of attention has been paid to the rapidity with which the mortality transition has been under way in the region over the past several decades. Japan's unprecedented mortality transition is a good illustration. Japan's life expectancy at birth in 1960 was 65.3 years for men and 70.2 years for women, and these two values were the lowest life expectancies among the OECD member countries at that time (Mason and Ogawa 2001). However, by the mid-1970s, Japanese life expectancy for both sexes combined became one of the highest among the OECD members. In 2013, Japan's male life expectancy at birth exceeded 80.2 years to become the fourth highest in the world, while its female life expectancy rose to 86.6 years, the highest in the world (National Institute of Population and Social Security Research 2015). As regards South Korea and Taiwan, the corresponding figures for females in 2013 were 85.1 and 82.8 years, respectively, and for males, 78.5 and 76.4 years (Statistics Korea n.d.; Department of Statistics, Ministry of the Interior, Republic of China (Taiwan) n.d.).

Because of such long-term transformations in both fertility and mortality, the age structures of the three East Asian economies have been shifting to a marked extent. In the case of Japan, the proportion of those aged 65 and over increased from 4.9 per cent in 1950 to 24.1 per cent in 2014, which indicates that Japan's population is currently the oldest in the world. In sharp contrast, the number of those aged below 15 has been declining for 33 consecutive years from 1982 to 2014, and Japan now has fewer children than at any time in the past 100 years (Statistics Bureau, Ministry of Internal Affairs and Communications, Japan 2015).

Moreover, although Japan's elderly population reached the 10 per cent level in 1984 and was the last to do so among the industrialised nations, Japan became the first industrialised country in which the aged comprise more than 20 per cent of the total population. The length of time required for the increase from 10 to 20 per cent was only 21 years. Compared with European countries such as Sweden and Norway, Japan is ageing approximately three times as fast. In addition, in the first half of the 21st century, both South Korea and Taiwan are projected to age faster than Japan despite the fact that the onset of the population ageing phenomena there came with a delay compared to Japan, with Taiwan catching up with Japan by 2054, and South Korea by 2059 (Ogawa et al. 2015)

What can the National Transfer Accounts (NTA) do?

With a view to analysing a host of socioeconomic and demographic problems caused by age structural transformation, the NTA Global Project, an international collaborative research project, was launched a few years after the turn of the century. At present, a total of 46 countries, including Australia, are participating. The project's principal objective is to develop the NTA, a methodological system for measuring economic flows across age groups, for each of the member countries.

Societies take different approaches to reallocating resources from surplus to deficit ages, and there are two possible methods. One is reliance on capital markets. Namely, individuals accumulate capital during their working lives and, when they are no longer productive, they support their consumption in old age by relying on capital income (interest, dividends, rental income, profits, etc.) and by liquidating their assets. The other method relies on transfers from those at surplus ages to those at deficit ages. Some of these transfers are mediated by the public sector, but many are private transfers, of which familial transfers are most important. The material needs of young children are fulfilled mostly by their parents, which is true everywhere in the world. In most Asian societies, familial transfers between adult children and the elderly are also very important. Some of these transfers are between households, but intra-household transfers seem to be of more importance, since family members in Asia tend to form multigeneration households that involve large intergenerational transfers.

The NTA provides a comprehensive framework for estimating consumption, production, and resource reallocations by age. The accounts are constructed so as to be consistent with and complementary to the National Income and Product Accounts (NIPA). The NTA are being constructed with sufficient historical depth to allow for analysis of key features of the transfer system, and can also be projected into the future and thus enable us to analyse the economic and policy implications of future demographic changes. Furthermore, sectoral disaggregation allows the analysis of public and private education and health care spending. It should be noted, however, that no gender differentiation is incorporated in the NTA system, except in an experimental way.

It is worth noting that a comprehensive volume containing numerous NTA country reports, and several chapters on the methodological basis of NTA and intercountry comparative analysis on selected topics, has already been published (Lee and Mason 2011). Furthermore, an NTA manual was published by the United Nations Population Division in 2013, intended for national experts and planners who are interested in constructing the NTA system for their country.

Calculating the private and public costs of children and the elderly

(a) Plausible theoretical links between the costs of children and the elderly

According to the data gleaned in the three most recent rounds (2002, 2005, 2010, Kaneko et al. 2008 and NIPSSR 2011) of the Japanese National Fertility Survey conducted by the National Institute of Population and Social Security Research (NIPSSR), the high cost of children remains the most important reason for having fewer children among married women of reproductive age below 50. The survey respondents were asked to select as many possible replies as they wished from 13 precoded responses in order to explain why they did not intend to have their ideal number of children. The response category that attracted the largest number of responses was 'because rearing and educating children requires too much money'.

The foregoing result is consistent with what Becker's economic theory of fertility (1960, 1981) states. According to an essential idea of the Becker model, if parents spend a greater amount of resources on a child, they derive greater satisfaction because the child is of 'higher quality'. In Becker's fertility model, to increase the amount of satisfaction in the conditions where there is a higher private cost for having children, the parents opt for the substitution of quality for quantity of children, thus operating to decrease fertility. Consequently, Becker's model suggests that there exists a trade-off between the number of children in the family and the quality of children. It should also be stressed that, besides private costs of children, public spending on children may also play an important role in determining the quality and quantity of children parents have. For example, subsidising the quality of children reduces the private cost of acquiring high-quality children, thus leading to higher fertility.

More importantly, the trade-off between spending and the number of children is related to generational equity. Preston (1984) has raised the possibility that population ageing will lead to a decline in the welfare of children relative to the welfare of the elderly. In Japan, the cost of the elderly has been rising in parallel with the cost of children, partly owing to the maturity of the pension programs (Ogawa and

Retherford 1997; Ogawa, Chawla and Matsukura 2010). In addition, as a consequence of the increased political power of the elderly induced by rapid population ageing, and due to the fact that the Japanese government's budgetary resources are severely constrained, it is highly conceivable that a 'crowding out' effect between the resources directed to the young and to the elderly might be occurring.

(b) Age-specific profiles of per capita private and public consumption for children and the elderly

Before proceeding any further, it should be pointed out that a fuller explanation of the NTA's basic concepts, containing the crucial computational assumptions, definitions of other key variables, and the theoretical consideration behind each key equation is available on the NTA website (www.ntaccounts.org). In this subsection, therefore, we confine ourselves to discussing primarily how the direct public and private costs of rearing children and supporting the elderly are computed in the NTA system.

In NTA, consumption, both private and public, is comprised of education, health, and other consumption (food, clothing, housing, durables, etc.). Moreover, because the young population, particularly at school ages, has little or no labour income, its consumption is virtually equal to the direct costs of raising children. In contrast, the direct living costs of the elderly need to be calculated as a difference between their consumption and labour income. In addition, it should be noted that, although the foregone income is an important part of the costs to be incurred in rearing children and taking care of elderly persons, it falls outside the scope of this paper.

The age-specific profile of the per capita private education cost is estimated by applying a regression equation to the micro-level data gathered in a nationally representative household income and expenditure survey. In the case of Japan, the equation is applied to the six rounds (1984, 1989, 1994, 1999, 2004 and 2009) of the National Survey of Family Income and Expenditure (NSFIE), carried out by the Statistics Bureau of Japan. Similarly, the age-specific profile of the per capita private health care cost is also estimated on the basis of the same survey data, using a similar regression equation.

Furthermore, the age-specific profile of the per capita cost of private consumption, excluding private education and health, is estimated by a relatively simple *a priori* method, as shown below:

$$\alpha(a) = 1 - 0.6 \cdot D(4 < a < 20) \cdot \frac{20 - a}{16} - 0.6 \cdot D(a \leq 4) \quad (1)$$

Where $\alpha(a)$ = equivalence scale of age group a and $D(z)$ is a dummy variable that takes the value of 1 when condition z is met, but is otherwise zero. The computed equivalence scales at varying ages are as follows: 0.4 for the age group 0–4, and 1.0 for the age group 20 and over, whereas the scale values for the age group 5–19 increase linearly with age.

Now, let us discuss the public costs of children and the elderly. The age-specific profile of the per capita public education cost is computed by utilising the published data on the government expenditure for each level of education and the number of pupils and students at each level of education in 1984, 1989, 1994, 1999, 2004 and 2009. The age-specific profile of the per capita health care expenditure is estimated on the basis of published government data concerning age-specific outpatient and inpatient costs per case and age-specific incidence of receiving such medical treatments. In the case of per capita expenditure on public consumption in general (e.g. government employees' salaries, road maintenance costs, national defence, etc.), we assume that every person consumes equally, and simply divide the total annual expenditure for each component of public consumption, except for education and health, by the total population.

Using these computed results for age-specific profiles of various components of consumption, we estimate the age-specific profile of per capita consumption for 1984, 1989, 1994, 1999, 2004 and 2009, private and public sectors combined. In Figure 1, we have plotted for illustrative purposes the estimated results of per capita total consumption only for three selected years (1984, 1994 and 2009). For comparative purposes, we have also plotted the corresponding age-specific profiles of per capita production (labour income) for the three selected years. (For a more detailed methodological explanation pertaining to the per capita production profiles, see Ogawa, Mason, Chawla and Matsukura 2010). It should be also noted that these estimated results are expressed in terms of year 2000 constant prices.

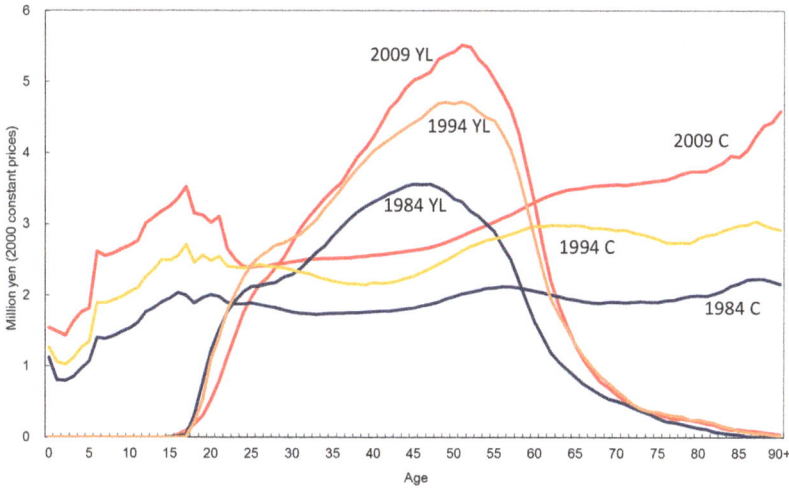

Figure 1. Age specific profiles for per capita consumption (C)
and production (YL): Japan, 1984, 1994 and 2009
Source: Provided by author.

A few points of interest can be derived from this graphical exposition. First, by drawing upon information contained in Figure 1, we can calculate the size of income-consumption deficits by age in 1984, 1994 and 2009. Throughout the time under review, as shown in Figure 2, there are sizeable income-consumption deficits at both young and older lifecycle stages. Obviously, these lifecycle deficits (LCD) must be covered, with reallocations coming largely from the surplus of income generated at the lifecycle surplus stage during the current period or from assets accumulated during previous periods.

Second, it is also worth noting in Figure 1 that the age at which an average individual shifts from a net consumer to a net producer gradually increased from 23 years old in 1984 to 25 in 1994, and 29 in 2009. At the other end of the lifecycle, the age transition from a net producer to a net consumer was postponed only marginally from 58 years old in 1984 to 60 in 2009. The fact that the shift in the crossing age at the later stage of lifecycle was relatively small is attributable to the existence of the mandatory retirement age. (It should be noted, however, that as a result of a new legislation, the retirement age in Japan was gradually raised from 60 to 65 between 2006 and 2013.)

Third, the age-profiles of per capita consumption were rising almost continuously over time. The 1984 and 1994 age-profiles show a mildly shaped double hump, being high at both young and older ages. The first peak corresponds to the high costs of the young, while the second peak is related to the high costs shouldered by household heads under multigenerational living arrangements. In addition, it is worth noting that the amount of per capita consumption rose distinctly among those aged 65 and over in 2009. This can be accounted for by the implementation of the Long-term Care Insurance (LTCI) scheme, starting from the year 2000. In-home care for the frail elderly, which had until then been informally provided by family members, thus became formalised as a part of the market economy. As a result, Japan's per capita consumption profiles have, over time, become more similar to those of the United States, Sweden and Costa Rica, among the NTA member countries (Tung 2011).

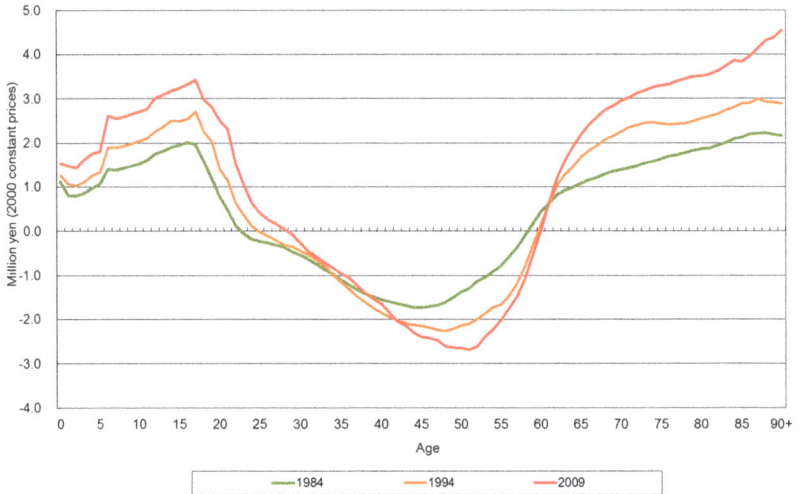

Figure 2. Lifecycle deficits: Japan. 1984, 1994 and 2009
Source: Provided by author.

(c) Changing pattern of lifecycle deficits and total reallocations

As is widely described in numerous publications pertaining to the system of NTA, the accounts measure intergenerational flows for a certain period of time (usually a calendar or fiscal year), and are governed by the following relationship:

$$y^l + y^A + t_g^+ + t_f^+ = C + S + t_g + t_f \quad (2)$$

Where y^l = labour income; y^A = asset income; t_g^+ = public transfer inflows; t_f^+ = private transfer inflows; C = consumption; S = saving; t_g = public transfer outflows to the government; and t_f = private transfer outflows. Rearranging terms in Equation (2), the LCD, which is the difference between consumption and production, is matched by age reallocations consisting of reallocations through assets and net transfers, as expressed below:

$$\underset{\text{Lifecycle deficit}}{C \quad y^l} = \underset{\text{Asset reallocations}}{y^A \quad S} + \underset{\text{Net public transfers}}{t_g^+ \quad t_g} + \underset{\text{Net private transfers}}{t_f^+ \quad t_f} \quad (3)$$

Net transfers

Age reallocations

Furthermore, to gain further insight into Equation (3), we can express the mathematical relationship by using the relevant data for 2009 as illustrated in Figure 3. In this graphical exposition, the vertical scale represents age-specific per capita deficit, which corresponds to the difference between per capita consumption and per capita production at each age. It should be further noted that the graph indicating the age-specific aggregate-level deficit takes into consideration the number of persons at each age, thus showing a pattern substantially different from the one displayed in Figure 3.

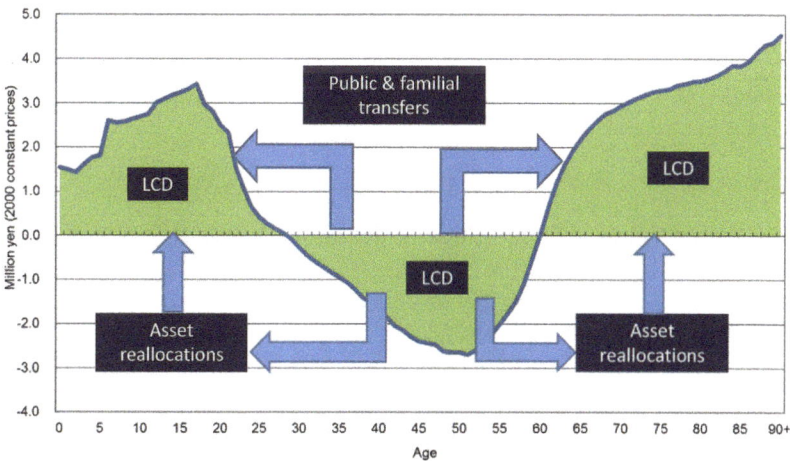

Figure 3. Total reallocations: Lifecycle deficits (LCD)

Source: Provided by author.

At this point, caution should be exercised with regard to the following two remarks. First, both 'familial transfers' and 'private transfers' are used interchangeably in this paper; both of them refer to private transfers received by households from any source, of which the predominant share is, surely, familial transfers. Second, although net private transfers are comprised of bequests and *inter vivo* transfers, the computation of the bequest component has not been completed at the time of writing. For this reason, bequests are excluded from the computational results reported here.

By applying the time-series data for Japan to Figure 3, we have produced Figure 4, which shows how the pattern of three components of reallocation of the LCD changed in Japan over the past 25 years. The three components are reallocations through assets, public transfers, and private transfers, measured on an annual basis. Panels A, B and C illustrate annual reallocations of the LCD observed in 1984, 1994 and 2009.

A brief comparison of the three panels reveals the following three important results. First, there was a marked increase in the impact of the rapid growth of the elderly population upon transfers over time. The amount of net total transfers given to the elderly aged 65 and over increased by 3.5 times from 1984 to 2009. Concretely, the amount of net public transfers to the elderly grew 5.4 times in real terms over this time period. It is also worth noting that the role of asset reallocations in financing the lifecycle deficits has become extremely important among the elderly population—the amount of asset-based reallocations increased by 12 times in real terms during 1984–2009. In the face of such phenomenal growth of the importance of asset-based allocations, however, the total amount of net public transfers dominated that of asset allocations in the elderly population in 2009.

Second, despite the shrinking of the young population, the total amount of net transfers to the population group aged 0–19 grew by 8 per cent during 1984–2009. It should also be added that the composition of the net transfers changed considerably over time. That is, during 1984–2009, the amount of net public transfers given to this age group rose by 37 per cent in real terms, while the corresponding figure for net familial transfers declined by 13 per cent.

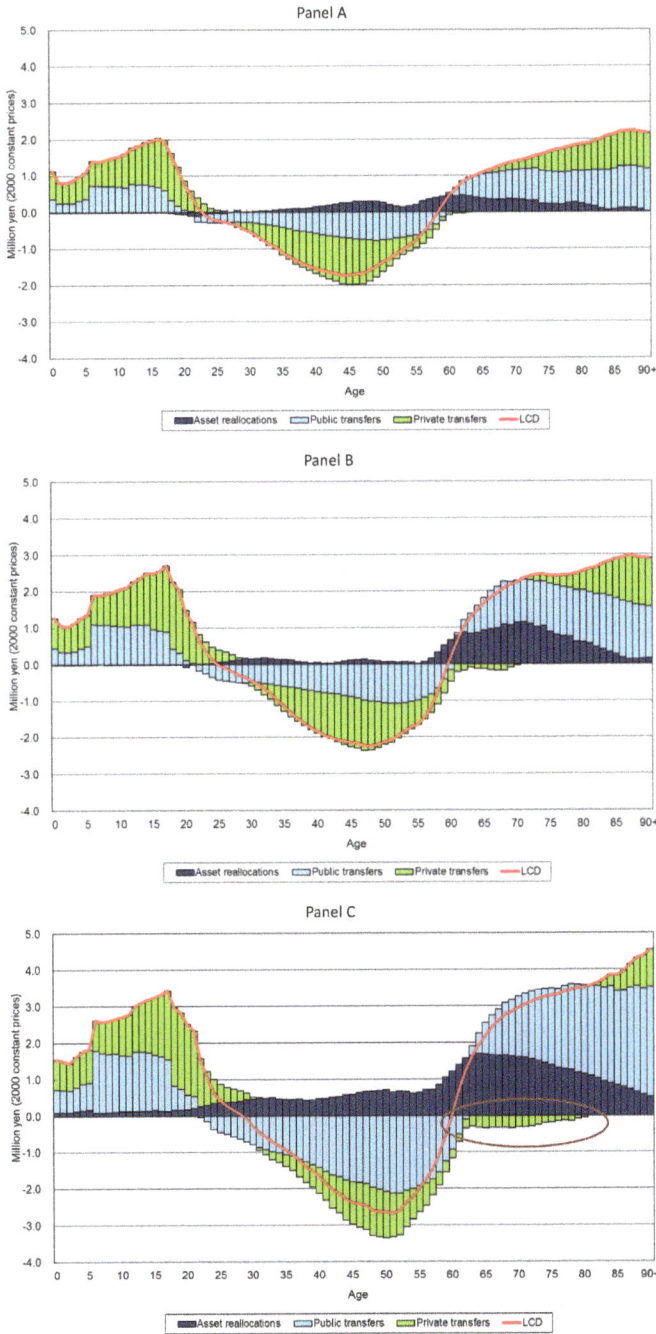

Figure 4. Changing pattern of three components of per capita reallocation of lifecycle deficit: Japan. (a) 1984, (b) 1994, and (c) 2004.

Source: Provided by author.

Third and more important, the net familial transfers are negative among relatively young elderly persons. As indicated by a circle in Panel C of Figure 4, this phenomenon is particularly pronounced in 2009 among the elderly in their 60s and 70s. This implies that the amount of financial assistance that the relatively young elderly persons provided to their adult children and/or grandchildren exceeded the monetary assistance from the latter to the former. It is also worth noting that the amount of these negative net familial transfers from the relatively young elderly to other age groups rose during the prolonged deflationary period beginning from the mid-1990s. Up until the early 2010s, the unemployment rate remained at a high level and labour income hardly grew at all in both nominal and real terms.

Rising per capita costs of children and the elderly in selected Asian countries

To facilitate our analysis in this section, we define the following two new variables: 'the child LCD' and 'the elderly LCD'. The former represents the per capita direct cost of raising children up to their self-sufficient ages, i.e. the age at which the age-specific LCD shifts from positive to negative, based upon the system of NTA. The latter represents the per capita direct cost of the elderly from the age at which they cease to be self-sufficient up to the age of their death. The per capita direct cost of the elderly corresponds to the sum of the age-specific LCD, computed as consumption minus production.

(a) Spending per child and the number of children in Japan and other selected Asian countries

As previously discussed, one of the most crucial concepts in the economics of fertility is the trade-off between the spending per child and the number of children, and this idea is fully embedded in Becker's model of fertility decision-making (Becker 1960, 1981). Becker's theory states that higher income leads to an increase in the demand for higher-quality children and a more modest increase in the demand for the number of children (quantity). But because higher-quality children are costly, this leads couples to substitute away from quantity. In other words, the basic trade-off has to do with private costs of children, i.e. costs borne by the fertility decision-makers (parents). Moreover, public spending on children may play an important role as well. For instance, with the provision of government subsidies for improving the quality of children, the private cost of acquiring high-quality children is likely to be reduced, which may result in raising fertility.

As mentioned in the previous section, the child LCD is the consumption of children (both public and private) minus the value of labour by children, i.e. the cost that children themselves cover. The child LCD is calculated for single years of age and can be used to construct a synthetic cohort measure of the cost of children. It represents the direct cost of children, assuming that they were raised from birth to adulthood consuming and producing at the same age-specific rates that prevailed in the year in question.

We normalise the child LCD by dividing it by the mean labour income of prime-age adults aged 30–49. This facilitates comparison across countries and also indirectly controls for the effects of income on child spending. In order to allow for mortality risks in childhood, we have also adjusted the normalised child LCD, by using appropriate life table values. Thus, the computed values can be interpreted as the years of prime-age adult labour devoted to rearing a child from birth to economic independence, or to the child's death, should that occur during childhood.

Using the computed results of the child LCD per person below a self-sufficient age and the mean per capita labour income of adults aged 30–49 for Japan, we have calculated the normalised per capita child LCD adjusted for survivorship up from birth to the self-supporting age in 1984, 1989, 1994, 1999, 2004 and 2009. The calculated values increased monotonically over time, namely, 9.6 years of labour income in 1984, 10.3 years in 1989, 10.9 years in 1994, 11.9 years in 1999, 13.0 years in 2004, and 14.1 years in 2009. In addition, we have carried out the same computation for Taiwan (1981–2005) and South Korea (1996–2010). In the case of Taiwan, the normalised per capita child LCD adjusted for survivorship increased almost continuously from 7.7 years in 1981 to 16.6 years in 2005. In the case of South Korea, the corresponding value rose linearly from 9.0 years in 1996 to 14.1 years in 2010. Besides these three East Asian countries, we have included in the analysis the normalised per capita child LCD adjusted for survivorship for the following five Asian countries: China in 2002 (6.5 years of the mean labour income), India in 2004 (9.0 years), Thailand over the period 1981–2004 (from 8.0 years to 10.4 years), the Philippines in 1999 (7.8 years), and Vietnam in 2008 (8.5 years).

In order to quantitatively examine the trade-off between spending on children and the number of children, we have pooled the results on the child LCD derived from the eight countries, and have linked them to the time-series data on TFR for each country under investigation. In the case of Japan, TFR declined considerably from 1.81 in 1984 to 1.37 in 2009. Taiwan's TFR declined substantially from 2.46 to 1.12 from 1981 to 2005, while South Korea's TFR fell from 1.60 to 1.22 during the period 1996–2010. In the case of Thailand, the TFR declined from 3.69 in 1981 to 1.66 in 2004. TFRs for the remaining four countries were as follows: 1.82 for China, 2.85 for India, 3.56 for the Philippines, and 2.08 for Vietnam.

In Figure 5, a total of 51 data points of the normalised per capita child LCD for the eight Asian economies for various years are plotted, coupled with the TFR for the corresponding years. As displayed in this graph, we have fitted the data by regressing the natural logarithm of the normalised per capita child LCD onto the natural logarithm of the TFR and, hence, the coefficient is the elasticity of the quality–quantity trade-off.

As is well-known, a coefficient of −1 implies that a 1 percentage point decrease in the number of children is accompanied by a 1 percentage point increase in the cost of children and, hence, the total change in spending by adults on childrearing remains constant. As presented in Figure 5, the estimated elasticity for the eight Asian countries combined is −0.698, implying that a 1 percentage point decrease in the TFR leads to a less than 1 percentage point increase in the total cost of childrearing per adult.

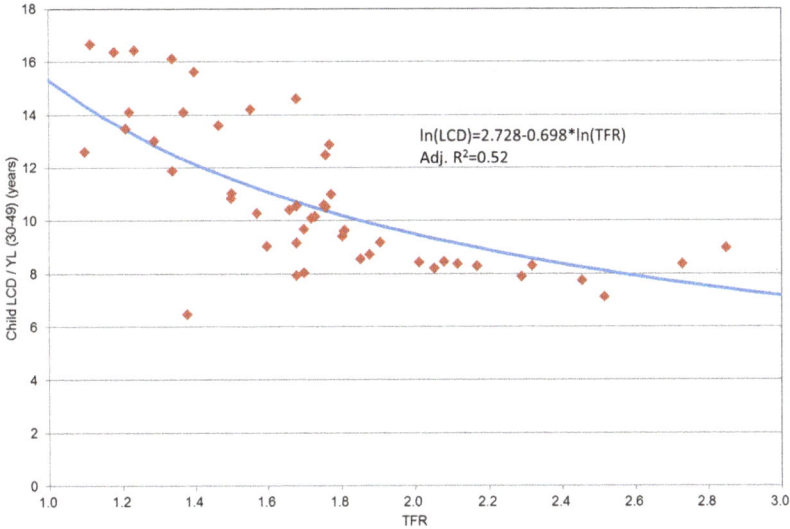

Figure 5. TFR versus normalised per capita LCD for children:
Selected Asian countries

Source: Provided by author.

This result has changed dramatically once we have undertaken a regression analysis, as displayed in Figure 6, by focusing on the relationship between the human capital component (education and health costs) of per capita child LCD and the TFR. It should be noted that, except for the fact that we have used the human capital component of the per capita child LCD in place of the per capita child LCD as a whole, all the data points plotted in Figure 6 have been constructed in the same manner as in Figure 5. The regression result indicates that the computed elasticity (−1.512) is much larger than the one shown in Figure 5 for the total cost of children. This elasticity is also much larger than the cross-sectional elasticity reported by Lee and Mason (2010). In addition, the goodness of fit, as measured by adjusted R^2, is better in the case of the computed result shown in Figure 6 than in Figure 5. Hence, the health and education components of per capita child LCD are more closely linked to fertility change than the other components of child LCD. This finding is consistent with the widely held view that human capital factors have been playing an important role in the relationship between economic growth and fertility change in Asian countries, particularly in East Asia (Ogawa, Retherford and Matsukura 2009; McDonald 2009).

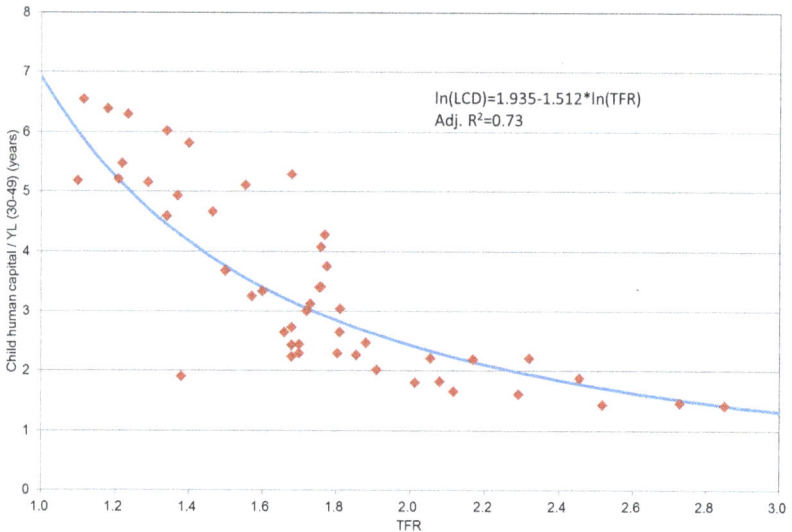

Figure 6. TFR versus normalised per capita human capital spending for children: Selected Asian countries
Source: Provided by author.

For the purpose of shedding more light on the nexus between human capital factors and fertility, we have conducted the following two additional regressions for the eight Asian countries. In one of them, we have fitted the data by regressing the natural logarithm of normalised per capita *public* human capital spending onto the natural logarithm of the TFR. In the other regression, the natural logarithm of normalised per capita *private* human capital spending has been regressed on the natural logarithm of the TFR. The results of these regressions, not detailed here, indicate that both the *public* and *private* components of human capital spending have fairly comparable association with fertility, i.e. the elasticity of −1.302 for *public* human capital spending and the elasticity of −1.618 for *private* human capital spending.

These computational results appear to be inconsistent with those obtained in the work recently undertaken by Lee and Mason. In their recent analysis of NTA data covering 19 countries (including not only Asian, but also European and Latin American countries), Lee and Mason (2010) have found that the quantity–quality trade-off is very strong for *public* spending (particularly on education) but not for *private* human capital spending. As displayed in Table 1, however, *private* human capital spending (particularly education) tends to be very large, and even exceeds *public* human capital spending in the Asian economies, particularly in such East and Southeast Asian countries as South Korea, Taiwan, China, and Vietnam. More importantly, it should be noted that primarily because East and Southeast Asia are 'success-oriented' societies, parents in this region are prone to spend a vast amount of financial resources on their children's education (McDonald 2008).

Table 1. Proportion of private spending in per capita educational costs for children and youths aged 0–24: Selected economies

Country	Year	Percentage
Sweden	2003	3.1
France	2001	5.0
Austria	2000	5.8
Slovenia	2004	8.7
Hungary	2005	11.1
US	2003	17.0
Costa Rica	2004	22.3
Japan	2009	26.0
India	2004	38.9
Chile	1997	39.4
Indonesia	2004	39.6
Uruguay	1994	46.4
Philippines	1999	48.2
South Korea	2005	51.6
Taiwan	2005	69.4
China	2002	71.2
Vietnam	2008	75.6

Source: Author's calculations.

The regression results presented thus far appear to conform to the view that there is a distinctive trade-off between the number of children and the combined (familial and public) spending per child in East Asia. Caution should be exercised, however, in interpreting these fitted results. It should be noted that all the regressions for the Asian countries are based upon a mix of cross-section and time-series data heavily dominated by Taiwan. Given such limitations, the fixes that are usually employed to deal with well-known statistical problems that limit the value of aggregate regression estimates are not practical in this case. Moreover, these regression results do not represent causal relationships. That is, the variable on the right-hand of the regressions is not necessarily an explanatory variable, while the variable on the left-hand of the regressions is not necessarily a dependent variable. Hence, the regressions estimated here should be treated only as descriptive device, thus making causal interpretation impossible.

(b) The nexus between the per capita child LCD and the per capita elderly LCD

In recent years, the cost of the elderly has also been rising in ageing Asia, particularly in East Asia (Takegawa 2005). A question therefore arises: is there a 'crowding out' effect between the resources going to the young and those allotted to the elderly? To shed some light on this question, we have calculated (1) how many years of the mean labour income of prime-age adults aged 30–49 is needed to finance the per capita LCD for a child, and (2) how many years of prime-age mean labour income is required to finance the per capita LCD for an elderly person. The data for the computation have been prepared for the same eight Asian countries in the same manner as in our foregoing analysis pertaining to the cost of children and fertility.

The computed results are plotted in Figure 7. The pattern emerging from this graph seems to roughly indicate that both the cost of a child and the cost of an elderly person tend to grow in the same direction, thus suggesting that there is no distinctive 'crowding out' effect in these eight Asian economies. (The simple correlation coefficient between the two variables shown in this graph amounts to 0.791.) These results seem to suggest that in these Asian countries, working-age adults are sandwiched by their elderly parents and their children, heavily relying on assets to meet their own material needs as well as their familial and social obligations to other generations.

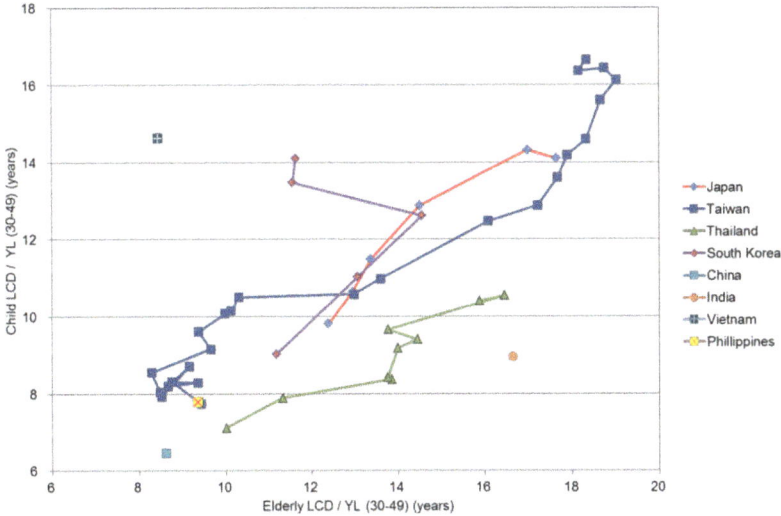

Figure 7. Relationship between the cost of children and the cost of the elderly: Selected Asian countries

Source: Provided by author.

For comparative purposes, we have calculated the cost of a child and the cost of an elderly person for NTA member countries in other regions. Although relevant graphs are omitted, the following two observations can be safely made. First, in both Latin America and Africa, we found virtually the same pattern as the one prevailing in the selected Asian countries. Second, European countries show a totally different pattern from these developing countries, and the cross-sectional data gleaned from the European countries involved in the NTA project indicates that there is no significant relationship between the costs of the two age groups.

Concluding remarks

In the present study, we have examined the relationship between the cost of raising children up to self-supporting ages and the number of children parents have, by drawing heavily upon the computed results for the eight selected Asian countries. The results suggest that the two variables in question have a negative association in the case of these eight Asian economies, and that the calculated elasticity is –0.698.

More importantly, as regards the per capita child human capital costs and the TFR, the calculated elasticity amounts to −1.512, which suggests that, in the eight Asian countries under examination, the health and education component of the per capita child LCD is more closely linked to changes in fertility than the other components of the per capita child LCD.

So, what can the Asian economies with below-replacement fertility do to restore their fertility levels in the years to come? The fact that higher-quality children are costly leads couples to substitute away from quantity. This basic trade-off relationship between the quality and quantity of children plays a crucial role in determining the private cost of children defrayed by parents. Moreover, *public* spending on children also plays a vital role in this respect. By subsidising the quality of children through public resources, for example, the cost of acquiring high-quality children is reduced, and consequently higher fertility is encouraged.

Apart from the provision of government subsidies for pronatalist purposes, the child LCD can also be reduced by lowering the self-supporting ages. One of the possible policy measures for this purpose is creating more stable full-time job opportunities for young workers. In the case of a shrinking population such as that of Japan, hourly labour productivity can be raised through better vocational and on-the-job training. In addition, greater women's labour force participation is another option, but methods for ameliorating the potential impact of female paid employment on fertility need to be carefully considered before implementing this policy option.

The trade-off between the cost of children and the number of children is important not only in terms of formulating effective fertility policies but also from the standpoint of generational equity. As hypothesised by Preston (1984), population ageing induced by reduced fertility and extended longevity should lead to a decline in the welfare of children relative to the elderly. However, contrary to Preston's hypothesis, one of the conclusions derived from our study is that the 'crowding out' phenomenon between children and the elderly competing for limited public and private resources could not be observed in the eight selected Asian countries in the past two decades or so.

Acknowledgements

This work has been supported by JSPS KAKENHI Grant Number 15H05692.

References

Becker Gary (1960). An economic analysis of fertility. In *Demographic and Economic Change in Developed Countries*, National Bureau of Economic Research Special Conference Series 11, Columbia: Columbia University Press, pp. 209–231.

Becker Gary (1981). *A Treatise on the Family*. Cambridge, Massachusetts and London, England: Harvard University Press.

Department of Statistics, Ministry of the Interior, Republic of China (Taiwan) (n.d). *Statistical Yearbook of Interior*. eng.stat.gov.tw/ct.asp?xItem=6503&CtNode=2202&mp=5.

Kaneko Ryuichi, Sasai Tsukasa, Kamano Saori, Iwasawa Miho, Mita Fusami and Moriizumi Rie (2008). Marriage Process and Fertility of Japanese Married Couples, *The Japanese Journal of Population*, 6(1): 24–50.

Lee Ronald and Mason Andrew (2010). 'Fertility, human capital, and economic growth over the demographic transition'. *European Journal of Population*, 26(2): 159–182.

Lee Ronald and Mason Andrew (Eds) (2011). *Population Aging and the Generational Economy: A Global Perspective*. Cheltenham, Northampton, Ottawa: Edward Elgar and International Development Research Centre.

Lutz Wolfgang, Sanderson Warren and Scherbov Sergei (2004). *The End of World Population Growth in the 21st Century: New Challenges for Human Capital Formation and Sustainable Development*. London and Sterling, VA: Earthscan.

Mason Andrew and Ogawa Naohiro (2001). Population, labor force, saving and Japan's future. In Magnus Blomström, Byron Gangnes, and Sumner La Croix (Eds) *Japan's New Economy: Continuity and Change in the Twenty-First Century*. Oxford: Oxford University Press, pp. 48–74.

McDonald Peter (2008). Low fertility as a macro-sociological issue: an application to East Asia. Paper presented at the International Conference on Low Fertility and Reproductive Health in East and Southeast Asia, organised by Nihon University Population Research Institute, in cooperation with WHO, UNFPA, IUSSP, and The Mainichi Daily Newspapers Tokyo, Japan, 12–14 November.

McDonald Peter (2009). Explanations of low fertility in East Asia: a comparative perspective. In Gavin Jones, Paulin Tay Straughan, and Angelique Chan (Eds) *Ultra-low Fertility in Pacific Asia: Trends, Causes and Policy Issues*. Abingdon: Routledge, pp. 23–39.

National Institute of Population and Social Security Research (NIPSSR) (2011). *Marriage Process and Fertility of Japanese Couples*. Tokyo: NIPSSR.

National Institute of Population and Social Security Research (NIPSSR) (2015). *Latest Demographic Statistics*, Population Research Series No. 333. Tokyo: NIPSSR.

Ogawa Naohiro, Chawa Amonthep and Matuskura Rikiya (2010). Changing intergenerational transfers in aging Japan. In Karen Eggleston and Shripad Tuljapurkar (Eds) *Aging Asia: The Economic and Social Implications of Rapid Demographic Change in China, Japan, and South Korea*. Baltimore: The Brookings Institution, pp. 43–62.

Ogawa Naohiro, Mason Andrew, Chawla Amonthep and Matsukura Rikiya (2010). Japan's unprecedented aging and changing intergenerational transfers. In Takatoshi Ito and Andrew K Rose (Eds) *The Economic Consequences of Demographic Change in East Asia*, NBER-EASE Vol. 19. Chicago and London: University of Chicago Press, pp. 131–160.

Ogawa Naohiro, Mason Andrew, Chawla Amonthep, Matsukura Rikiya and Tung An-Chi (2009). Declining fertility and the rising cost of children: What can NTA say about low fertility in Japan and other Asian countries? *Asian Population Studies*, 5(3): 289–307.

Ogawa Naohiro, Mason Andrew, Lee Sang-Hyop, Tung An-Chi and Matsukura Rikiya (2015). Very low fertility and the high costs of children and the elderly in East Asia. In Naohiro Ogawa and Iqbal Shah (Eds) *Low Fertility and Reproductive Health in East Asia*. New York and London: Springer, International Studies in Population, pp. 31–58.

Ogawa Naohiro and Retherford Robert (1997). Shifting costs of caring for the elderly back to families in Japan. *Population and Development Review*, 23(1): 59–94.

Ogawa Naohiro, Retherford Robert and Matsukura Rikiya (2009). Japan's declining fertility and policy responses. In Gavin Jones, Paulin Tay Straughan, and Angelique Chan (Eds) *Ultra-low Fertility in Pacific Asia: Trends, Causes and Policy Issues*. Abingdon: Routledge, pp. 40–72.

Preston Samuel H (1984). Children and the elderly: Divergent paths for America's dependents. *Demography*, 21(4): 435–458.

Retherford Robert D and Ogawa Naohiro (2009). Guest editors' introduction. *Asian Population Studies*, 5(3): 211–213.

Statistics Bureau, Ministry of Internal Affairs and Communications, Japan (2015). *Population Estimates*. Tokyo: Statistics Bureau, Ministry of Internal Affairs and Communications, Japan.

Statistics Korea (n.d). *Vital Statistics (number and rate)*, data downloaded from Korean Statistical Information Service, kosis.kr/eng/statisticsList/statisticsList/statisticsList_01List.jsp?vwcd=MT_ETITLE&parentId=A.

Takegawa Shogo (2005). Japan's welfare-state regime: welfare politics, provider and regulator. *Development and Society*, 34(2): 169–190.

Tung An-Chi (2011). Consumption over the lifecycle: an international comparison. In Ronald Lee and Andrew Mason (Eds) *Population Aging and the Generational Economy: A Global Perspective*. Cheltenham, Northampton, Ottawa: Edward Elgar and International Development Research Centre, pp. 136–160.

6
Facing the challenges
of an ageing society

Jan Pakulski

Since the mid-20th century the world's population has been ageing, most noticeably in the most advanced (developed) societies, with social consequences so profound that they justify forging the concept of the 'ageing society'. The ageing society emerges as a result of, principally, low fertility rates and decreasing mortality combined with increasing longevity. Sociologists and social demographers see such a society as a harbinger of a shift to the 'fourth stage' of demographic transition, whereby birth and death rates stabilise at a low level and longevity increases (Cardwell 2006). Parallel to these processes, there are some changes in the social structure, economy, culture and politics, as well as attempts by governments to devise strategies of adaptation-*cum*-modification to meet the challenges posed by rapid ageing, such as a proliferation of 'ageing problems', a shrinking labour force, escalating costs of pensions and aged-care services, and social-political conservatism. Australia's relative success in facing these challenges suggests the broader applicability of a general strategic model or policy template—described below as the '4Ps' (a modification of the 3P strategy suggested in Australian Intergenerational Reports)—to other developed countries, such as Poland, that are facing the challenges of ageing.

'Ageing society' refers to a specific type of society that emerges during demographic transition in which large shares of populations become old (65+) and very old (80+). Ageing societies share a number of similar challenges, such as widening individual 'problems of ageing' (poor health, loneliness, social isolation, impoverishment of old people); depletion of the labour force and an increasing dependency ratio, which together slow down growth; rising pension, aged-care and health costs and accompanying budgetary strains; and the increasing generational pressures of 'silver/grey lobbies' that contribute to rising conservatism, slow down reforms and threaten to skew the allocation of resources (e.g. United Nations 2001; Harper 2006; Harper and Hamblin 2014).

It is estimated that the proportion of such older (60+) people worldwide—at present around 12 per cent—will nearly double by 2050. Even in Australia, where the total fertility rate is relatively high (1.9), and where immigration of young people also remains high, thus 'cushioning' the impact of ageing, the proportion of people aged over 65 will double by mid-century from about 13 per cent to about 27 per cent, with centenarians constituting 0.01 per cent of the total population.[1] In Poland, where the process of ageing has been aggravated by a low (1.3) fertility rate and high emigration of young people, the anticipated change is more rapid and—potentially—more disruptive, with the population shrinking, an estimated 30 per cent of people reaching the retirement age by 2050, and the age dependency ratio more than doubling.

As would be expected, with the process of ageing accelerating in most developed societies, the attention paid to population ageing and the challenges that accompany it has been increasing. As the UNDESA Report (United Nations 2013) notes:

> Between 2005 and 2013, the percentage of Governments that considered population ageing as a major concern has increased in more developed regions (from 76 to 92 per cent) ... [with] more than 9 out of 10 Governments in Europe and North America considering population ageing as a major concern in 2013.

---

1   For these and other figures see Commonwealth of Australia (2015).

Yet, this increase is seldom accompanied by a debate about the 'population targets', as well as the nature and effectiveness of policy responses, which range from 'mitigation', typically in the form of pronatalist policies that aim at boosting fertility, to 'adaptation', typically in the form of boosting old age provisions and services. One generation after the ageing has been recognised as a source of serious challenges, there seems to be an emerging consensus that ageing poses urgent developmental and intergenerational problems, and that effective responses have to combine mitigation with adaptation, and that they have to be strategic in adopting a long-term perspective (e.g. Bloom et al. 2011; Harper and Hamblin 2014).

The trajectories of ageing, as well as the acuteness of problems that ageing engenders, differ between developed societies, but the similarities of the main challenges, as well as experiences of the initial stages of ageing, enable us to formulate some general 'lessons conclusions' in the form of a generally applicable strategic policy model. This policy model reflects the experiences and successes of Australia—a developed society that relatively successfully faces the process of ageing—but can be applied to other developed societies, especially those, like Polish society, facing more serious challenges and experiencing the problems of ageing more acutely.

Polish society is ageing fast and faces many more problems of ageing because it is ageing faster and is less affluent than Australia, and has prepared less for the demographic transition (Table 1). The median age today is 38, and it will have increased to 51 in 2050. The demographic dependency ratio (the ratio of people 65+ compared to those aged 15–64) is predicted to shoot up from 19 per cent (2010) to 36 per cent (2030) and then to 56 per cent in 2050. The current very low fertility rate (1.3 births per woman) is not likely to increase, because spending on pronatal policies is very low (1 per cent of GDP, compared to 3.3 per cent in neighbouring Germany), high child care and child-raising costs, and growing pressure on women to take employment and delay conception—or to emigrate. Poland has a much lower living standard than Australia, higher debt, and much more strain placed on the budget, and these factors limit its preparedness for ageing and restrict the field of manoeuvre for government. Yet, as argued below, these are problems shared, to various degrees, by all developed and ageing societies, and they do not prevent Poland from applying—with necessary modifications—the 4P strategic model.[2]

Table 1. International comparison of social-demographic indicators: Australia and Poland

Country	TFR 2005–10	Median age (years)	Population 65+ (%)	TDR (%)	Population 2010 [50] (millions)	AAPG (%) 2005–10	LFPR 2014 (%)
Australia	1.9	37 [45]	13.4	48	24 [40]	1.8	65
Poland	1.3	38 [51]	13.5	40	38 [32]	0.0	56

Source: Based on Commonwealth of Australia (2015: 9) and OECD (2013).

TFR=Total Fertility Rate; TDR=Total Dependency Ratio (aged 0–14 and 65+ per 100 aged 15–64); AAPG=Annual Average Population Growth; LFPR=Labour Force Participation Rate.

The focus of this chapter is on these general policy strategies—their overall pattern, rather than the detailed content and modes of implementation—and on the applicability of these strategies in developed societies with different ageing profiles and migration regimes. In order to highlight these strategies and discuss their broader applicability, we first discuss briefly:

• those challenges of ageing that generate the most concern and anxiety; and then

• the strategies that have been designed and partly tested with considerable success in Australia.

Ageing societies and their problems

One reason for widespread anxiety related to ageing has been poor anticipation. Until the 1980s, most social scientists in developed societies had anticipated the levelling of birth rates at or above reproduction levels, steady population growth, and even overpopulation. In fact, the mid-20th century ageing trends have proved persistent: birth rates have continued to fall throughout the late stages of modernisation, especially the Western-type modernisation that increasingly relied

2   For an overview of ageing and its social consequences in Australia, see Commonwealth of Australia (2015). For an overview in Poland see Devictor (2012) and OECD (2013). For the overall policy implication of ageing, see McDonald and Kippen (1999). For the impact of immigration on ageing in Australia, see McDonald and Kippen (2001a).

on the occupational activisation (participation) of women, and, consequently, on the delay of marriage and child-bearing. Moreover, the initially widely acclaimed pronatalist policies have proven costly, difficult to implement, and less effective than expected, thus resulting in their half-hearted embracement and application (e.g. Kaufmann 2011). At the same time, death rates have continued their 'secular decline', and longevity has been steadily increasing, resulting in a declining proportion of young and economically active people, and an increasing proportion of the aged (65+), usually 'retirees', and the very aged (80+) who increasingly suffer from dementia.

There have, of course, been some variations in the processes of ageing and its social consequences—principally between more affluent and less affluent societies, and between high immigration and low immigration ones—but the consequences of population ageing have been roughly the same in developed and developing societies, though, naturally, developed societies face these problems earlier than developing ones. The problems include, above all, the widening of 'ageing problems' (illness, loneliness, social isolation, dependency, impoverishment), shrinking of working populations combined with increasing dependency ratios (dependent/working), and increasing generational 'burdens' (rising costs of welfare and aged care, rapidly increasing health costs). All of these trends result in declining economic dynamism (diagnosed as an aspect of 'secular stagnation'), combined with the mobilisation of 'grey lobbies' and rising conservatism— all exacerbated by the Great Recession hitting the advanced societies, and by the misconceived responses of some recession-traumatised governments. These responses include anti-immigration campaigns and 'deficit-*cum*-debt' funding of welfare and aged-care services that have proven unsustainable and that amount to intergenerational 'burden shifting' (e.g. Harper 2006; Harper and Hamblin 2014; Torp 2013; Commonwealth of Australia 2015; Summers 2014).

Due to a combination of poor anticipation, misconceived initial responses, and the constraints of the Great Recession, ageing started to transform into a set of inter-related and spiralling problems. The net effect of all these problems has been a steep stratification of societies in their vulnerability to ageing problems, and a generally increasing awareness-*cum*-anxiety about the problems of an ageing society.

Five inter-related problems attract the attention of students of ageing societies. First and foremost is the high cost and dubious effectiveness of the major 'modifier'—pronatalist policies. These policies are expensive (e.g. 3.4 per cent of GDP in France; 3.9 per cent in Denmark), they often backfire (e.g. reducing participation of women in the labour force), their effectiveness differs widely, and their overall efficiency seems to depend on the design of the policy packages. Moreover, they seldom bring fertility close to the reproduction level, and are seen as only a part of the strategic policy response (e.g. Goldstone et al. 2013; Gray et al. 2008).

Second is a set of problems related to the spread—together with population ageing—of the typical afflictions of ageing: chronic illness (especially dementia and related conditions), loneliness, social isolation, dependency and impoverishment. These problems have been well diagnosed and analysed, so we add only that they are not just widening in scope, but are also gendered (women outlive men) and this requires some attention (seldom granted by decision-makers). When not tackled, these problems result in the formation of an 'aged underclass'.

Particularly worrisome—and challenging for policymakers—are problems related to the widening scope and mounting costs of aged care for dementia-afflicted aged. While the quality and cost of care at 'lower life expectancy' levels—when most people were dying from circulation/heart diseases and, if they survived those, then of cancer—could be sustained in affluent societies, dementia and related chronic diseases/conditions have proved extremely difficult and costly. Neither families nor medical facilities, nor even the expanding added care programs, are capable of providing adequate and effective care; added care often being required on a 24/7 basis by qualified staff. Similarly, loneliness and social isolation pose a growing, as well as a widening, problem, because they are reinforced by communication difficulties (often coming with illness), mobility limitations, lack of facilities, and—last but not least—decreasing family networks combined with high mobility of children and family members. Impoverishment has hit the ageing population not only as a result of limitations to welfare budgets, but also due to the financial vulnerability of the aged: they are much less capable of managing their finances, become vulnerable to fraud, and are frequently exploited by unscrupulous care providers. These factors contribute to the rapidly widening 'dependency syndrome'—declining capacity of the aged to sustain their autonomy—which quickly translates into care needs and costs, as well as a growing frustration and anger among the dependent aged, whose dignity is reduced.

Perhaps the most widely publicised—especially at a time of intensified deficit fears and budgetary strains—are the problems related to, and generated by, workforce shrinking and pension costs. They concern, above all, the shrinking and ageing labour force and the related increase in the 'dependency ratio' and pension burden.[3] These problems—in fact a whole galaxy of inter-related problems—have been well diagnosed and analysed. If unmitigated, they threaten the standard of living of new generations, as well as the integrity of governmental budgets (lowering revenue, a declining tax base and wealth generation, increasing budgetary costs, etc.) (e.g. Bloom et al. 2011; Harper and Hamblin 2014; Commonwealth of Australia 2015).

Closely linked is the problem of spiralling welfare (including aged care and health) expectations and costs. The historically expanding welfare state generates its own self-propelling—and unsustainable, according to some critics—dynamics. At the core are growing welfare ('social') rights, regularly translated into entitlements, and their accompanying public expectation—particularly high in the baby boom generations—that these rights-*cum*-entitlements will expand in scope and quality. Such an expectation trajectory is fed by the culture and politics of welfare. The former creates norms and standards associated with the notion of social development: higher development = more extensive, intensive and costly services. The latter (the 'demand side') feeds into the regular 'promises' of further expansion and improvement of services made by most parties and most political candidates in the process of electoral competitions (the 'supply side'). Both feed into the spiralling costs and into politically delegitimising effects ('broken promises' and declining trust provoking populist backlash). This is particularly dangerous in societies in which the aged welfare constituencies increase in absolute and relative terms. And it is

---

3   Thus, among EU members, the old age dependency ratio (number of people aged 65+ as a percentage of 20–64 years old) increased from 22 in the mid-1980s to 30 today, and is estimated to skyrocket to 55 in 2050 (United Nations 2013).

dangerous because the very cost of welfare provisions, both generally and 'per unit', has been increasing, while the willingness to address this problem has not (e.g. Harper and Hamblin 2014; Torp 2013).

Spiralling welfare costs require prompt reactions and long-term mitigations. Otherwise welfare will transform into a 'burden' easily passed to the next generation (as public debt, pension obligations, anticipated cost of mitigation, etc.). This is easy—and dangerous— because the issue of intergenerational equity (distribution of burdens) has not been absorbed into the political debates over social fairness and justice. Forthcoming generations, as cynics say, have no vote, and little political influence, and they are regularly burdened by unsustainable debts and mitigation costs (e.g. the costs of environmental mitigations). This is the case with the 'post–baby boom' generations in most Western societies. These generations face not only escalating welfare costs, an increasing 'dependency rate', and stagnating growth, but also the 'triple whammy' of mounting (public and private) debts, rising costs of living, and massive (though hard to calculate) burdens of environmental modifications. It is as if the ageing baby boomers in advanced societies have lost not only the capacity for anticipation, but also a sense of what is fair to their descendants.

The fourth set of problems of ageing concerns the costs and burdens of health care. These deserve a special mention because of their magnitude and rate of acceleration—higher than other welfare costs—as well as their declining manageability. The fast acceleration is the result of expanding expectations and demands, as well as— and increasingly—the changing nature of ageing chronic conditions (like dementia). Ageing chronic conditions are those that cannot be cured, and require expensive treatment (e.g. Alzheimer Disease International 2014). Moreover, hopes of a prolonged healthy life, due to 'morbidity and mortality compression', now appear to have been exaggerated. The 'market' cost-inflation is also relevant: costly medicines, costly procedures, costly care, all resulting from the demand for high-cost 'niche' treatments (for the affluent aged) becoming a 'mass' expectation and demand.

With the ageing of the labour force, there is an accompanying problem of declining entrepreneurialism, innovativeness and productivity, which affects the associated developmental dynamism of advanced societies. This danger has been recently and separately diagnosed in the most rapidly ageing societies, such as Japan and South Korea, and in the Western advanced societies ('secular stagnation'). It seems that developed societies enter an unexpected slow-down in their economic dynamism that is, at least partly, related to ageing. They tend to become less dynamic and innovative, and more conservative and routine-prone than younger societies with youthful and expanding labour forces. That poses a number of problems, especially in the context of competitive globalisation.

One should also point to the problems coded into the fashionable—but seldom effective—mitigation strategy labelled, variously, 'family-friendly', 'fertility-raising' or 'pronatalist'. Such strategies consist of creating incentives to have more children through 'revaluing the traditional roles' of women as mothers (the domain of the conservatives) and/or offering payments, services and facilitations to families with children. While the unwanted side-effects, wrong targeting and (dubious) cost-effectiveness of such strategies have been widely discussed, the unintended consequences and 'ironic side-effects' deserve attention. Perhaps the most damaging unintended consequence is the reduction of opportunities for women—opportunities for careers, self-realisation and the financial independence and dignity associated with them. Poorly designed pronatal policies may also undermine the very 'medicine' for workforce depletion, namely labour force participation by women (e.g. Harper 2006).

Finally, one should mention the sociocultural changes that accompany ageing. While it is fashionable to stress the advantages and benefits of ageing—declining criminality and violence, peaceful conservatism, etc.—the problems associated with those very tendencies should also be kept in mind. Ageing societies turn more conservative and more crime/violence fearing. This may reduce aggressive behaviour, but also increases the irrational fear of crime—and makes pressures for (inevitably expensive and often socially divisive) security measures, such as gated communities, harder to resist. Conservatism of age typically aids conservative parties, and spawns conservative policies that cement the status quo and reduce the pressures for early, costly, but necessary reforms. Yet such reforms are essential for effective social and political adjustment.

This brings us to the central topic of effective policy strategies. Such strategies, we argue, have to be 'learned', rather than 'invented'. They work better when adopted from successful 'policy leaders', rather than derived from party ideologies under pressure of crises. Obviously, the effective strategies have to be complex and systemic—like the problems themselves—and must combine preventive, mitigating and adjusting measures. Perhaps most importantly, they should be bi-partisan and long-term strategies that are propelled by prudent anticipation backed by social science, rather than short-term ('reactive') political opportunism that gets hold of political parties competing for votes in greying electorates. The 'should' in the last sentence is to be interpreted as advocacy for 'best practice' and for 'successful/effective outcomes'. I want to argue that the strategic approach to the problem of an ageing society will be improved by monitoring diverse policy outcomes and by learning from 'the relative successes' of such societies as Australia.

The Australian strategy: '4Ps'

Australian decision-makers, it is argued here, combine mitigation with adaptation in a strategy—referred to as '3Ps' (see Commonwealth of Australia 2002, 2007, 2010 and 2015)—that proves comprehensive and effective in mitigating the dangers of ageing and countering the key anxiety-generating problems of an ageing society. This effectiveness is highlighted in a comparison with Poland, a society that faces wider and more serious challenges related to population ageing, and, at the same time, a society that illustrates the broader applicability of the Australian strategic model template (expanded to 4Ps). The '4Ps' of the strategy's shorthand name stand for the four elements of the policy template: people, productivity, participation and (added) provisions. The first three are well known, and have been discussed in previous Intergenerational Reports (Commonwealth of Australia 2002, 2007, 2010 and 2015).

It should be stressed that the 4Ps strategy is by no means a problem-free 'model ideal', or that the policies pursued by Australian governments are necessarily successful in implementing the model template. Rather, we argue that the policy strategy outlined below: (i) addresses the key challenges, problems and threats posed by ageing; (ii) does this in a comprehensive and sustainable manner by combining modification with adaptation; and (iii) has been partly but successfully 'tested' through an application that has reduced the scope of some problems.

Therefore, we can learn from this relative success by generalising the strategy—or rather those elements that seem to be most important for successful mitigations and adaptations. Such strategic policy 'model templates', though, it should be remembered, can never be copied 'verbatim' without appropriate adjustments. Rather, implementation requires careful adaptation to the 'local idiom'—careful grafting rather than mechanical copying.

Population: Rejuvenating immigration and immigrant integration

This is the most important and the most effective element of the proposed strategic model template. Rejuvenating immigration—which has to be controlled and selective to play this role—is rare and difficult to sustain. Moreover, in order to 'work' as a 'moderator of ageing', it has to be backed by policies facilitating the integrative adaptation of immigrants; this is labelled '(integrative) multiculturalism' in Australia (e.g. McDonald and Kippen 2001a).

Australia is not only a high-immigration society, but also a permanent-, selected- and young-immigration society. Since 2005, immigration levels have increased to around 220,000 per annum—reaching around 300,000 in 2008–09 and then declining again to 150,000–180,000—adding nearly 1 per cent of the total population per year. Most of these immigrants are selected for desirable skills, education and swift integration into the labour force and society. Importantly, nearly nine out of every 10 immigrants are aged under 40, with the median age within the 20–24 range. A growing proportion of immigrants come through Australian educational institutions, which facilitates social and economic integration and high incomes. The key facilitator of swift integration, though, is a strategy of multiculturalism that encourages integration, reduces mal-integration, and minimises discrimination. Altogether, this immigration-*cum*-integration strategy provides the main and most effective mitigation of the problems of ageing, though its maintenance becomes more difficult with the less-controlled inflow of immigrants and refugees from less developed regions and their more difficult experiences of integration. Nevertheless, population projections—based on current/recent migration, fertility and mortality rates—show a steady (1.3 per cent) and balanced growth of population, with a slow rate of ageing, and the dependency ratio falling gradually from about 4.5 today to about 2.7 in the 2050s.

Poland represents a very different pattern with very low fertility, prevailing out-migration and medium-level unemployment—all ripe for policy reforms. The out-migration of young and skilled men and young and highly educated women, in particular, exacerbate the problems caused by the process of ageing-*cum*-labour force depletion. The greatest 'population loss' has been in the 24–29 age group—among men with secondary and vocational education and among women with tertiary education. This is why the old age dependency ratio, which at present is not much different from Australia's (20–22 per cent) is expected to grow to 55 per cent in the next generation—a level similar to that anticipated in Germany, Italy and Spain (Okólski and Topińska 2012; *The Economist* 2009).

Yet, increasing immigration from the East gives Poland wide scope for policy manoeuvres. With fast growth (over 3 per cent), rapidly increasing living standards and declining unemployment, Poland has become an attractive destination to her eastern neighbours, especially Ukraine—a country experiencing economic and political crises and with a much lower standard of living. Ukraine and Belarus have similar languages and cultures and can count on the sympathy of Polish people, which facilitates integration. Moreover, Poland harbours residues of the multiculturalism it inherited from the 16th–18th-century Jagiellonian Commonwealth with similarities to the Australian 'integrative multiculturalism', which can therefore serve as a moral political idiom in legitimising mass immigration.

Productivity: Monitoring and sustaining high efficiency

The negative effects of a shrinking labour force can be effectively mitigated, as the Australian example shows, by monitoring and promoting productivity increases. The key role of the Australian Productivity Commission and Australian Workforce and Productivity Agency in monitoring productivity nationwide, and the role of reforms increasing the productivity of the (shrinking) labour force have been discussed widely in the policy literature. Here we would like to stress the overall direction of the reforms, including 'productivity agreements' replacing 'workplace warfare', and the adaptive reforms of education (including mass upskilling of the workforce) providing a backbone for productivity boosting reforms that have proved so crucial in sustaining economic growth, income increases and a high standard of living.

The key component of the productivity increases (between 1.5 per cent and 2.2 per cent per year) in Australia has in recent decades been growing *labour* productivity. This has been sustained by reforms that boost competition, by harnessing innovations, absorbing new technologies and utilising as a springboard the educational revolution that accompanied a shift in production towards the service sector and its high-tech, high-skill end. *Capital* productivity, by contrast, has been declining, mainly because of massive investment in the declining mining/mineral boom. The success in increasing labour productivity—through a mixture of labour market and workplace reforms, education/training, and support for innovation—indicates that it could become an effective 'cushion' against the ageing-related shrinking of productive labour.

The danger of declining productivity—be it due to the fading impact of reforms, the declining inflow of educated and skilled migrants, high ('boom-windfall') profitability, low unemployment or high/ uncompetitive labour costs—can be countered only by the continuous monitoring and boosting of productivity across all sectors of the economy, as well as by promoting a 'culture of high productivity' across society. The latter encounters two serious barriers: the rising tide of conservatism, partly as a result of the ageing population, and the pressures of high consumption and leisure expectations of the (ageing) baby boom generation. In this context, one should stress that the highest productivity growth in Australia occurred in the post–World War II decades and was achieved by a highly liberal war generation. Since the beginning of this century, this growth has floundered; Australia is ranked 50th on total productivity growth. The generational shift, a conservative-complacent cultural wave, and the mining boom that brought with it an enormous jump in investment and windfall profitability, all lowered the reformist pressures and growth in productivity, while an increased inflow of educated and skilled immigrants helped to sustain productivity increases.

Poland is well placed in respect of productivity growth. Labour productivity in Poland remains much lower than in Australia, but it has also been increasing much faster (around 25 per cent in the last five years, compared with around 6 per cent in the last five years in Australia) (PRP 2013; Commonwealth of Australia 2015; Trading Economics 2014). This growth is high in both industry and services, coincides with increasing education and technological absorption, and follows the steady increase in exports. Most importantly, this growth is seen as sustainable, reflecting intense reforms and steady industrial-*cum*-service growth, and therefore opens the way for effective cushioning of the effects of ageing in the forthcoming decades. However, the 'productivity dividend' badly needs social-political reinforcement in the form of a 'social contract' between the government, trade unions, and employer organisations. Such a contract—followed by reforms—should not be difficult to develop considering the still strong residues of national solidarism created by the Solidarity movement and post-communist reforms.

As Devictor (2012: 6) points out:

> Experience suggests that increasing labour productivity is also a complex, multidimensional task. It involves efforts in areas such as: the quality of education (basic education, professional training, higher education, life-long learning, etc.); the business environment, to support job creation and innovation; labour regulations, to help jobs move towards more productive and growing firms; economic transformation in sectors where productivity remains low, including agriculture; etc. This is an agenda that needs to be pursued regardless of demographic trends, but that the aging of society makes even more pressing.

Participation, employment and unemployment

One of the successful measures expanding the labour force and reducing the 'socioeconomic' impact of ageing—that typically brings a decline in the number of working persons—has been the high participation rate. Australia had one of the highest participation rates of people aged 15+ among the OECD countries in 2013, and this rate is predicted to stay at a high level for the next 40 years, while migrant participation will be falling, and female participation increasing. Australian women have doubled their proportion in the labour force within one generation (to the current 59–65 per cent in all adult cohorts) and this growth is likely to continue. Another aspect of the Australian strategy of cushioning the impact of ageing through participation is the gradual extension of working time through incentives to professionals to continue their work, and the phasing in of the increase of the retirement age to 70 (by 2030). Thus the steady increase in participation rates, combined with prolonged employment, offers to Australian society another buffer against the impact of sudden ageing and its labour- and growth-depleting consequences.

The biggest challenge comes from another aspect of participation: hours worked. The volume of work and the level of unemployment have a large impact on economic outcomes; and that forms a formidable challenge, because the number of hours worked has been falling with a shift to part-time and temporary employment, especially among women and older workers. Women often prefer part-time employment because it is easier to square with their home/parental duties. Older workers are tempted to ease their load, especially when it does not adversely affect their superannuation funds and pensions. The decline in working hours is likely to continue with the expansion of the female and old labour forces, thus threatening the integrity of the participation strategy.

A similar threat comes from increasing unemployment, or rather decreasing employment. 'Postmodern' (increasingly service) economies shed low-skill and secure jobs, and create more fickle jobs demanding high social and technical skills (see Summers 2014). This means that unemployment is likely to become a chronic condition for large low-skill segments of 'postmodernising' populations, even in countries like Australia, where the labour force is highly skilled, flexible and mobile. In the light of trends in the most developed societies, the assumption of low (5 per cent) and stable unemployment in the Australian Intergenerational Report must strike us as highly optimistic—or as a harbinger of increasing public employment (straining the welfare budget).

Participation rates in Poland are lower than in Australia, doubtless due to more rapid ageing and higher unemployment (see Table 1). The share of people 65+ is expected to nearly double by 2030, and almost triple by 2050, while the trend in participation in the 15–64 age cohorts had been less favourable, declining until 2007–08 and then increasing only slightly. But these trends are reversible, and, in fact, are starting to change. Participation rates, especially among women, has stabilised on the low level, and it is hard to predict how it is likely to be affected by the newly introduced child bonuses and by the promised lowering of the retirement age. Thus, while unemployment has been falling and the number of hours worked has been increasing, one should not assume the continuing increase trend in workforce participation rates in Poland, especially among women.

This opens the way for many-fold reforms boosting participation even further. The current (and minor) rise in female participation can be easily reinforced because it has followed a rapid increase in female education and—though less strong—growth in employment opportunities in the public sector. That may bode well for the future of female participation in Poland—and for the cushioning effect against ageing. Second, as shown by the experience of almost all developed societies, 'if you live longer, you have to work longer'. Government attempts to increase the retirement age have been quite successful, though they follow disastrous incentives for early retirement of 'uniformed services', and an equally imprudent decision by the opposition Law and Justice (PiS) party to 'restore'—when in government—the 'old' retirement age of 60 (women) and 65 (men). The biggest challenge is to increase participation by older (over 55) workers. Only 35 per cent of 55–64-year-old persons in Poland are employed (compared with the EU average of 51); this requires facilitations (such as upskilling) and incentives (such as tax breaks).

Provisions: Pensions and superannuation funds

The fourth P is most challenging in its design and most difficult in its implementation. It consists of policies that secure financial and fiscal sustainability for old-age pensions and welfare services, and that implies not only balanced budgets (extremely rare among developed societies) but also savings preventing future financial squeezes and over-runs. In negative terms, such policies prevent the impoverishment of, and degradation of services for, the aged, including health/medical services. When faced with the unanticipated and rapid ageing of populations, governments face the challenge of expanding old-age pension provisions without creating deficits, debts and budgetary strains that, in turn, easily create or fuel social divisions and political tensions (e.g. Kendig et al. 2013). In Japan, a country that best illustrates the escalating costs of old-age pensions and aged care, the connected health and care costs—left untackled until recently—have been increasing geometrically: 6 per cent of GNP in 1970, 18 per cent in 1992, 22 per cent in 2013, and are expected to have increased to 27 per cent by 2025 (Ogawa 2014). Australia has largely avoided such dramatic fiscal pressures, though one estimate of budgetary deficit related to old-age pensions and aged-care services has been $40 billion and $13 billion respectively.

Broadly defined, provisions also include (i) financial adaptation (*cum*-cost-containment) of the growing number of aged, increasing longevity, and growing expectations of the ageing baby boomers; and (ii) the expansion of aged care and services, including the adaptation of the entire living environment to the specific needs of the aged. It ranges from trivial—like accessible housing and parking—to more sophisticated, such as easily driven cars, internet medicine, means-tested concessions and sophisticated information provision. Such services work if they are driven by the principle of widening and lengthening participation and the social benefits that participation brings to society and individuals, rather than by the self-serving needs-assessment of professional workers, who often create perverse incentives for dependency and the associated budget strain.

Australia has a relatively small deficit (2.5 per cent of GDP) and net public debt (around 15 per cent of GDP). The government has managed to contain the escalating costs through the monitoring and topping up of pension funds (including the $109 billion Future Fund to cover public service pensions), the building up of a strong ($1.8 trillion) superannuation system, with compulsory contributions rising to 12 per cent, the creation of private–public 'partnerships' in service provision (HACC[4], PACE[5]), the expansion of the 'user pays' principle combined with phased-in means-testing, and the expansion of market-regulated old-age services. To this policy set may be added a facilitation-*cum*-incentive for co-funding old age services by pensioners with high-value but 'frozen' assets through various forms of 'liquidification', such as reverse mortgages.

---

4   Home and Community Care.
5   Positive Action towards Career Engagement.

Poland, like most EU economies, is less prepared for a massive increase in old-age provisions (PRP 2013). The pension system has been reformed, but the country's superannuation-like open pension funds (OFE) have been emasculated. As Devictor (2012: 10) notes:

> The funding of the pensions system is obviously a key concern. Poland went through a full restructuring of its system over a decade ago and is reasonably well prepared. Yet, there remain uncertainties over the pension levels that will be provided in the medium-term. Under Poland's notional account pension system accumulated contributions are divided by life expectancy: thus, as life expectancy increases, benefits automatically decrease (unless people retire later) and the question is whether they will remain adequate. Some countries, such as Sweden, Italy, or Latvia, are also grappling with these issues.

Restoring private retirement funds, together with providing incentives (tax and otherwise) for saving for retirement, would not only restore balance between the 'three pillars' of old-age financial provisions (public pensions, superannuation, dedicated private savings), but also reduce future budgetary burdens, which are unfairly and unrealistically high at present. This can be done in an 'Australian way', through a mixture of incentives and regulations, partly because consumption levels in Poland are very high, and are unlikely to be lowered by incentives to save more and by regulations facilitating saving for retirement.

Is there a place for the 'Fifth P'', namely pronatalist measures, understood as policy designed to increase fertility rates and promote parenthood? The answer—based on the experiences of Australia, other developed societies and Poland—seems to be a qualified 'yes'. Australia may be seen as a moderate success in increasing fertility rates without high costs and 'perverse incentives' that reduce employment (participation) of women. But one has to keep in mind the reservations and qualifications mentioned above. Pronatal policies are very expensive, their effectiveness is dubious, and they often produce unintended consequences, some of them quite perverse (like reducing procreation choices or discouraging women from seeking employment). Taxing the childless (discredited in communist Poland), reducing access to contraceptives (discredited in communist Romania) or direct payments to mothers (discredited everywhere) are examples of poor strategies and policies pregnant with perverse effects.

They work only as a 'part of the policy mix', when designed in a way that limits perverse effects (e.g. welfare dependency, discouragement of employment)—and, obviously, when they are affordable and do not unduly 'burden' employers and/or the next generation. Examples of such well-designed measures include tax breaks for child-rearing expenses, parental leave, subsidised child care, etc. They are flexible, easily adjustable, and—most importantly—they have proven effective in raising fertility without reducing freedom and/or breaking government budgets.

Conclusions: Facing the challenges of ageing societies

The meta-principle of policy strategy suggested here may be formulated as 'follow the best practice' and 'emulate success'. Australia's response to population ageing seem to closely approximate such a best practice—it is comprehensive, complex, sustainable, long-term—and it has shown considerable success in facing the numerous challenges of an ageing society. Hence this attempt to 'generalise it' and 'forge out of it' a general strategic model that can be applicable to other highly developed societies, as exemplified by Poland.

Let us summarise the key elements of the complex strategy for facing the challenges of an ageing society that we have 'extracted' (necessarily selectively) from the Australian strategic policy set under the label of '4Ps':

- systematic monitoring of 'old age problems' (poor health, loneliness, social isolation, dependency, impoverishment)—their scope, intensity and social distribution;
- systematic monitoring of 'ageing society problems': economic dynamism, shrinking of working populations combined with increasing old age dependency ratios (dependent/working), and increasing generational 'burdens'; rising costs of welfare and aged care; rapidly increasing health costs, formation and mobilisation of 'grey lobbies', and rising conservatism;
- selective and rejuvenating immigration combined with integrative multiculturalism that includes incentives for, and facilitations of, swift employment and social engagement;

- systematic monitoring and promotion of productivity combined with reforms that boost productivity, such as 'productivity agreements' and productivity enhancement (education, skilling, investment in technologies, etc.);
- encouraging high labour force participation, especially among women and older workers, as well as encouraging longer employment, especially among highly skilled workers and professionals, and reducing unemployment, especially among young people;
- building up the self-funding component of pensions through strengthening of superannuation and encouragement of individual saving for old age. This also includes incentives for co-funding of old-age pensions and services from inheritable assets;
- containment of welfare and old-age care costs through the expanding use of 'partnerships' between families, volunteers, private service providers, philanthropic organisations and government bodies in provision and through the continuous rationalisation (qualitative) of old-age care;
- adaptation of the environment and 'living infrastructure' (houses, flats, roads, cars, shops, public spaces) for the use of all age cohorts.

The success of all of these strategies, it seems, depends on three factors. The first consists of stringing all these elements together, reducing inconsistencies, and 'testing' the model in practice in order to identify its 'sticking points', strengths and weaknesses early. The second—mentioned only briefly but extremely important—consists of adapting the strategic 'model' to the specific conditions of place and time. In social policy, as in transplant surgery, grafts that are not carefully prepared are often rejected. The third condition, hardly mentioned above, concerns the political presentation and promotion that, in turn, secure systematic implementation. This is to a large extent dependent on public information, education and systematic generation of political approval and good will. Public information and education, as the practice shows, are easily provided in highly educated advanced societies. The biggest barriers are short-termism—the best friend of demagogic opportunists—and sectional (ideological generational, age group, class, partisan) biases. When faced with the problems of an ageing society, conservative politicians tend to resort to 'traditionalist' strategies, such as 'pronatalism' aimed at 'restoring' traditional gender roles and identities, often at the expense of women's rights—an obvious illusion in the contemporary world.

Socialists often want to return to the communist-era restrictions on individual liberties and human rights by promoting state direct interventions, and they often promote popular but expensive policies with dubious returns (e.g. shortening working time, 'baby bonuses', etc.). Liberal-minded politicians are prone to another illusory belief—that it is enough to 'restore' individual responsibility, restrict public welfare, deregulate, cut entitlements and build up 'market driven individualism' in order to encourage rational conduct and the accompanied social-demographic balance. Such a strategy, as can be seen in Europe and America, does not work either. Instead, this kind of strategy exacerbates and masks, rather than mitigates, the problems of an ageing society. So do the strategies routinely embraced by the socialist left—expansion of services at the cost of mounting deficits and crippling debts, increasing taxation and, generally, pushing the burden onto the shoulders of coming generations. Therefore, the best chance of success is offered by removing policy strategies from the realm of ideological and partisan competition, making them supra-ideological (based on proven success), bi-partisan, or at least by removing them from the agenda of daily partisan contests.

References

Alzheimer Disease International (2014). Five Country Alzheimer's Disease Survey. Report of Key Findings. www.alz.co.uk/research/statistics. Accessed March 2015.

Beard John, Biggs Simon, Bloom David, Fried Linda, Hogan Paul, Kalache Alexandre and Olshansky Jay (Eds) (2011). *Global Population Ageing: Peril or Promise*. Geneva: World Economic Forum.

Bloom David, Boersch-Suppan Axel, McGee Patrick and Seike Atsushi (2011). *Population Aging: Facts, Challenges, Responses*. PGDA Working Paper No. 7. Program on the Global Demography of Aging, www3.weforum.org/docs/WEF_GAC_GlobalPopulation Ageing_Report_2012.pdf. Accessed December 2014.

Cardwell John (2006). *Demographic Transition Theory*. Dordrecht: Springer.

Devictor Xavier (2012). *Poland: Aging and the Economy*. Opinion piece, 14 June, The World Bank. www.worldbank.org/en/news/opinion/2012/06/14/poland-aging-and-the-economy.

Goldstone Jack, Kaufmann Eric and Toft Monica Duffy (eds) (2013). *Political Demography. How Population Changes Are Reshaping International Security and National Politics.* Oxford: Oxford University Press.

Gray Matthew, Qu Lixia and Weston Ruth (2008). *Fertility and Family Policy in Australia.* Research Paper No. 41, Australian Institute of Family Studies.

Harper Sarah (2006). *Ageing Societies: Myths, Challenges and Opportunities.* London: Hodder Arnold.

Harper Sarah and Hamblin Kate (Eds) (2014). *International Handbook of Ageing and Public Policy.* London: Edward Elgar.

Commonwealth of Australia (2002). *Intergenerational Report: 2002–03.* Canberra: Department of Treasury.

Commonwealth of Australia (2007). *Intergenerational Report: 2007.* Canberra: Department of Treasury.

Commonwealth of Australia (2010). *Australia to 2050: Future Challenges. The 2010 Intergenerational Report.* Canberra: Department of Treasury.

Commonwealth of Australia (2015). *2015 Intergenerational Report: Australia in 2055.* Canberra: Department of Treasury. www. treasury.gov.au/PublicationsAndMedia/Publications/2015/2015-Intergenerational-Report. Accessed March 2015.

Department of Treasury (n.d.). Australia's Demographic Challenges— the economic implications of an ageing population. demographics. treasury.gov.au/content/_download/australias_demographic_ challenges/html/adc-04.asp. Accessed March 2015.

Kaufmann Eric (2011). *Shall the Religious Inherit the Earth: Demography and Politics in the Twenty-first Century?* London: Profile Books.

Kendig Hal, Wells Yvonne and O'Laughlin Kate (2013). Australian baby boomers face retirement during the global financial crisis, *Journal of Ageing and Public Policy*, 25: 264–280.

Lee Ronald (2003). The Demographic Transition: Three Centuries of Fundamental Change, *Journal of Economic Perspectives*, 17(Fall): 167–190.

McDonald Peter and Kippen Rebecca (1999). Ageing: the social and demographic dimensions. In *Policy Implications of the Ageing of Australia's Population*, Conference Proceedings, 18–19 March 1998, Productivity Commission and Melbourne Institute of Applied Economic and Social Research, pp. 47–70.

McDonald Peter and Kippen Rebecca (2001a). The impact of immigration on the ageing of Australia's population. In M Siddique (Ed) *International Migration into the 21st Century*, Cheltenham: Edward Elgar, pp. 153–177.

McDonald Peter and Kippen Rebecca (2001b). Labour supply prospects in 16 developed countries, 2000–2050, *Population and Development Review*, 27(1): 1–32.

Ogawa Naohiro (2014). *Population Ageing in Japan and Its Financial Consequences*. Paper presented at the session on Population Ageing Academy of the Social Sciences in Australia, Canberra, 11 November 2014.

Okólski Marek and Topińska Irena (2012). *Social Impact of Emigration and Rural-Urban Migration in Central and Eastern Europe*, Final Country Report—Poland. Berlin: GVG.

Organisation for Economic Co-operation and Development (OECD) (2013). *Demographic Transition and an Ageing Society: Implications for local labour markets in Poland*, Report. www.oecd.org/cfe/leed/Poland%20Report_V8.1%20FINAL.pdf.

Pracodawcy Rzeczypospolitej Polskiej (PRP) (2013). Starzejace sie spoleczenstwo jako wyzwanie ekonomiczne dla europejskich gospodarek, Raport, Pracodawcy Rzeczypospolitej Polskiej. docplayer.pl/4071703-Raport-starzejace-sie-spoleczenstwo-jako-wyzwanie-ekonomiczne-dla-europeiskich-gospodarek.html. Accessed 2 October 2015.

Productivity Commission (2013). *An Ageing Australia: Preparing for the future*. Research Report. Canberra: Productivity Commission.

Summers Lawrence H (2014). US Economic Prospects: Secular Stagnation, Hysteresis, and the Zero Lower Bound, *Business Economics*, 49(2): 65–73.

The Economist (2014). *Age Invaders*, 26 April. www.economist.com/news/briefings/21601248-generation-old-people-about-change-global-economy-they-will-not-all-do-so.

The Economist (2009). *Healthcare Strategies for an Ageing Society*, Economist Intelligence Unit, 7 May.

Torp Cornelius (Ed) (2013). *Ageing in the 20th Century*. Cambridge: Cambridge University Press.

Trading Economics (2014). Poland Productivity. www.tradingeconomics.com/poland/productivity. Accessed March 2015.

United Nations (2001). *World Population Ageing: 1950–2050*. New York: Department of Economic and Social Affairs Population Division.

United Nations (2013). *World Population Ageing 2013*, New York: Department of Economic and Social Affairs Population Division. www.un.org/en/development/desa/population/publications/pdf/ageing/WorldPopulationAgeing2013.pdf. Accessed March 2015.

Websites

Alzheimer Disease International, www.alz.co.uk/research/statistics. Accessed March 2015.

Dementia and Alzheimer Disease, www.alzheimer-europe.org/Dementia. Accessed March 2015.

HACC–Home and Community Care Program, www.health.wa.gov.au/hacc/home/whatis.cfm. Accessed March 2015.

Knoema, knoema.com/PDYGTH/labour-productivity-growth-in-the-total-economy?country=1000240-poland. Accessed March 2015.

PACE, www.ncbi.nlm.nih.gov/pubmed/9033525. Accessed March 2015.

Polskie Towarzystwo Alzheimerowskie. alzheimerpolska.pl.

Wikipedia, Population Ageing, en.wikipedia.org/wiki/Population_ageing. Accessed March 2014.

Part 3. Improving health and wellbeing

7

Social research and actions on ageing well

Hal Kendig and Colette Browning

Why do researchers and advocates use the holistic term 'ageing well'? The term encompasses positive and constructive views of ageing, health, and wellbeing. It recognises 'ageing' as a lifelong, normal experience for everyone rather than being limited to those who are (often pejoratively) termed old. 'Wellness' as viewed by older people is grounded in a sense of feeling good as well as maintaining or recovering good physical and mental health as a resource for daily living. Ageing well is increasingly viewed as a major goal for health and care practitioners, as well as for older people themselves. A multidisciplinary approach to health recognises the influences of social factors and allows for active pursuit of better experiences of ageing.

A social perspective brings us beyond the 'problems' approach to ageing (which can cast responsibilities onto individuals) to focus more on opportunities and societal responses. This constructive approach is beginning to complement and at times challenge dominant biomedical and 'decrement' constructions of ageing. Yet the entrenched stereotype (and in *some* cases the reality) of individual ageing as an inevitable process of degeneration, continues to underpin much of the personal and public concern for treatment and care of vulnerable older individuals. This negative discourse is often promulgated by health professions and organisations, particularly when seeking resources for their work treating disease and meeting care needs. Alarmist images of population ageing as a 'tsunami' or 'demographic doomsday' are invoked by governments seeking justifications for their fiscal strategies. In the ongoing contests of ideas and interests, progressive researchers and advocates are finding common ground in 'reimaging' ageing positively.

The chapter begins with international and national concepts of ageing well and directions for action. We then present a body of Australian research on ageing well including the context and funding that has enabled these studies to be conducted. Qualitative accounts provide older people's own viewpoints while survey findings highlight social variability and the improvability of ageing. The next section provides examples of applied studies that have better connected research and action, informing new approaches to policies and services. The chapter concludes by considering ways in which advocacy organisations that represent older people are promoting ageing well.

Conceptualising ageing well and action directions

Much of the research and policy discussion on healthy ageing is now centred on the widely accepted World Health Organization (WHO) definition: 'Health is a state of complex physical, mental and social well-being and not merely the absence of disease or infirmity.' It's comprehensive *World Report on Ageing and Health* (WHO 2015) sets further initiatives in healthy ageing and wellbeing building on a substantial evidence base. WHO conceptualises the related concept of 'active ageing' as 'the process of optimising opportunities for health, participation, and security in order to enhance quality of life as people age' (WHO 2002: 12). It also established and now facilitates the global 'age-friendly communities', which guides applied local research and action aiming to facilitate active ageing (Kendig and Phillipson 2014).

International research is demonstrating that processes of ageing are amenable to a range of bio-psychosocial influences, with many of them being changeable and hence improvable. The origins of the ageing well concept can be traced back to ideas on 'successful ageing', as initiated nearly two decades ago by Rowe and Kahn (1987) in their US-based challenge to the view that old age necessarily equates to loss and disability. They take an aspirational approach (rather than 'usual' ageing focus), defining 'successful ageing' as a multidimensional concept with the three components of 'avoiding disease', 'engagement in life', and 'maintaining high cognitive and physical functioning'. The research literature subsequently burgeoned with Cosco et al. (2014) identifying 105 empirical studies with a range of operational definitions—most have a biomedical focus but increasingly they also have psychosocial and lay components.

There has been extensive commentary and criticism of the 'successful ageing' concept and its terminology. In our own work, we have preferred the term 'ageing well', because 'successful ageing', in its original formulation, implicitly defines nearly all older people as 'unsuccessfully ageing'. This is clearly at odds with the good quality of life reported by most older people, notwithstanding their having some health problems (Kendig et al. 2014). A range of commentators have pointed out that 'successful ageing' focuses on individuals to the exclusion of structural, social, gender and cultural explanations of their circumstances. We have demonstrated the widely varying concepts of ageing well, for example between Calvinist religions in the West and Buddhism in the East (Kendig and Browning 2010). Katz and Calastanti (2014) take a critical approach, observing that successful ageing 'fails to acknowledge social relations of power, environmental determinants of health, and the bio politics of health inequalities' (p 29). They highlight the importance of social exclusion, as well as the lifelong accumulation of advantage or disadvantage (Dannefer 2003) that is central to inequalities in later life, including poor access to health care.

The original formulators of 'successful ageing' have responded to these debates. They presented a case for research and action on 'Successful Aging of Societies' in their special issue of *Dædalus: Journal of the American Academy of Arts & Sciences* (Rowe 2015). Contributors reviewed the importance of ageing for productivity; the benefits and potential of an ageing society; healthy ageing as a human right; and prevention as a core responsibility of health systems. This Successful Ageing of Society initiative brought US mainstream ageing and health research, and its dominant epidemiological and clinical traditions, closer to European political economy and social determinants perspectives (see Chapter 1) that are informing critical approaches to social action on ageing.

Phillipson (2013), writing from the UK, provides a sociological paradigm for understanding how ageing societies generate age-related inequalities in the evolving welfare state. Health providers and professionals—as well as socioeconomic groups and governments—form interest groups that influence as well as benefit from public action in health and welfare services. The social practices that underlie these relationships form power structures influencing, in the instance of health, the subsidies and regulation of the industries and professions and the priority issues they represent to the public. Phillipson makes a case that the structured dependency of old age, the traditional focus of ageing in the welfare state, is shifting to new recognitions as political and economic pressures intensify along with population ageing and uncertain economic prospects. Health can be viewed as a dimension of his general argument that preparing for ageing populations requires 'rebuilding institutions', developing 'new pathways for later life', and 'recognising new forms of solidarity'.

Further sociological conceptions are informing proactive ways of thinking about ageing. Kohli and Arza's (2011) observation on pension reform in Europe would apply equally to ageing and health: they comment on the 'power of ideas' that are employed by interest groups to portray difficult and interest-laden reforms as being 'inevitable'. Drawing on social gerontology and social welfare practice, Scharf and Keating (2012) raise theoretical issues and review evidence on the global challenge of moving 'from exclusion to inclusion in old age'.

In Australia, Fine (2014a) has applied a political economy perspective to how population ageing has been portrayed as a cause of economic deterioration and as a rationale for cutting health and social expenditure in Australia and other G20 countries. He also examines ways in which longevity has accentuated gender and age inequalities in caregiving, and the social constructions of care, by the ageing field as contrasted with the disability movement (Fine 2014b). Stebbing and Spies-Butcher (2015) also apply a political economy perspective, in their case to interpret the implications of declining home ownership rates in later life and ways in which they can combine with related public subsidies, accelerating inequalities of economic wellbeing between social classes, age groups, and cohorts.

A valuable Australian commentary on 'ageing well', Aberdeen and Bye (2013) observe the 'silence' of critical sociology in Australia in the face of what Asquith (2009) has termed 'neoliberal policies of positive ageing'. They comment that, in contrast to scholarship in the Northern Hemisphere, Australian gerontology had developed (with a few exceptions) in a functionalist tradition focused on individual adjustment and economic priorities of government. They observe a predominance of biomedical research and very little political economy, feminist, or other theoretical perspectives. Mendes (2013) provides an Australian critique of 'Active Ageing: A right or a duty?'

The paucity of critical Australian studies in ageing arises in part because the Australian Research Council (ARC) and National Health and Medical Research Council (NHMRC) provide funding primarily for large-scale empirical research more than critical scholarship. Available research funding on ageing supports the medical and health fields more than the humanities and social sciences. Australian research is underway to inform action on ageing well, inclusive of social as well as health dimensions, however, a plurality of disciplinary viewpoints is yet to develop very far.

Australian research on ageing well

Our research on ageing well began more than 25 years ago thanks to the vision and support of the Victorian Health Promotion Foundation (VicHealth), which recognised the value of improving health status across the life-course (Kendig and Browning 2010). The Foundation funded what eventually became the Melbourne Longitudinal Surveys on Ageing (MELSHA), subsequently funded by the NHMRC and then the 'Healthy and Productive Ageing' Stream in the ARC Centre of Excellence in Population Ageing Research (CEPAR). (See Chapter 1 for these and other longitudinal studies.)

Each of the studies reviewed below has yielded findings from older people that can inform action on ageing well and provide a balance of evidence along with that from other interest groups. The studies provide guidance as to directions for health promotion in the community as well as interventions when people are at risk in later life.

Older people's views and experiences

Older people's views can contrast notably with portrayals of them as clients or patients in health systems, subjects in experiments, or respondents in surveys. Rigorous qualitative studies, while difficult to fund at a significant scale, can seek out a range of voices, hear people on their own terms, and bring balance and insights into multidisciplinary studies of ageing.

Public attitudes are among the most powerful social influences on ageing well. Others' expectations of ageing people can not only influence the scope of their social opportunities but more fundamentally influence their conceptions of themselves, their capacities, and their value. An early qualitative study explored ageing individuals' perceptions of their 'social treatment' by others in everyday life, ranging from affirmation of 'normal ageing' to the ageism, demoralisation, and exclusion of being made to 'feel old' (Minichiello et al. 2000, 2012). The study found that ageist attitudes were most pronounced in terms of older people's experiences in the health system and employment.

These findings accord with US evidence that negative attitudes can impact on ageing self-stereotype, which in turn can predict preventive health behaviours, functional health and survival (Levy and Myers 2004). Research from the Australian Longitudinal Survey on Ageing (ALSA) in Adelaide concluded 'we have shown that the psychological resources of expectancy of control and self-esteem are important for the maintenance of older adults' self-perceptions of ageing when physical functioning is declining' (Sargent-Cox et al. 2012). ALSA researchers also identified the importance of a 'sense of purpose as a psychological resource for ageing well' (Windsor et al. 2015; see also Chapter 9).

When beginning our own VicHealth-supported study several decades ago, we conducted and reviewed qualitative investigations of older people's life goals and the significance health had for them (Kendig et al. 2014). They speak of life and health ideals centred around keeping active, feeling well, a positive outlook, and capacities to maintain their independence and make ongoing contributions. While good health is in part viewed as an absence of disease or functional limitations, the older people generally viewed health as a valued resource in which they invest, for example, through good eating and staying physically active. Many report having made adaptations to their lives and homes that have enabled them to maintain their health and ways of life, notwithstanding mounting frailty. We concluded that health is a critical resource for older people in maintaining continuity in their sense of self and continuing to live in their own homes in the community.

Listening to older individuals reveals some systematic variations in their stories. Gender is prominent as seen in the contrasting 'his' and 'her' versions. Women are more likely to view health as a means of enabling social participation, while men focus more on their continuing physical capacities and contributions. Older individuals have 'health identities' and view themselves as successful 'survivors' (Walker-Birckhead 1996). While care needs to be taken to avoid cultural stereotypes, Chinese Australians have reported the importance of physical activity, healthy eating and successful children for their own wellbeing (Browning et al. 2011).

Locale studies

Locale studies can provide rich insights into the many ways in which the features of place and community can influence ageing well. Winterton and Warburton (2012) report, from their study of ageing in two Victorian rural areas, on the significance of 'place' and historical context of rural living; the life choices (human agency) made over people's lifetimes; and ways in which 'ageing in the bush' can reinforce successful ageing. A qualitative study of older men in rural Victoria found that their work, family, and ethnic identity were important resources for health and wellbeing, although rural locations imposed significant barriers to accessing services (Radermacher and Feldman 2015).

The importance of place was reinforced in Mackenzie et al.'s (2015) Sydney-based analysis of older people's subjective views on their homes and plans for moving or adapting them. Those who most strongly identified with their homes and felt connected to their neighbours and their communities had more positive perceptions of their homes and communities. Housing policies and urban design were recommended as important to maintain independence and adaptability as people age.

An NHMRC-funded ethnographic study of homeless older men in inner Sydney (Russell et al. 2001; Quine et al. 2004) found that many were proactive and capable in securing safe shelter, food, companionship, and other necessities for health and independence. This research underscored the value of action with vulnerable older people at a local level within accommodation and service contexts.

A qualitative study of older gay men in Sydney found that many had experienced positive changes since the 1970s, with greater public and private acceptance, but some expressed a loss of gay community as they grew older and experienced HIV-related stigma within the gay community (Lyons et al. 2015). The authors comment that broader community understanding of this potentially vulnerable group would facilitate quality of life and quality of care.

Population findings

The MELSHA study followed a cohort of older people living in the community from 1994 to 2010 (Browning and Kendig 2010; Kendig et al. 2014). Respondents had a strong focus on positive health actions, notably physical activity, healthy eating, and social activity. Healthy actions were encouraged most by spouses (especially wives), with friends and adult children also being significant. Education, income, and other aspects of social class were related to positive health behaviours and risk factors for serious illness.

At baseline, more than 70 per cent were 'ageing well' as defined by continuing to live in the community independently (that is not in residential aged care), with good self-rated health and psychological wellbeing. Subsequent survival was related to low levels of reported strain in daily life and higher levels of social activity, while entry to residential aged care was predicted by being underweight and having low levels of social activity (Kendig et al. 2010). Significant lifestyle predictors of continuing to age well included physical activity, nutrition, not being underweight, social support, low strain, and not smoking (Kendig et al. 2014). These lifestyle factors, which are potentially improvable, are major risk factors for chronic disease and important targets for health promotion late in life. Gender differences in the findings underscore the importance of tailoring promotion efforts to men and women.

Another longitudinal study based in Melbourne (Hodge et al. 2013) reported similar predictors of ageing successfully. A Sydney cross-sectional study found that physically active lifestyles (and less sitting time) were associated with good self-rated health and quality of life among ageing people (Rosenkranz et al. 2013).

The Healthy Retirement Project, funded by the Victorian Health Promotion Foundation, followed individuals through retirement transitions since the late 1990s (De Vaus et al. 2007). Most managed the transitions with continuing good health and wellbeing; many had freely chosen retirement and found that it enabled changes to healthier ways of life and improved health and wellbeing. Some adverse outcomes were apparent, particularly for working-class men and those who had been forced to retire by employers or through ill-health. Socioeconomic resources and opportunities for choice were found to be critical to a rewarding and independent life after retirement and managing the life transitions. A national analysis of women's adjustment to retirement, conducted a generation later, found a two-stage process (Zhu and He 2015): first, there were significant and lasting increases in life satisfaction just after retirement; and then ongoing decline through later years.

The Ageing Baby Boomer in Australia (ABBA) project, funded by an ARC Linkages grant with National Seniors Australia (NSA), provided evidence on this new cohort entering later life. As discussed in Chapter 2, there is great diversity among the boomers, who exemplify both continuity and change as compared to earlier cohorts. Focus group interviews and a national survey found that to varying degrees boomers reject ageist expectations, overwhelmingly evince a fierce desire to remain independent and contributing, and have a strong 'generational stake' in their children's and grandchildren's futures. Health promotion is a priority for the many boomers who have significant behavioural risks (notably obesity and sedentary lifestyles) that predispose them to diabetes and other chronic diseases (Humpel et al. 2010). The global financial crisis significantly reduced boomers' life satisfaction, especially for those still employed with fewer socioeconomic resources, and increased expectations to work longer. (Kendig et al. 2013). NSA drew on the study to produce popular reports used to inform National Seniors membership and in advocacy to government.

The Life History and Health Survey (Kendig et al. 2016), funded by an ARC Discovery project and now CEPAR, is examining how productivity, health, and wellbeing on entry to later life are influenced by earlier life experiences. Childhood advantage or disadvantage during the early post-war era—in terms of (parents') socioeconomic resources, educational attainment and health—was found to predispose work and family pathways through adulthood that had continuing influences on wellbeing on entry to later life. The findings suggest the value of investment in human capital from childhood onward throughout life.

Only 5 per cent of Aboriginal people are aged 60 years or more, as a result of high birth rates and life expectancies estimated at 15 to 20 years less than other Australians. The Koori Growing Old Well Study in urban and regional NSW (Radford et al. 2014) found that the dementia rate in Indigenous communities was three times that of non-Indigenous communities. Indigenous Australians face a 'cascade' of risk factors across the life-span, including low birth weight, removal from family, education, head injuries, alcohol misuse, smoking and inactivity. Another study developed specialised assessment tools that took cultural and social context into account in assessing dementia and cognitive capacities among older Indigenous people in remote areas (Smith et al. 2008.) Efforts to 'close the gap' in Indigenous life expectancy are directed overwhelmingly to younger people while older people 'age without longevity' (Cotter et al. 2012). Clapham and Duncan (2016) have reviewed initiatives by Indigenous people themselves to support ageing well in their own communities.

Migration and ethnicity are major factors in cultural orientations and life experiences, yet diversity of ageing in these terms has received relatively less research attention. The Melbourne Collaborative Study (a large prospective survey) has examined from mid-life onward variation in lifestyles and risk factors for those born in Italy and Greece as compared to the Australian born (Hodge et al. 2007). Dietary patterns were found to be associated with cultural background—e.g. fruit and white bread consumption was a larger component of the diet among these groups (and meat a smaller component)—which would have influenced their risk of diabetes and other chronic disease. A study of older men in Sydney (Waern et al. 2015) found that the Italian and Greek migrants were at higher risk compared to the Australian born for poor nutrition and higher alcohol intake. While low income is a greater risk, the authors suggest 'the need for nutritional education targeted at older men from culturally and linguistically diverse backgrounds' (p 819).

It can be difficult to conduct surveys on social factors in the health of older people from culturally and linguistically diverse (CALD) background as researchers need to understand the cultural context and translation. This knowledge is a priority, given that by 2026 about 25 per cent of people aged over 80 years will come from diverse cultural backgrounds (Productivity Commission 2013).

Research for practice, services, and policy to promote ageing well

It is important to reflect on what we would term the 'political economy' of knowledge and the ways in which interest groups shape research funding and directions—and hence the available knowledge. While valuable scholarship can be produced relatively independently, larger-scale efforts in applied multidisciplinary research, yielding rewards in the careers for university staff as well as public benefits, depend critically on funding, particularly from the ARC and the NHMRC. As we have explained elsewhere (Kendig and Browning 2010), targeted ARC and NHMRC funding has been essential in building the knowledge base in line with the National Research Priority:

> *Ageing well, ageing productively*: Developing better social, medical and population health strategies to improve the mental and physical capacities of ageing people.

Our knowledge in this priority area has been built with a cornerstone of strategic research funding including the NHMRC/ARC Ageing Well/ Ageing Productively Research Program, the ARC/NHMRC Research Network in Ageing Well, the ARC Centre of Excellence in Population Ageing (CEPAR) (which has a research strand on Ageing Well, Ageing Productively). ARC Linkage programs funded on the basis of social and commercial benefit (as well as research and investigator quality) have also been important. The future direction of these programs, and indeed all ARC and NHMRC funding, faces considerable uncertainties at present as government deliberates on ways in which research can best contribute to Australia's national development.

Research funding is inevitably driven by government priorities and other interests, as well as researchers' own priorities, and these can change. Current ageing research, as evidenced particularly by recent NHMRC grants and special initiatives, has shown a shift towards relatively more research on age-related diseases, notably 'problems' such as dementia. Observing a similar trend in the US 25 years ago, Estes and Binney (1989) warned of the 'biomedicalization of aging'. When ageing is cast as a medical problem, this risks an imbalanced knowledge base that yields less understanding of potential action on the environmental, social and economic drivers of wellbeing in old age.

National research funding has been supplemented by philanthropic organisations that have a primary concern for informing social actions that may follow from understanding the needs and experiences of disadvantaged older people. Philanthropic foundations have been at the forefront of funding innovative research on action to improve quality of life:

> social change philanthropy focuses on the root causes of social, economic and environmental injustices; includes people impacted by injustices as decision-makers; and makes philanthropy more accessible and diverse (Lord Mayor's Charitable Foundation 2012).

Governments also fund research to inform specific issues for policy or service applications.

There are multiple ways in which research-based knowledge can inform social action on ageing well and the health of older people. The traditional approach is that researchers independently design and conduct studies, publish in peer-reviewed journals, and then this information is eventually identified in literature reviews before devising health programs or interventions. This mainstream, and indeed usual, approach provides some quality assurance through peer review but it relies on uncoordinated connections between research and action. The process may also take years, from planning to conducting and utilising research. Research commissioned by philanthropic organisations or by government, however, may not be disseminated through peer-reviewed journals and as such the utility of this type of 'grey' literature may not be fully realised.

Program grants (such as the VicHealth-initiated MELSHA studies), Linkages grants such as the ABBA project reviewed earlier, and the CEPAR Ageing Well/Ageing Productively research strand augment traditional research approaches in several ways. Longer-term partnerships, between researchers and those who will use the knowledge, can build collaborations in setting study directions and make joint investments attentive to mutual, complementary interests, and each can learn from the other while conducting the research. Researchers can release information reports and working papers fairly quickly, for timely applications by their partners, while articles take more time as they undergo the lengthy peer-review process for scholarly audiences. With consultancies, researchers conduct evaluations and other studies (often with short time-frames) according to objectives set in contractual terms by their research partners, with attendant risks to quality and independence that require careful terms in contracts.

We now turn to some examples of the ways in which Australian social science research has been contributing to actions on ageing well in specific policy arenas.

Research-informed actions in the health arena

In an earlier commentary for the Academy of Social Sciences in Australia (Kendig and Browning 2011), we reviewed the research base and priority contributions to healthy ageing policy and programs. Our research-informed submissions on the value of comprehensive health promotion and integrated health care for older people were used to reinforce recommendations from the 2009 National Health and Hospital Commission Report. However, national action continued to focus on single diseases and behaviours with little attention to older people. Eventually, in March 2016, the Prime Minister and Minister of Health announced 'A healthier Medicare for chronically-ill patients' that was said to 'revolutionise the way we care for Australians with chronic diseases and complex conditions—aiming to keep them out-of-hospital and living happier and healthier lives at home'. An accumulation of evidence and submissions and growing appetite for health reform, precipitated by the forthcoming election, appears to have eventually contributed to some action on a difficult and long-standing priority wrought by Commonwealth–state tensions on funding.

Applied research has also been important in recognising self-care as a core component of health promotion and clinical care. After trial efforts in self-management were proved to be effective, Medicare now funds general practitioners to work in collaboration with other health professionals to implement Chronic Disease Management Plans (Browning and Thomas 2015). However, health assessments for older people have continued to focus on identifying 'problems' without providing much in the way of resources for general practitioners and other health professionals to work with patients to assist with changing health behaviours as preventive health measures before the onset of these conditions and their associated morbidity. Many years earlier Byles et al. (2004) had found that while health assessment for veterans and war widows resulted in higher quality of life, they also increased the probability of residential aged-care placement. These are instances where our *health systems* are not set up to provide integrated solutions to assist older people to age well.

An area of successful research translation has been with falls-prevention interventions. Clemson et al. (2004, 2012) developed model risk-reduction for falls interventions building self-efficacy, behavioural changes, and home adaptations. The programs were proven to be effective in reducing injuries and hospitalisation. The NHMRC funded the core research while the NSW State Government has supported the production of training manuals and program implementation. Benefits are anticipated in restraining costs to governments as well as better quality of life outcomes for older people.

Actions in the aged and community care arenas

Applied research on ageing well also has contributed to reforms of aged and community care. After reviewing literature (including MELSHA findings), and extensive consumer and industry consultations, the Productivity Commission outlined major new directions in its commissioned *Caring for Older People* report, which led to the 2013 Living Longer, Living Better legislative reforms now being implemented.[1] The Australian Department of Social Services (2012, 2015) is implementing Consumer-Directed Care (CDC) programs informed by a government-funded evaluation of pilot programs (KPMG 2012) that examined impacts on the wellbeing of older people and carers, promoting independence, enabling choice and maintaining community engagement. The usefulness of this consultancy was limited, however, by its delayed release. There is a small related academic literature (Low et al. 2012) and ARC Linkages studies are underway.

Practice-based research also has demonstrated the case for prevention as well as re-enablement (Lewin et al. 2014) in the design and implementation of the national Home Care Packages Program. This work has been supported by a partnership between Curtin University and the Silver Chain (an aged-care provider). Qualitative research and consultations by innovative community-care providers, such as the ACH Group's (2011) *Good Lives for Older People*, have focused on person-centred care building self-help capacities and quality of life. Partnerships with local universities in Adelaide are furthering this work with the support of ARC Linkages funding.

Actions in the culturally and linguistically diverse community arena

A study funded by the Lord Mayor's Charitable Foundation (Feldman and Radermacher 2014) examined barriers and capacities to enhance ageing well in Chinese, Greek and Italian communities. This provided the basis for future engagement by the Foundation to progress social change. The RDNS Dementia Care in the Community project was funded by the Lord Mayor's Charitable Foundation. This project conducted research in the area of a 'key worker' to advocate for and support CALD clients with dementia and their carers. This approach is now being investigated with other at-risk older people in the community. Similarly, a project by the UNSW Social Policy Research Centre, in partnership with the Benevolent Society (SPRC 2010), identified number of issues for people from CALD backgrounds, including loss of homeland and status within the family, isolation

---

1   livinglongerlivingbetter.gov.au.

and vulnerability due to changes to traditional networks and poor English skills leading to poorer access to services and communication problems.

Actions in the age-friendly communities arena

Research has demonstrated the value of the WHO Age Friendly Cities approach for facilitating local action to improve wellbeing and address inequalities (Kendig et al. 2014). In Canberra, an ANU survey (funded by the ACT Government) reported on older people's views on their priorities for improving their neighbourhoods and city and the vulnerabilities of groups, including older residents living in public housing and older women living alone. Findings have been reviewed by subsequent community assemblies, informed modest actions such as improvements to the bus system, and yielded academic journals as well as National Seniors publications (Pearson et al. 2012). This work follows the WHO age-friendly cities initiative and further work on implementation is being led by Councils on the Ageing (COTA) (Australia) working closely with the International Federation on Aging (see below).

Consumer advocacy and ageing well

National and international advocacy organisations provide essential leadership in action on ageing well initiatives. COTA (Australia) was founded to 'protect and promote the wellbeing of older Australians'.[2] COTA has played a key part in building the National Aged Care Alliance (NACA): 'a body of peak national organisations in aged care, including consumer groups, providers, unions and health professionals, working together to determine a more positive future for aged care in Australia'.[3] COTA and NACA have been influential advocates for consumer-directed care as per legislation now being introduced to the Australian Parliament (February 2016).[4]

---

2   www.cota.org.au.
3   www.naca.asn.au.
4   www.cota.org.au/australia/NewsList/2016/older-australians-welcome-more-choice-and-control-in-delivery-of-home-care.aspx.

The National Seniors Association (NSA) is a large representative organisation with strong grassroots membership and involvement in policy. It's Productive Ageing Centre, working with the Department of Social Services:

> aims to play a pivotal role in bridging the gap between traditional academic researchers in ageing, the community and decision-makers. Our broad research purpose is to "emphasise the positives of ageing and an ageing society, as well as flag the challenges (nationalseniors. com.au/be-informed/research).

NSA is partnering with Per Capita and NAB Bank in convening a coalition of interests taking action on their Blueprint for an Ageing Australia.[5] The Blueprint argues for action recognising that with increased longevity we now have '25 extra years of high quality living with new opportunities for productive work, unprecedented leisure, teaching and learning, and fulfilling relationships with family and friends'.

The Australian Association of Gerontology (AAG) has the mission of 'expanding knowledge on ageing'.[6] The AAG plays a pivotal role in relating research to action, and in advocacy and coordination to build research capacities and translate findings into practice and educational programs. It is the principal point for Australia's engagement with the International Association of Gerontology and Geriatrics (IAGG),[7] and it auspices the International Longevity Centre (ILC) (Australia) as part of the international network of ILCs.[8] Other important contributors in ageing networks are provider organisations including Aged and Community Services in Australia (ACSA)[9] and Leading Aged Services Australia (LASA).[10]

International developments in ageing also are forming coalitions and they provide valuable resources and support for Australian initiatives. In addition to leadership by the WHO (as reviewed above), international organisations are forming networks for advocacy on behalf of the interests of older people:

---

5   percapita.org.au/wp-content/uploads/2014/11/BlueprintForAnAgeingAustralia.pdf.
6   www.aag.asn.au.
7   www.iagg.info/.
8   www.ilc-alliance.org/index.php/members/details/ilc-australia.
9   www.agedcare.org.au/.
10   www.lasa.asn.au/.

- The United Nations' *Transforming our World: The 2030 Agenda for Sustainable Development* set as its Goal 3: 'To ensure healthy lives and promote wellbeing for all at all ages' (UN 2015). It also is leading action to establish a Convention on the Human Rights of Older People. The UN continues to work towards the 2002 UN Second World Assembly on Ageing Declaration that had set three priority directions to achieve 'a society for all ages': 1) the active participation of older people in development that would benefit all citizens; 2) the promotion of health and wellbeing as people age; and 3) the provision of enabling environments to support healthy ageing.

- The World Economic Forum is a 'comprehensive and integrated platform to strategically shape global, regional, national, and industry agendas'. It's Global Agenda Council on Ageing Society, comprised of leading international organisation on ageing, highlighting the challenges ahead in *Global Population Ageing: Peril or Promise* (Beard et al. 2011), and in 2015 launched a campaign on how longevity can create markets and drive economic growth.[11]

- The International Federation on Ageing (IFA) (a network of non-government organisations, industry, and academia, and individuals in 70 countries) has a mission to 'influence age-related policies that improve the lives of older people'.[12]

- Help Age International, while its work focuses mainly on developing countries, aims to 'work with our partners to ensure that people everywhere understand how much older people contribute to society and that they must enjoy their right to health care, social services and economic and physical security'.[13] Its Global Age Watch provides comparable data on the quality of life and other country 'performance indicators'. Appendix 1 benchmarks Australia with comparator countries

- In the United States, eight of the leading ageing-focused organisations have formed the Frameworks Institute 'to create a better public understanding of older adults' needs and contributions to society—and subsequently to improve the lives of all people as they age.[14] The partner organisations include AARP Inc. (representing 40 million older people), the knowledge-based Gerontological Society of America, and organisations representing service providers and professionals, and grant-funding bodies.

---

11   www.weforum.org/communities/global-agenda-council-on-ageing.
12   www.ifa-fiv.org/about/.
13   www.helpage.org/.
14   www.frameworksinstitute.org/aging.html.

The Institute's influential report, *Aging, Agency, and Attribution of responsibility: Shifting Public Discourse about Older Adults* (O'Neil and Haydon 2015), identifies media and advocacy narratives on ageing including 'the throw-away generation', 'Vibrant Senior', 'Demographic Crisis', 'Aging Workers', 'Government and Solution' and 'Government as Problem'.

Conclusion

Evidence and ideas-based action is underway on ageing well. Constructive images of ageing are being championed by advocates, notably COTAs and NSA along with AAG, the Australian Human Rights Commission (AHRC 2015), and researchers and service providers who seek out older people's views. Research can suggest priorities and inform effective directions for achieving ageing well. In the short-term, research findings on fundamental concepts such as ageing well are unlikely to have much influence among the contests of interest groups in the broader economy and public policy. Over the longer-term, however, the values-based ageing well approach, embedded in the experiences and aspirations of older people themselves, can be an important investment in positive approaches to ageing people and an ageing society.

References

Aberdeen Lucinda and Bye Lee-Anne (2013). Challenge for Australian Sociology: Critical ageing research—ageing well? *Journal of Sociology*, 49(1): 3–21.

ACH Group (2011). *Good Lives for Older People*. Annual Report 2010/2011, South Australia: Aged Care and Housing Group Inc.

Asquith Nicole (2009). Positive Ageing, Neoliberalism and Australian Sociology. *Journal of Sociology,* 45(3): 255–269. doi:10.1177/1440783309335650.

Australian Department of Social Services (2012). *Evaluation of the consumer-directed care initiative*, Final Report, January, Canberra: Australia Government. www.dss.gov.au/sites/default/files/documents/10_2014/evaluation-of-the-consumer-directed-care-initiative-final-report.pdf.

Australian Department of Social Services (2015). *National Home Care Packages Programme*. Canberra: Australia Government. www.dss.gov.au/our-responsibilities/ageing-and-aged-care/programs-services/home-care-packages.

Australian Human Rights Commission (AHRC) (2015). *National Prevalence Survey of Age Discrimination in the Workplace: The prevalence, nature and impact of workplace age discrimination amongst the Australian population aged 50 years and older*. Sydney: AHRC Report.

Beard John, Biggs Simon, Bloom David, Fried Linda, Hogan Paul, Kalache Alexandre and Olshansky Jay (Eds) (2011). *Global Population Ageing: Peril or Promise*. Geneva: World Economic Forum.

Browning Colette and Kendig Hal (2010). Cohort profile: The Melbourne Longitudinal Studies on Healthy Ageing Program. *International Journal of Epidemiology,* 39(5): e1–e7. doi: 10.1093/ije/dyq137.

Browning Colette and Thomas Shane (2015). Implementing chronic disease self-management approaches in Australia and the United Kingdom. *Frontiers in Public Health*, 27 April. doi: 10.3389/fpubh.2014.00162.

Browning Colette, Zeqi Qiu, Thomas Shane and Yang Hui (2011). *Cultural conceptualisations of ageing in Chinese elders*. Healthy Ageing Research Unit Report, Monash University.

Byles Julie, Tavener Meredith, O'Connell Rachel, Nair Balakrishnan, Higginbotham Nick, Jackson Claire, McKernon Mary, Francis Lyn, Heller Richard, Newbury Jonathan, Marley John and Goodger Brendan (2004). Randomised controlled trial of health assessments for older Australian veterans and war widows. *Medical Journal of Australia*, 181(4):186-190.

Clapham Kathy and Duncan Cathy (2016). Indigenous Australians and Ageing: Responding to Diversity in Policy and Practice. In Kate O'Loughlin, Colette Browning and Hal Kendig (Eds), *Ageing in Australia: Challenges and Opportunities*. New York: Springer.

Clemson Lindy, Cumming Robert, Kendig Hal, Swann Megan, Heard Robert and Taylor Kirsty (2004). The effectiveness of a community-based program for reducing the incidence of falls in the elderly: A randomized trial. *Journal of the American Geriatrics Society*, 52(9): 1487–1494.

Clemson Lindy, Fiatarone Singh Maria, Bundy Anita, Cumming Robert, Manollaras Kate, O'Loughlin Patricia and Black Deborah (2012). Integration of balance and strength training into daily life activity to reduce rate of falls in older people (the LiFE study): Randomised parallel trial. *BMJ* 345: 1–15.

Cosco Theodore Prina Matthew, Perales Jaime, Stephan Blossom and Brayne Carol (2014). Operational definitions of successful aging: A systematic review. *International Psychogeriatrics*, 26(3): 373–381.

Cotter Phillipa, Condon John, Barnes Tony, Anderson Ian, Smith Leonard and Cunningham Teresa (2012). Do Indigenous Australians age prematurely? The implications of life expectancy and health conditions of older Indigenous people for health and aged care policy. *Australian Health Review*, 36(1): 68–74.

Dannefer Dale (2003). Cumulative advantage/disadvantage and the life course: Cross-fertilizing age and social science theory. *Journals of Gerontology Series B: Psychological Sciences and Social Sciences,* 58(6): S327–S337.

de Vaus David, Wells Yvonne, Kendig Hal and Quine Susan (2007). Does gradual retirement have better outcomes than abrupt retirement? Results from an Australian panel study. *Ageing and Society*, 27(5): 667–682. doi 10.1017/S0144686x07006228.

Estes Carroll and Binney Elizabeth (1989). The biomedicalization of aging: Dangers and dilemmas. *The Gerontologist*, 29(5): 587–596. doi: 10.1093/geront/29.5.587.

Feldman Susan and Radermacher Harriet (2014). *Ageing well in three culturally and linguistically diverse (CALD) communities.* Summary Report, Lord Mayor's Charitable Foundation. Global Agenda Council on the Ageing (2012–2014), p 2.

Fine Michael (2014a). Intergenerational perspectives on ageing, economics and globalisation. *Australasian Journal on Ageing,* 33(4): 220–225. doi: 10.1111/ajag.12208.

Fine Michael (2014b). Nurturing Longevity: Sociological constructions of ageing, care, and the body. *Health Sociology Review,* 23(1): 33–42.

Hodge Allison, English Dallas, Giles Graham and Flicker Leon (2013). Social connectedness and predictors of successful ageing. *Maturitas* 75(4): 361–366. doi: 10.1016/j.maturitas.2013.05.002.

Hodge Allison, English Dallas, O'Dea Kerin, and Giles Graham (2007). Dietary Patterns and Diabetes Incidence in the Melbourne Collaborative Cohort Study. *American Journal of Epidemiology,* 165(6): 603–610. doi: 10.1093/aje/kwk061.

Humpel Nancy, O'Loughlin Kate, Wells Yvonne and Kendig Hal (2010). The health of Australian baby boomers. *Australasian Journal on Ageing,* 29(1): 8–13. doi: 10.1111/j.1741-6612.2010.00412.x.

Katz Stephen and Calastanti Toni (2014). Critical perspectives on successful aging: does it 'appeal more than it illuminates'? *The Gerontologist,* 55(1): 26–33. doi: 10.1093/geront/gnu027.

Kendig Hal and Browning Colette (2010). A Social View on Healthy Ageing: Multi-disciplinary Perspectives and Australian Evidence. In D Dannefer and C Phillipson (Eds) *The Sage Handbook of Social Gerontology.* London: Sage Publications, pp. 459–471.

Kendig Hal and Browning Colette (2011). Directions for ageing well in a healthy Australia. *Dialogue,* Academy of the Social Sciences in Australia, Canberra, 31(2): 22–30.

Kendig Hal, Browning Colette, Pedlow Robert, Wells Yvonne and Thomas Shane (2010). Health, social and lifestyle factors in entry to residential aged care: An Australian longitudinal analysis. *Age and Ageing,* 39(3): 342–349. doi: 10.1093/ageing/afq016.

Kendig Hal, Browning Colette, Thomas Shane and Wells Yvonne (2014). Health, lifestyle, and gender influences on aging well: An Australian longitudinal analysis to guide health promotion. *Frontiers in Public Health*, 2 July. doi: 10.3389/fpubh.2014.00070.

Kendig Hal, Loh Vanessa, O'Loughlin Kate, Byles Julie and Nazroo James (2016). Pathways to well-being in later life: Socioeconomic and health determinants across the life course of Australian baby boomers. In H Kendig and J Nazroo (Eds) Life Course Influences on Inequalities in Later Life: Comparative Perspectives. Special Issue, *Journal of Population Ageing*, 9(1). doi: 10.1007/s12062-015-9132-0.

Kendig Hal and Phillipson Chris (2014). Building Age-Friendly Communities: New Approaches to Challenging Health and Social Inequalities. In N Denison and L Newby (Eds) *'If you could do one thing...' Nine local actions to reduce health inequalities*. British Academy Policy Centre, pp. 102–111.

Kendig Hal, Wells Yvonne, O'Loughlan Kate and Heese Karla (2013). Australian Baby Boomers Face Retirement During the Global Financial Crisis, *Journal of Aging & Social Policy*, 25(3): 264–280, doi: 10.1080/08959420.2013.795382.

Kohli Martin and Arza Camila (2011). The Political Economy of Pension Reforms in Europe. In R Binstock and L George (Eds) *Handbook of Aging and the Social Sciences* (7th edition). San Diego: Academic Press, pp. 251–264.

KPMG (2012). *Evaluation of the consumer-directed care initiative — Final Report*. Canberra: Department of Health and Ageing.

Levy Becca and Myers Lindsay (2004). Preventive Health Behaviors Influenced by Self-perceptions of Aging. *Preventive Medicine* 39: 625–629.

Lewin Gill, Allan Janine, Patterson Candice, Knuiman Matthew, Boldy Duncan and Hendrie Delia (2014). A comparison of the home-care and healthcare service use and costs of older Australians randomised to receive a restorative or a conventional home-care service. *Health and Social Care in the Community*, 22(3): 328–336.

Ley The Hon Sussan (2016). A Healthier Medicare for chronically-ill patients. Media Release, www.health.gov.au/internet/ministers/publishing.nsf/Content/health-mediarel-yr2016-ley021.htm.

Lord Mayor's Charitable Foundation (2012). *Inspiring Philanthropy.* www.lmcf.org.au/.

Low Lee-Fay, Chilko Natalie, Gresham Meredith, Barter Sarah and Brodaty Henry (2012). An update on the pilot trial of consumer-directed care for older persons in Australia. *Australasian Journal on Ageing*, 31(1): 47–51. doi: 10.1111/j.1741-6612.2011.00572.x.

Lyons Anthony, Croy Samantha, Barrett Catherine and Whyte Carolyn (2015). Growing old as a gay man: How life has changed for the gay liberation generation. *Ageing and Society*, 35(10): 2229–2250. doi: 10.1017/ S0144686X14000889.

Mackenzie Lynette, Curryer Carrie and Byles Julie (2015). Narratives of home and place: Findings from the Housing and Independent Living Study. *Ageing and Society*, 35(8): 1684–1712 doi: 10.1017/ S0144686X14000476.

Mendes Felismina (2013). Active Ageing: A right or a duty? *Health Sociology Review*, 22(2): 174–185.

Minichiello Victor, Browne Jan and Kendig Hal (2000). Perceptions and consequences of ageism: Views from older persons. *Ageing and Society*, 20: 253–278.

Minichiello Victor, Browne Jan and Kendig Hal (2012). Perceptions of ageism: Views of older people. In J Katz and S Spurr (Eds) *Adult Lives: A Life Course Perspective*. Bristol: The Policy Press, pp. 332–340.

National Aged Care Alliance (NACA) (2015). Enhancing the quality of life of older people through better support and care. ACT: NACA Blueprint Series, June. www.naca.asn.au/.

O'Neil Moira and Haydon Abigail (2015). *Aging, Agency, and Attribution of responsibility: Shifting public disclosure about older adults*, Framing Aging, Framework Institute www.frameworksinstitute. org/aging.html.

Pearson Elissa, Windsor Tim, Crisp Dimity, Butterworth Peter and Anstey Kaarin (2012). *Neighbourhood characteristics and ageing well—a survey of older Australian adults.* NSPAC Research Monograph No. 2. Canberra: National Seniors Productive Ageing Centre.

Phillipson Chris (2013). *Ageing.* Cambridge: Polity Press.

Productivity Commission (2013). *An Ageing Australia: Preparing for the Future.* Research Paper Overview (November), Canberra: Productivity Commission.

Quine Susan, Kendig Hal, Russell Cherry and Touchard Denise (2004). Health promotion for socially disadvantaged groups: The case of homeless older men in Australia. *Health Promotion International*, 19(2): 157–165.

Radermacher Harriet and Feldman Susan (2015). 'Health is their heart, their legs, their back': Understanding ageing well in ethnically diverse older men in rural Australia. *Ageing and Society*, 35(5): 1011–1031. doi: 10.1017/S0144686X14001226.

Radford Kylie, Mack Holly, Robertson Hamish, Draper Brian, Chalkley Simon, Daylight Gail, Cumming Robert, Bennett Hayley, Jackson Pulver Lisa and Broe Tony (2014). The Koori Growing Old Well Study: Investigating aging and dementia in urban Aboriginal Australians. *International Psychogeriatrics*, 26(6): 1033–1043. doi: 10.1017/S1041610213002561.

Rosenkranz Richard, Duncan Mitch, Rosenkranz Sara and Kolt Gregory (2013). Active lifestyles related to excellent self-rated health and quality of life: Cross sectional findings from 194,545 participants in the 45 and up study. *BMC Public Health*, 13: 1071. doi: 10.1186/1471-2458-13-1071.

Rowe John (2015). Successful Aging of Societies. *Dædalus: Journal of the American Academy of Arts & Sciences*, Spring: 5–12. doi:10.1162/DAED_a_00325.

Rowe John and Kahn Robert (1987). Human aging: usual and successful, *Science*, 237(4811): 143–149. doi: 10.1126/science.3299702: 2.

Russell Cherry, Touchard Denise, Kendig Hal and Quine Susan (2001). Foodways of disadvantaged men growing old in the inner city: Policy issues from ethnographic research. In D Weisstub, D Thomasma, S Gauthier and G Tomossy (Eds) *Aging: Culture, health, and social change*. Dordrecht, The Netherlands: Kluwer Academic Publishers, pp. 191–215.

Sargent-Cox Kerry, Anstey Kaarin and Luszcz Mary (2012). Change in Health and Self-Perceptions of Aging over 16 years: The Role of Psychological Resources. *Health Psychology*, 31(4): 423–432.

Scharf Thomas and Keating Norah (Eds) (2012). *From Exclusion to Inclusion in Old Age: A Global Challenge (Ageing and the Lifecourse)*. Policy Press: University of Bristol.

Smith Kate, Flicker Leon, Lautenschlager Nicola, Almeida Osvaldo, Atkinson David, Dwyer Anna and LoGiudice Dina (2008). High prevalence of dementia and cognitive impairment in Indigenous Australians. *Neurology*, 71(19): 1470–1473. doi: 10.1212/01.wnl. 0000320508.11013.4f.

Social Policy Research Centre and the Benevolent Society (SPRC) (2010). *Supporting older people from culturally and linguistically diverse backgrounds*. Research to Practice Briefing 4. Sydney: University of New South Wales and the Benevolent Society.

Stebbing Adam and Spies-Butcher Ben (2015). The decline of a homeowning society? Asset-based welfare, retirement and intergenerational equity in Australia. *Housing Studies* 31(2). doi: 10.1080/02673037.2015.1070797.

United Nations (UN) (2015). *Transforming our World: The 2030 Agenda for Sustainable Development,* A/RES/70/1. United Nations.

Waern Rosilene, Cumming Robert, Blyth Fiona, Naganathan Vasikarin, Allman-Farinelli Margaret, Le Couteur David, Simpson Stephen, Kendig Hal and Hirani Vasant (2015). Adequacy of nutritional intake among older men living in Sydney, Australia: Findings from the Concord Health and Ageing in Men Project (CHAMP). *British Journal of Nutrition*, 114(5): 812–821. doi: 10.1017/ S0007114515002421.

Walker-Birckhead Wendy (1996). *Meaning and Old Age: Time, Survival and the End of Life*, Lincoln Papers in Gerontology No. 35, Melbourne: Lincoln Gerontology Centre, La Trobe University.

Windsor Tim, Curtis Rachel and Luszcz Mary (2015). Sense of Purpose as a Psychological Resource for Aging Well. *Developmental Psychology*, 51(7): 975–986. doi: 10.1037/dev0000023.

Winterton Rachel and Warburton Jeni (2012). Ageing in the bush: the role of rural places in maintaining identity for long-term rural residents and retirement migrants in north-east Victoria, Australia. *Journal of Rural Studies*, 28(4): 329–337.

World Economic Forum (2015). *How 21st-Century Longevity Can Create Markets and Drive Economic Growth*, Global Agenda, 5 October, Geneva: World Economic Forum.

World Health Organization (WHO) (2002). *Active Ageing: A Policy Framework*, National World Assembly on Ageing. Madrid, Spain: WHO. apps.who.int/iris/bitstream/10665/67215/1/WHO_NMH_NPH_02.8.pdf.

World Health Organization (WHO) (2015). *World Report on Ageing and Health*. WHO. www.who.int/ageing/publications/world-report-2015/en/.

Zhu Rony and He Xiaobo (2015). How does women's life satisfaction respond to retirement? A two-stage analysis, *Economics Letters*, 137: 118–122. doi: 10.1016/j.econlet.2015.11.002.

8

Enhancing cognitive capacities over the life-span

Kaarin J Anstey

Cognitive capacities refer to memory, thinking, reasoning, problem-solving, planning and processing speed and are also broadly described as aspects of human intelligence. Early psychologists used the term 'intelligence' to refer to what was viewed as a form of 'innate' cognitive ability that was thought to be relatively fixed throughout life and strongly genetically based. However, over the past 50 years, this collection of cognitive abilities has been viewed increasingly in a fluid and dynamic way, recognising that there are strong environmental and experiential influences on cognitive development, as well as genetic influences (Horn 1987).

In order to think about enhancing cognitive function over the life-course we must make the assumption that cognitive abilities and their development are not fully predetermined (Baltes 1993). Genetic research has shown that heritability of intelligence increases through adulthood from about 20 per cent in younger adults up to around 80 per cent in old age.

However, this applies to level of cognitive function in old age; the rate of cognitive decline does not seem heritable (Deary 2012). Moreover, studies on heritability have used traditional psychometric tests of ability and have not examined more dynamic measures such as neuroplasticity. Variability within individuals may provide scope for improvement and optimising cognitive function (Ackerman 1987).

For several decades it has been recognised that different cognitive abilities appear to be vulnerable to different experiences and neurological conditions (Dixon 2011; Tucker-Drob 2009). Abilities such as reasoning, information processing speed and the higher-level planning and executive function appear to decline more with normal ageing and have been described as 'fluid' abilities or 'mechanic abilities' (Baltes 1987). Abilities involving the accumulation of knowledge and expertise appear to increase slowly through adulthood and are less vulnerable to ageing (Baltes 1987; Horn and Cattell 1967). These have been described as crystallised or pragmatic abilities.

At the societal level, the value of cognitive abilities can be viewed as a form of 'cognitive capital' that enriches a nation's capacity to be innovative and productive, and contributes significantly to wealth. Hence there are both individual- and society-level perspectives to consider in relation to optimising cognitive function.

Why should we aim for optimal cognitive function in an ageing society?

There are at least three important reasons for research into optimising cognitive development and cognitive health, and the translation of these research findings for public policy. First, as mentioned above, cognitive capital is a resource for society that enables productivity in both the paid and unpaid workforce (Beddington et al. 2008). Greater overall cognitive capital will lead to increased employment and economic benefits. Second, better cognitive function in earlier life reduces the risk of an individual developing cognitive impairment in later life, reduces the risk of dementia and is associated with greater longevity (Deary et al. 2004). Individuals with better cognitive function will take longer to decline to the point where they are impaired. Third, better cognitive function helps individuals age well (Starr et al. 2003). Cognitive function enables many aspects of everyday life, such as managing finances, planning travel, and managing medical conditions.

Hence, optimising cognitive function will improve quality of life for individuals and societies and reduce the economic burden of health-care provision as individuals are able to maintain self-integrity and self-care for longer.

Cognitive decline, cognitive impairment and dementia—a continuum

Importantly, with increasing life expectancy the integrity of the brain and cognition into very old age has become a new focus for research. There is a direct link between cognitive ageing and dementia, with researchers often seeing cognitive function, cognitive impairment and dementia on a continuum (Figure 1), whereas 20 years ago these were often viewed as distinct domains of research. There is much focus on dementia, and the public generally fear developing dementia (Kim et al. 2015; Zeng et al. 2015). However, it is less widely recognised that cognitive impairment that is not severe enough to meet criteria for dementia affects approximately 10 per cent of adults in their 60s (Anstey et al. 2013a) and 20 per cent of adults aged 70 and older, about three to four times the number of older adults who have dementia (Plassman et al. 2008). A large proportion of older adults with Mild Cognitive Impairment ultimately develop dementia (Farias et al. 2009) and hence Mild Cognitive Impairment is a strong risk factor for dementia.

Mild Cognitive Impairment impacts on quality of life and the capacity for independent living (Anstey et al. 2013b).

In our epidemiological study, the PATH Through Life, we found that adults aged in their 60s with Mild Cognitive Impairment reported higher rates of difficulties with instrumental activities of daily living such as reading maps, shopping, making telephone calls, and taking medications (Anstey 2013b). Hence, with an ageing population, it is crucial that we identify and implement methods to enable individuals to enhance their cognitive abilities and maintain them into very old age. Ideally, a minimal number of adults will experience cognitive impairment in their old age and few will develop dementia.

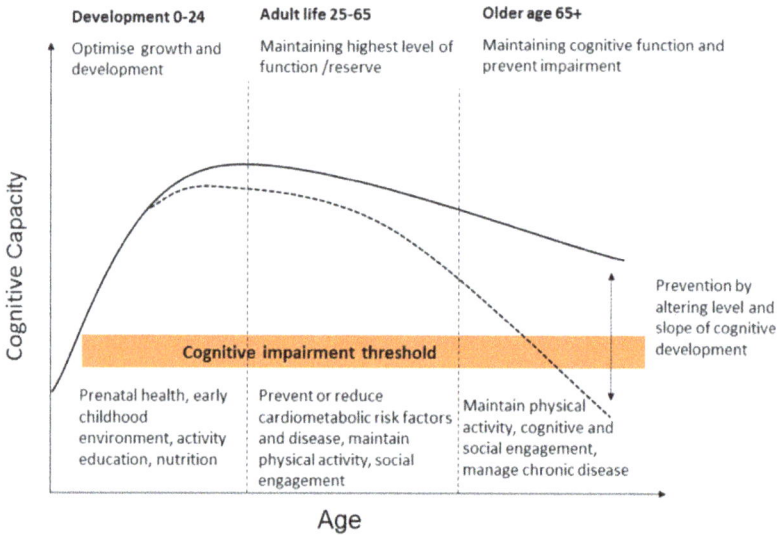

Figure 1. Schematic representation of the trajectory of cognitive development over the life-course

Capacity may vary according to lifestyle, environment, education and health.

Source: Provided by author.

Life-course perspective

When ageing research focuses exclusively on older adults, for example analysing data from studies of adults aged over 70 years, the contributions of earlier life are often overlooked. In the case of cognitive ageing, the starting point for an individual's cognitive development is prenatal, but the critical point for understanding their trajectory is the peak of cognitive ability reached in the mid-20s and then the rate of decline in cognitive abilities that commences in late-middle age. It is widely recognised that a life-course perspective needs to be taken into account for the development of cognitive abilities over the life-course (Baltes et al. 1999). Cognitive function in late life is influenced by the accumulation of the impacts of risk factors, insults to the brain, neuropathology, and cognitively enhancing activities that may provide some buffer against the impact of risk factors.

Figure 1 presents a schematic representation of cognitive development over the life-course, showing that cognitive impairment is on a continuum with normal age-related cognitive decline. The schematic illustrates the trajectory for cognitive growth, showing the peak in the mid-20s for fluid abilities, and the general stability of cognitive function in middle-age, followed by decline in late life. It is clear from this figure that increasing the peak of cognitive function in young adulthood will improve cognitive function for the remainder of the adult life-course. And hence, optimal cognitive ageing requires investment in early cognitive development (Anstey 2014). Similarly, maintaining cognitive function in middle-age will contribute to adults ageing well, minimising risk of cognitive impairment. The fact that cognitive function in late life is the accumulation of both cognitive growth in childhood and early adulthood, and the degree of maintenance through middle-age, means that a life-course approach needs to be taken to cognitive ageing at a public policy and health promotion level.

Taking a life-course approach to optimal cognitive ageing requires focusing different elements of the cognitive trajectories over the life-course and developing appropriate interventions for different ages or phases. Typically, cognitive function is stable in middle-age apart from the slowing of reaction time and processing speed. However, by the mid-60s, decline in cognitive function may start to occur. The age at which cognitive abilities start to decline and the rate of decline are influenced by a range of risk and protective factors. An example of how both level and slope of cognitive function may be associated with specific risk factors is shown in Figure 2. This depicts the adult life-course cognitive data from the PATH Through Life project for smokers and non-smokers. Smokers perform more poorly at each age, and, in the oldest cohort, are starting to show a faster rate of decline in processing speed than non-smokers.

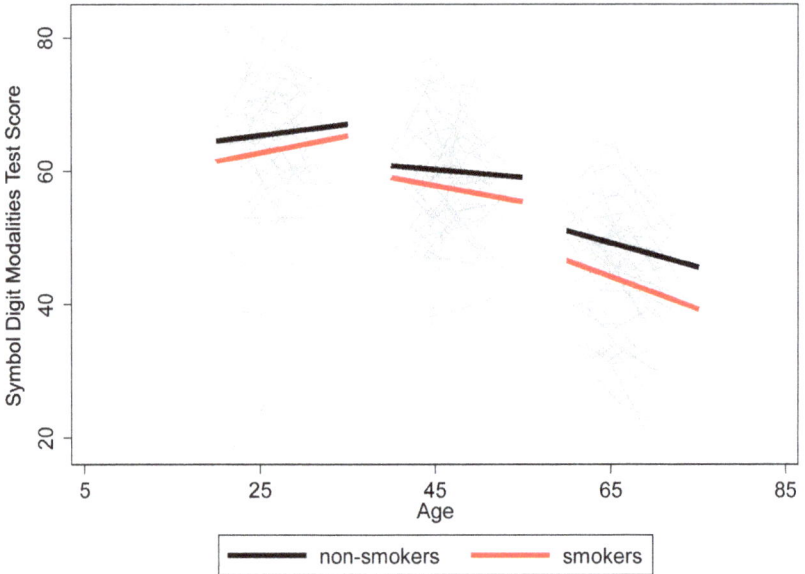

Figure 2. Processing speed ability for smokers and non-smokers aged in their 60s over eight years

Smokers show lower level and faster decline.

Source: Provided by author.

Cognitive reserve

The 'building of intelligence' in early life through enriched environments and education that promote peak functioning is related to another key concept described by psychologists as 'cognitive reserve' (Stern 2009). This 'reserve' provides individuals with a buffer to sustain their cognitive function when they develop neuropathology or experience diseases or stressors that impact on the brain and subsequent cognitive capacity. The idea of cognitive reserve was introduced originally to account for the finding at autopsy that some individuals who presented with Alzheimer's pathology did not have dementia. In a well-known study of 137 nursing home residents of whom 79 per cent were demented prior to death, 55 per cent had Alzheimer's pathology, 11 per cent had other neuropathology and 11 per cent had no neuropathology (Katzman et al. 1988). Of patients with dementia, 9 per cent had no neuropathology. This study demonstrated that there is no direct correlation between neuropathology and dementia and such results have been replicated numerous times over the past two decades. Those without dementia, but who had neuropathology associated with Alzheimer's disease, had more neurones and intact pyramidal neurones and heavier brains than controls. It was therefore postulated that some individuals have a type of 'reserve' capacity, originally described as 'brain reserve' (Richards and Deary 2005; Stern 2002, 2006).

More recent research has used functional Magnetic Resonance Imaging (MRI) to explore the idea of brain and cognitive reserve (e.g. Stern et al. 2005; Stern et al. 2008). Greater activation of specific brain regions during a working memory task has been associated with higher levels of education (Sandry and Sumowski 2014; Sumowski et al. 2014). The idea of cognitive reserve developed from this research to explain the fact that individuals with higher levels of education and higher IQ appear to be at lower risk of dementia and more resilient to the impact of neuropathology on cognitive function. At present, we do not know the full potential of the human brain in terms of how much we can intervene to build cognitive reserve. It is likely that cognitive reserve can be enhanced by cognitive and physical training throughout adulthood.

Neuroplasticity

Neuroplasticity is related to cognitive reserve and is another key concept for understanding how we may optimise cognitive function (Petrosini et al. 2009; Whalley et al. 2004). Neuroplasticity refers to the capacity of cerebral neural pathways to grow and adapt to environmental exposures, behavioural changes, and specific cognitive and brain training (May 2011). This means that intellectually stimulating activities may maintain and even improve brain function during adulthood, potentially contributing to cognitive reserve and reducing the risk of dementia. Support for the benefit of a cognitively engaged lifestyle has been seen in studies linking lifestyle cognitive activity to the reduced risk of dementia (Fratiglioni et al. 2004). Results from the largest cognitive training study, the ACTIVE trial, have also shown benefits of an intervention that trained older adults in either memory, processing speed or reasoning skills as well as everyday function (Willis et al. 2006). Importantly, long-term follow-up of participants trained on reasoning or processing speed showed cognitive benefits were maintained after 10 years (Rebok et al. 2014). Adults who participated in speed of processing training were also less likely to have given up driving over the follow-up period (Edwards et al. 2009).

In another cognitive training study, middle-aged and older adults used the speed of processing training paradigm from the ACTIVE trial and benefits were found for speed of processing training conducted both at home and by groups in a laboratory (Wolinsky et al. 2013). The benefits translated into between two and five years of prevented cognitive decline on standardised cognitive tests. Most cognitive training research has focused on older adults and children with attention deficit disorders; results typically demonstrate that cortical thickness can be increased through intensive repetitive cognitive exercises (Kueider et al. 2012). Research into music training has also demonstrated cognitive and brain benefits in children, but the long-term impact of musical training in childhood is not yet known (Lappe et al. 2011). Research in older adults has shown that there are brain changes associated with memory training (Engvig et al. 2010).

Brain training research in general has been criticised as improvements are only noted on those cognitive capacities focused on in the training; the transfer of benefit to everyday function has rarely been demonstrated. A number of empirical issues relating to dosage, frequency, intensity and type of training have not yet been resolved. Nevertheless, the field is part of a broader movement that will lead to discoveries about how to optimise cognitive function in ways that potentially will persist into late life.

Multidomain influences on cognitive development require a multidisciplinary approach—the CHELM Model

Influences on cognitive function draw from several different domains, including genetics, environment, sociodemographic factors, health behaviour, and disease (Fotuhi et al. 2012). Developments in education, neuroscience, medicine and psychology have each contributed to an emerging framework for understanding cognitive abilities over the life-course. These also speak to potential areas where interventions may be conducted to reduce risk of cognitive decline, and even promote or improve cognitive abilities.

Interventions to address the influences on cognitive development may occur at multiple levels, from changing individual behaviour to changing public policy relating to education, health care or the environment (Fratiglioni and Qiu 2011). Ultimately, the better our society facilitates optimal cognitive development and maintenance, the better we will age as individuals and as a society (Beddington et al. 2008).

A framework for optimising cognitive function is required to pull together the multidomain nature of impacts on cognitive function that will ultimately lead to the level of cognitive ability an individual has in old age (Anstey 2014). I have previously proposed the Cognitive Health Environment Lifestyle Model to depict a framework for understanding influences on cognitive function that may guide policy and intervention.

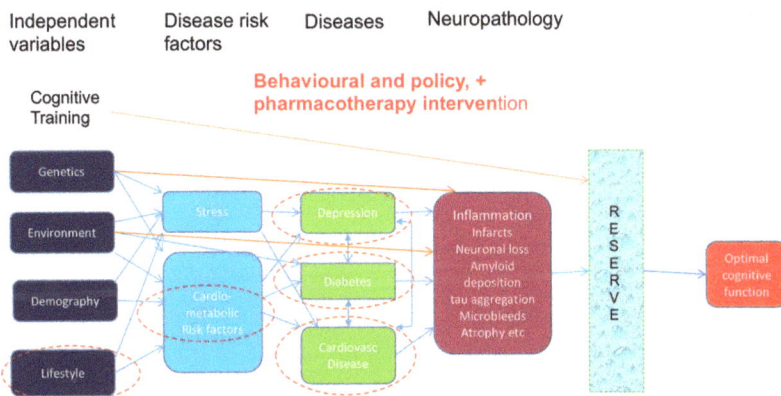

Figure 3. The Cognitive Health Environment and Life Course Model
Source: Adapted from Anstey (2014).

This model depicts how various domains influence cognitive outcomes, providing a framework for interventions at the levels of public policy, lifestyle and behavioural changes, and pharmacotherapy.

According to the CHELM framework, intervention can occur through public policy, non-pharmacological behaviour change interventions, pharmacological interventions and activities to develop cognitive reserve. Public policy interventions are required to address environmental and contextual influences on cognitive development and cognitive function. These include ensuring as many children as possible receive high-quality education to develop brain structure and brain reserve. Retaining children in school and promoting lifelong learning and occupational training can be influenced by public policy in relation to the provision of education and the maintaining of standards of education.

Public policy is also important for addressing environmental influences such as air pollution in large cities, and the impact of the built environment on the lifestyle behaviours that ultimately impact on the brain and cognition. Environmental factors influencing cognition may, for example, include the design of environments, access to high-quality unprocessed food and access to sporting facilities that encourage individuals to engage in activities that promote health and wellbeing and ward off disease. Establishing building and design codes that take into account the health and capacities of communities and populations with specific needs will ultimately lead to gains in cognitive capital as well as reduced prevalence of chronic diseases. Hence, our society's approach to a broad range of issues and inequality can be viewed in terms of how such factors impact on the cognitive health of individuals, which in turn contribute to how well individuals will age.

Behavioural interventions are required to address risk factors for chronic disease that are also linked to brain and cognitive health. These include sedentary behaviour (Lautenschlager et al. 2010), diet quality (Ashby-Mitchell et al. 2015), smoking (Anstey et al. 2007) and unhealthy alcohol drinking (Anstey et al. 2009). While Body Mass Index (BMI) is not a health behaviour it is a medical condition that may be influenced by health behaviour as well as medical treatment. Both low BMI (underweight) and high BMI (overweight and obese) in middle-age have been linked to increased risk of Alzheimer's disease and dementia (Anstey et al. 2011).

Emerging research in the field of dementia risk reduction is focusing on developing ways of reducing behaviours that increase the risk of cognitive decline and dementia. For example, we have developed an online dementia risk-reduction intervention called Body Brain Life (BBL) (Anstey et al. 2013a). BBL includes seven modules, two of which educate individuals about dementia and dementia risk reduction. Another five modules address individual health behaviours using behavioural change principles and techniques such as goal-setting and self-monitoring. Other more intensive interventions to improve cognitive decline have involved walking groups, personal exercise prescription and individual dietary prescription and support (Ngandu et al. 2015; Richard et al. 2012).

Preliminary results from one large European risk-reduction trial has shown that two years post-intervention, cognitive function was improved in the intervention group compared with a control group that received usual care (Ngandu et al. 2015). As depression is an established risk factor for dementia, behavioural interventions to reduce depression are also an avenue for dementia risk reduction. Protective behaviours that reduce risk of dementia include increasing social engagement (Fratiglioni et al. 2004), cognitive engagement (Wilson et al. 2002) and eating fish (Fotuhi et al. 2009).

Pharmaceutical interventions are also appropriate to treat conditions that increase the risk of dementia. These include hypertension, diabetes, heart disease and depression. Recent studies have identified cardiovascular risk factors in young adults influence cognitive ability (Aberg et al. 2009), and cardiovascular risk factors in middle-age influence dementia outcomes in late life (Kivipelto et al. 2001). Other medical conditions linked to cognitive function and decline include head injury and diabetes. However, research is now looking beyond purely medical and health explanations for individual differences in cognitive function.

Environmental factors are of increasing concern in the domain of public health in relation to respiratory function, and there is now evidence for air pollution being associated with poorer cognitive function and Alzheimer's pathology (Calderon-Garciduenas et al. 2012).

There is growing evidence that a range of pesticides and other chemicals are associated with cognitive deficits, yet this area of research is currently limited due to a lack of high-quality data (Zaganas et al. 2013). Environmental factors relating to diet may affect entire populations, in addition to historical effects such as major societal stressors and traumas.

Our society still traditionally views early life as the period during which individuals undertake their education and vocational training. However, research on brain development combined with increasing longevity suggests that our perspective on education needs to change. Participation in education at various points during adulthood may have influences on the brain that we have not yet imagined. Bringing all our knowledge together and creating the best possible public policy for cognitive health is likely to promote genuine increases in the numbers of adults who age well, and reduce the prevalence of late life dementia.

Future directions

Research into factors that reduce cognitive capacity and methods of optimising cognitive capacity is relatively new and many fundamental questions remain unanswered. For example, little is known about how interventions at specific ages may influence longer-term cognitive outcomes, and whether this again differs by sex and genetic risk profile. We still do not know the optimal dosage of most interventions, or for how long they need to be administered. Often cohort studies are limited by the initial measures included in the study, by short follow-up periods or attrition. Intervention studies are typically limited by highly selected and unrepresentative samples, and short follow-up periods, with few interventions lasting as long as two years. In the context of cognitive function over the life-course it is possible that interventions may need to be administered for decades or even lifelong, to demonstrate their potential. Cognitive change in healthy adults is very slow and hence it is difficult to detect the effects of interventions with small samples and over short time-frames.

In addition to unanswered questions about interventions, there are also unanswered questions about the sub-populations in whom they may be trialled. We do not know which interventions may be effective in adults who already have some degree of cognitive impairment and the extent of neural plasticity possible in adults with dementia. Many of our hypotheses relating to optimising cognitive function are based on observational research that links risk and protective factors to better cognition. However, to date there has not been enough research to confirm whether risk modification will lead to reversibility of cognitive decline or improvement. With increasing longevity, it is unknown whether the same risk profiles associated with cognitive decline in say adults in their 80s will be associated with cognitive decline in adults in their 90s or beyond 100. Some recent research has suggested that the increased longevity associated with lack of risk factors (e.g. non-smoking) may actually increase the time spent with cognitive impairment over the entire life-span because adults simply live longer and age is the greatest risk factors for cognitive decline (Anstey et al. 2014). Altogether, there is a need for a major research effort in enhancing cognitive capacities over the adult life-course that will have major benefits for individuals and societies.

Acknowledgements

This work is funded by NHMRC Fellowship 1002560 and the ARC Centre of Excellence in Population Ageing Research CE110001029.

References

Aberg Maria, Pedersen Nancy, Toren Kjell, Svartengren Magnus, Backstrand Bjorn, Johnsson Tommy, Cooper-Kuhn Christine, Aberg David, Nilsson Michael and Kuhn George (2009). Cardiovascular fitness is associated with cognition in young adulthood. *Proceedings of the National Academy of Sciences of the United States of America*, 106(49): 20906–20911.

Ackerman Phillip (1987). Individual differences in skill learning: An integration of psychometric and information processing perspectives. *Psychological Bulletin*, 120(1): 3–27.

Anstey Kaarin (2014). Optimizing cognitive development over the life course and preventing cognitive decline: Introducing the Cognitive Health Environment Life course Model (CHELM). *International Journal of Behavioral Development*, 38(1): 1–10.

Anstey Kaarin, Bahar-Fuchs Alex, Herath Pushpani, Rebok George and Cherbuin Nicolas (2013). A 12-week multidomain intervention versus active control to reduce risk of Alzheimer's disease: Study protocol for a randomized controlled trial. *Trials*, 14: 60.

Anstey Kaarin, Cherbuin Nicolas, Budge Marc and Young Jennifer (2011). Body mass index in mid life and late-life as a risk factor for dementia: A meta-analysis of prospective studies. *Obesity Reviews*, 12(5): e426–e437.

Anstey Kaarin, Cherbuin Nicolas, Eramudugolla Ranmalee, Sargent-Cox Kerry, Easteal Simon, Kumar Rajeev and Sachdev Perminder (2013b). Characterizing mild cognitive disorders in the young-old over 8 years: Prevalence, estimated incidence, stability of diagnosis, and impact on IADLs. *Alzheimer's and Dementia*, 9(6): 640–648.

Anstey Kaarin, Kingston Andrew, Kiely Kim, Luszcz Mary, Mitchell Paul and Jagger Carol (2014). The influence of smoking, sedentary lifestyle and obesity on cognitive impairment-free life expectancy. *International Journal of Epidemiology*, 43(6): 1874–1883. doi: 10.1093/ije/dyu170.

Anstey Kaarin, Mack Holly and Cherbuin Nicolas (2009). Alcohol consumption as a risk factor for dementia and cognitive decline: Meta-analysis of prospective studies. *American Journal of Geriatric Psychiatry*, 17(7): 542–555.

Anstey Kaarin, von Sanden Chwee, Salim Agus and O'Kearney Richard (2007). Smoking as a risk factor for dementia and cognitive decline: A meta-analysis of prospective studies. *The American Journal of Epidemiology*, 166(4): 367–378.

Ashby-Mitchell Kimberly, Peeters Anna and Anstey Kaarin (2015). Role of dietary pattern analysis in determining cognitive status in elderly Australian adults. *Nutrients*, 7(2): 1052–1067.

Baltes Paul (1987). Theoretical propositions of life-span developmental psychology: On the dynamics between growth and decline. *Developmental Psychology*, 23(5): 611–626.

Baltes Paul (1993). The aging mind: Potential and limits. *The Gerontologist*, 33(5): 580–594.

Baltes Paul, Staudinger Ursula and Lindenberger Ulman (1999). Lifespan psychology: Theory and application to intellectual functioning. *Annual Review of Psychology*, 50: 471–507.

Beddington John, Cooper Cary, Field John, Goswami Usha, Huppert Felicia, Jenkins Rachel, Jones Hannah, Kirkwood Tom, Sahakian Barbara and Thomas Sandy (2008). The mental wealth of nations. *Nature*, 455(7216): 1057–1060.

Calderon-Garciduenas Lillian, Kavanaugh Michael, Block Michelle, D'Angiulli Amedeo, Delgado-Chavez Ricardo, Torres-Jardon Ricardo, Gonzalas-Maciel Angelica, Reynoso-Robles Rafael, Osnaya Norma, Villareal-Calderon, Guo Ruixin, Hua Zhoawei, Zhu Honghi, Perry George and Diaz Phillipe (2012). Neuroinflammation, hyperphosphorylated tau, diffuse amyloid plaques, and down-regulation of the cellular prion protein in air pollution exposed children and young adults. *Journal of Alzheimer's disease*, 28(1): 93–107.

Deary Ian (2012). Intelligence. *Annual Review of Psychology*, 63: 453–482.

Deary Ian, Whiteman Martha, Starr John, Whalley Lawrence and Fox Helen (2004). The impact of childhood intelligence on later life: Following up the Scottish mental surveys of 1932 and 1947. *Journal of Personality and Social Psychology*, 86(1): 130–147.

Dixon Roger (2011). Enduring theoretical themes in psychological aging: Derivation, functions, perspectives, and opportunities. In KW Schaie and SL Willis (Eds) *Handbook of the Psychology of Aging* (7th edition). San Diego: Academic Press, pp. 3–23.

Edwards Jerri, Myers Charlsie, Ross Lesley, Roenker Daniel, Cissell Gayla, McLaughlin Alexis and Ball Karlene (2009). The longitudinal impact of cognitive speed of processing training on driving mobility. *The Gerontologist*, 49(4): 485–494.

Engvig Andreas, Fjell Anders, Westlye Lars, Moberget Torgeir, Sundseth Oyvind, Larsen Vivi and Walhovd Kristine (2010). Effects of memory training on cortical thickness in the elderly. *NeuroImage*, 52(4): 1667–1676.

Farias Sarah, Mungas Dan, Reed Bruce, Harvey Danielle and DeCarli Charles (2009). Progression of mild cognitive impairment to dementia in clinic- vs community-based cohorts. *Archives of Neurology*, 66(9): 1151–1157.

Fotuhi Majid, Do David and Jack Clifford (2012). Modifiable factors that alter the size of the hippocampus with ageing. *Nature Reviews Neurology*, 8(4): 189–202.

Fotuhi Majid, Mohassel Payam and Yaffe Kristine (2009). Fish consumption, long-chain omega-3 fatty acids and risk of cognitive decline or Alzheimer disease: A complex association. *Nature Clinical Practice Neurology*, 5(3): 140–152.

Fratiglioni Laura, Paillard-Borg Stephanie and Winblad Bengt (2004). An active and socially integrated lifestyle in late life might protect against dementia. *The Lancet Neurology*, 3(6): 343–353.

Fratiglioni Laura and Qiu Chengxuan (2011). Prevention of cognitive decline in ageing: Dementia as the target, delayed onset as the goal [Comment]. *The Lancet Neurology*, 10(9): 778–779.

Horn John (1987). A context for understanding information processing studies of human abilities. In PA Vernon (Ed) *Speed of information processing and intelligence*. Norwood, NJ: Ablex, pp. 201–238.

Horn John and Cattell Raymond (1967). Age differences in fluid and crystallized intelligence. *Acta Psychologica*, 26(2): 107–129.

Katzman Robert, Terry Robert, DeTeresa Richard, Brown Theodore, Davies Peter, Fuld Paula, Renbing Xiong and Peck Arthur (1988). Clinical, pathological, and neurochemical changes in dementia: A subgroup with preserved mental status and numerous neocortical plaques. *Ann Neurol*, 23(2): 138–144.

Kim Sarang, Sargent-Cox Kerry and Anstey Kaarin (2015). A qualitative study of older and middle-aged adults' perception and attitudes towards dementia and dementia risk reduction. *Journal of Advanced Nursing*, 71(7): 1694–1703. doi: 10.1111/jan.12641.

Kivipelto Miia, Helkala Eeva, Laakso Mikko, Hanninen Tuomo, Hallikainen Merja, Alhainen Kari, Soininen Hilkka, Tuomilehto Jaakko and Nissinen Aulikki (2001). Midlife vascular risk factors and Alzheimer's disease in later life: Longitudinal, population based study. *The British Medical Journal*, 322(7300): 1447–1451.

Kueider Alexandra, Parisi Jeanine, Gross Alden and Rebok George (2012). Computerized cognitive training with older adults: A systematic review. *PLoS One*, 7(7): e40588.

Lappe Claudia, Trainor Laurel, Herholz Sibylle and Pantev Christo (2011). Cortical plasticity induced by short-term multimodal musical rhythm training. *PLoS One*, 6(6): e21493.

Lautenschlager Nicola, Cox Kay and Kurz Alexander (2010). Physical activity and mild cognitive impairment and Alzheimer's disease. *Current Neurology and Neuroscience Reports*, 10(5): 352-358.

May Arne (2011). Experience-dependent structural plasticity in the adult human brain. *Trends in Cognitive Sciences*, 15(10): 475–482.

Ngandu Tiia, Lehtisalo Jenni, Solomon Alina, Levalahti Esko, Ahtiluoto Satu, Antikainen Riitta, Bäckman Lars, Hänninen Tuomo, Jula Antti, Laatikainen Tiina, Lindström Jaana, Mangialasche Francesca, Paajanen Teemu, Pajala Satu, Peltonen Markku, Rauramaa Rainer, Stigsdotter-Neely Anna, Strandberg Timo, Tuomilehto Jaako, Soininen Hikka and Kivipelto Miia (2015). A 2-year multidomain intervention of diet, exercise, cognitive training, and vascular risk monitoring versus control to prevent cognitive decline in at-risk elderly people (FINGER): A randomised controlled trial. *The Lancet*, 385(9984): 2255–2263.

Petrosini Laura, De Bartolo Paola, Foti Francesca, Gelfo Francessca, Cutuli Debora, Leggio Maria and Mandolesi Laura (2009). On whether the environmental enrichment may provide cognitive and brain reserves. *Brain Research Reviews*, 61(2): 221–239.

Plassman Brenda, Langa Kenneth, Fisher Gwenith, Heeringa Stephen, Weir David, Ofstedal Mary, Burke James, Hurd Michael, Potter Guy, Rodgers Willard, Steffens David, McArdle John and Wallace Robert (2008). Prevalence of cognitive impairment without dementia in the United States. *Annals Internal Medicine*, 148(6): 427–434.

Rebok George, Ball Karlene, Guey Lin, Jones Richard, Kim Hae-Young, King Jonathan, Willis Sherry (2014). Ten-Year Effects of the advanced cognitive training for independent and vital elderly cognitive training trial on cognition and everyday functioning in older adults. *Journal of the American Geriatrics Society*, 62(1): 16–24.

Richard Edo, Andrieu Sandrine, Solomon Alina, Mangialasche Francesca, Ahtiluoto Satu, Moll van Charante Eric, Coley Nicola, Fratiglioni Laura, Neeley Anna Stigsditter, Vellas Bruno, van Gool Willem and Kivipelto Miia (2012). Methodological challenges in designing dementia prevention trials—the European Dementia Prevention Initiative (EDPI). *Journal of the Neurological Sciences*, 322(1–2): 64–70.

Richards Marcus and Deary Ian (2005). A life course approach to cognitive reserve: A model for cognitive aging and development? *Annals of Neurology*, 58(4): 617–622.

Sandry Joshua and Sumowski James (2014). Working memory mediates the relationship between intellectual enrichment and long-term memory in multiple sclerosis: An exploratory analysis of cognitive reserve. *Journal of the International Neuropsychological Society*, 20(8): 868–872.

Starr John, Deary Ian and Macintyre Sally (2003). Associations with successful ageing in the 'Healthy old people in Edinburgh' cohort: Being well, fit and healthy. *Aging Clinical and Experimental Research*, 15(4): 336–342.

Stern Yaakov (2002). What is cognitive reserve? Theory and research application of the reserve concept. *Journal of the International Neuropsychological Society*, 8(3): 448–460.

Stern Yaakov (2006). Cognitive reserve and Alzheimer disease. *Alzheimer Disease and Associated Disorders*, 20: 112–117.

Stern Yaakov (2009). Cognitive reserve. *Neuropsychologia*, 47(10): 2015–2028.

Stern Yaakov, Habeck Christian, Moeller James, Scarmeas Nikolaos, Anderson Karen, Hilton John, van Heertum Ronald (2005). Brain networks associated with cognitive reserve in healthy young and old adults. *Cerebral Cortex*, 15(4): 394–402. doi: 10.1093/cercor/bhh142.

Stern Yaakov, Zarahn Eric, Habeck Christian, Holtzer Roee, Rakitin Brian, Kumar Arjun, Flynn Josephm Steffener Jaron and Brown Truman (2008). A common neural network for cognitive reserve in verbal and object working memory in young but not old. *Cerebral Cortex*, 18(4): 959–967.

Sumowski James, Rocca Maria, Leavitt Victoria, Dackovic Jelena, Mesaros Sarlota, Drulovic Jelena, DeLuca John and Filippi Massimo (2014). Brain reserve and cognitive reserve protect against cognitive decline over 4.5 years in MS. *Neurology*, 82(20): 1776–1783.

Tucker-Drob Elliot (2009). Differentiation of cognitive abilities across the life span. *Developmental Psychology*, 45(4): 1097–1118.

Whalley Lawrence J, Deary Ian, Appleton Charlotte and Starr John (2004). Cognitive reserve and the neurobiology of cognitive aging. *Ageing Research Reviews*, 3(4): 369–382.

Willis Sherry, Tennstedt Sharon, Marsiske Michael, Ball Karlene, Elias Jeffrey, Koepke Kathy, Morris John, Rebok George, Unverzagt Frederick, Stoddard Anne and Wright Elizabeth (2006). Long-term effects of cognitive training on everyday functional outcomes in older adults. *The Journal of the American Medical Assocation*, 296(23): 2805–2814.

Wilson Robert, Mendes de Leon Carlos, Barnes Lisa, Schneider Julie, Bienias Julia, Evans Denis and Bennett David (2002). Participation in cognitively stimulating activities and risk of incident Alzheimer disease. *The Journal of the American Medical Assocation*, 287(6): 742–748.

Wolinsky Fredric, Vander Weg Mark, Howren Bryant, Jones Michael and Dotson Megan (2013). A randomized controlled trial of cognitive training using a visual speed of processing intervention in middle aged and older adults. *PLoS One*, 8(5) e61624.

Zaganas Ioannis, Kapetanaki Stefania, Mastorodemos Vassileios, Kanavouras Konstantinos, Colosio Claudio, Wilks Martin and Tsatsakis Aristidis (2013). Linking pesticide exposure and dementia: What is the evidence? *Toxicology*, 307: 3–11.

Zeng Fan, Xie Wan-Ting, Wang Yan-Jiang, Luo Hong-Bo, Shi Xiang-Qun, Zou Hai-Qiang, Zeng Yue-Ring, Li Ya-Fei, Zhang Shao-Rong and Lian Yan (2015). General public perceptions and attitudes toward Alzheimer's disease from five cities in China. *Journal of Alzheimer's Disease*, 43(2): 511–518.

9

Social engagement in late life

Tim D Windsor, Rachel G Curtis and Mary A Luszcz

Gerontologists and older adults agree that remaining socially engaged into late life represents a hallmark of ageing well. It is now well established that having diverse, supportive social networks can promote physical and mental health. Social network members can have a positive influence on health behaviours (e.g. a friend or relative encouraging exercise or medication adherence), provide support during times of need, and allow opportunities for social interactions that create positive emotional experiences (Berkman 1995; Thoits 2006). The past decade has also seen increasing research interest in the possibility that social engagement protects against cognitive decline and dementia (e.g. Fratiglioni et al. 2004; Hertzog et al. 2008; Windsor et al. 2014). Individuals who remain active and socially engaged across the retirement transition and into late life are also best placed to continue making a strong social and economic contribution; a factor likely to prove critical in successfully navigating some of the challenges of population ageing.

This chapter draws on theory and empirical research from social gerontology and life-span developmental psychology to outline a number of key factors that influence older adults' social engagement (Bowling and Dieppe 2005; Rowe and Kahn 1987). Where appropriate, we supplement discussion of international research with our own findings from the Australian Longitudinal Study of Ageing (ALSA; Luszcz et al. 2014) to provide a uniquely Australian perspective on key factors that influence social activity in late life. Finally, we discuss issues of relevance to public policy, outlining intervention programs designed to reduce social isolation in older adults, discussing the economic contribution made by older adult volunteers, and noting the challenges and opportunities associated with promoting social engagement among oldest-old adults who may be experiencing more significant health and cognitive limitations.

What predicts social engagement among older adults?

International studies have consistently shown that social networks tend to become smaller, and social engagement declines with advancing age (Lang and Carstensen, 1994). These findings are mirrored in the Australian context, as shown in Figure 1, which displays results of analysis using the ALSA.[1] Here we see that older participants report lower levels of social activity engagement, and show a steeper average rate of decline in social activity engagement over 18 years.

Researchers have tended to explain declines in social engagement with advancing age in terms of either ageing-related changes in resources, or social motivation (Windsor et al. 2011). Resource-based explanations tend to focus on how changes in one's repertoire of abilities or external 'assets' may have flow-on effects on the nature or extent of social activities or participation. They acknowledge that shrinking networks in later life are in part due to the loss of network members that occurs through the death of family and friends, and also focus on how declining health and mobility (including restricted access to private and public transport) can adversely affect social activity (e.g. Pinquart 2003).

1   Estimates used to generate Figure 1, as well as additional findings based on the ALSA that are reported subsequently, are based on a series of multi-level growth models that examined associations of age, gender, partner status, physical and cognitive health, socioeconomic status, positive affect, and subjective life expectancy with levels, and rates of change in social activity. Interested readers are invited to contact the first author for details of the analysis and results.

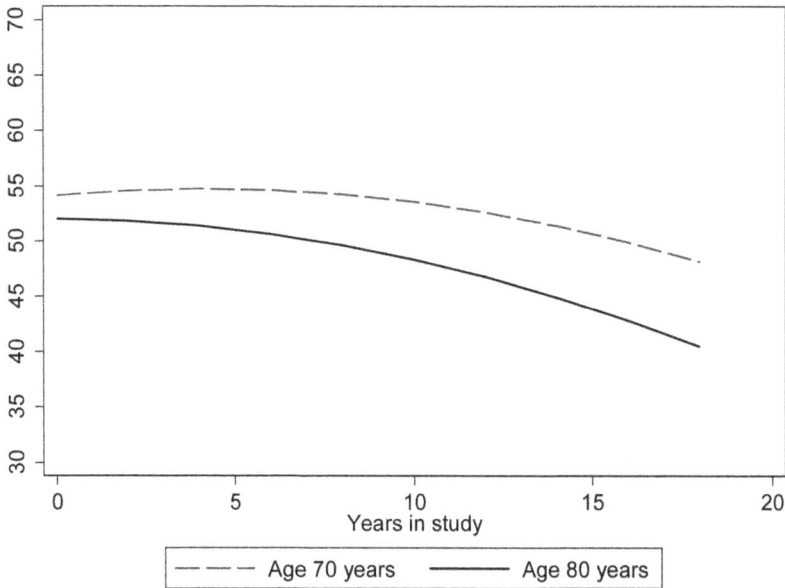

Figure 1. Social activity level change age as people grow older, Australian Longitudinal Study of Ageing

Estimated average trajectories of change in social activity for ALSA participants aged 70, and aged 80 at baseline. Older adults showed lower initial levels of social activity engagement, and this age differential increased in size over time.

Source: Provided by author.

Surviving to the 'fourth age' or oldest-old adulthood (e.g. ages 85 and above) might be regarded as a major achievement in and of itself. However, whereas the third age for many is a period of vitality and engagement, the fourth age is more typically accompanied by significant declines in health and functioning (Baltes and Smith 2003). In turn, losses in mobility, energy, and cognitive and sensory functioning may adversely affect levels of out-of-home activity and social contact among the oldest-old (Pinquart 2003). Various empirical studies have linked poor health with reduced social activity among older adults. For example, a population-based study of adults aged 57–85 found that those who were more socially disconnected also reported poorer health (Cornwell and Waite 2009). Complementing this finding, another cross-sectional study of adults aged 65–85 indicated that social connectedness (but not social support availability) was associated with better self-reported health (Ashida and Heaney 2008).

Cognitive health is also likely to be an important resource in driving levels of social activity engagement in older adulthood. To date, research has tended to focus on the extent to which maintaining levels of social engagement provides opportunities for cognitive enrichment that could help to maximise cognitive performance potential (e.g. Hertzog et al. 2008). However, it is also likely that normal and pathological cognitive ageing curtails social engagement. For example, dementia (particularly Alzheimer's disease) is preceded by a long pre-clinical phase characterised by milder cognitive deficits believed to reduce capacity around activities of daily living as well as precipitating withdrawal from social and leisure activities (Stoykova et al. 2011). The importance of health and cognition as enablers of late life social engagement is supported by results of our ALSA analysis, which showed that measures of disability and cognitive impairment were robust predictors of levels of activity engagement after controlling for a range of sociodemographic and individual difference (positive affect, subjective life expectancy) variables.

In addition to ageing-related changes in health and cognitive capacity, sociostructural factors such as social disadvantage are also relevant to social engagement. Theoretical perspectives, concerned with the link between socioeconomic status (SES) and health, recognise social disadvantage as resulting in fewer opportunities to accumulate the economic, behavioural and psychosocial resources believed to protect against health risk (e.g. Gallo 2009). For example, financial hardship may necessitate living in disadvantaged neighbourhoods where levels of social cohesion, trust, and reciprocity are low (Chen and Miller 2013). Low neighbourhood cohesion might be particularly disadvantageous to older adults living alone and in poor health, who might otherwise rely on their neighbours for support (Laporte et al. 2008).

Different structural opportunities established early in life might also have implications for the establishment and maintenance of social networks throughout adulthood. For example, individuals with higher educational attainment may have greater opportunities to develop communication, cognitive, and social skills, which in turn facilitate forming and maintaining relationships (Broese Van Groenou and Van Tilburg 2003). Empirical research generally supports the premise that, among older people, those with low SES report smaller networks with fewer non-kin relationships relative to those with higher SES (e.g. Antonucci 2001; Smith and Baltes 1998; Wenger 1995).

For example, a large study of older Dutch adults found that low SES older adults reported smaller networks, and lower levels of support from non-kin, relative to those with high SES (Broese Van Groenou and Van Tilburg 2003), and our own analysis of ALSA points to those who are better educated engaging in more social activity.

Explanations that focus on motivation for decreasing social engagement recognise the extent to which older adults play a deliberate role in shaping their own social development. According to socioemotional selectivity theory (SST; Carstensen and Lockenhoff 2003), recognition of one's mortality, or limits to time remaining, become more salient with advancing age, and this results in a re-prioritisation of goals. Specifically, future-oriented goals (e.g. acquiring knowledge to create opportunities) that are well served by larger, more diverse social networks are replaced by present-oriented goals (e.g. maximising the quality of emotional experiences in the here and now) that are better served by smaller, more close-knit networks. Thus, older adults may reduce their levels of engagement with more peripheral social network members in order to spend their remaining time with those who are most important to them.

Ageing-related changes in motivation and social behaviour described by SST have been invoked to account for the better quality of emotional experience frequently reported by older, relative to younger, adults (e.g. Charles and Carstensen 2009; Windsor et al. 2011), and the findings that older adults typically report smaller social networks, but at the same time greater satisfaction with their networks (Lang and Carstensen 1994). Consistent with SST, in the ALSA, perceptions of more time remaining to live are associated with greater social activity engagement; however, this relationship is accounted for to a large degree by individual differences in disability and cognitive limitations. Thus, the ALSA findings provide some broad support for SST, but also suggest that both perceived limits to time remaining and decreases in social engagement could result from underlying declines in functional and cognitive capacities.

Our brief coverage of the relevant literature above highlights the broad range of factors that facilitate, or inhibit older adults' social engagement. Among these various influences, physical health and cognitive capacity are central. This is important from a policy perspective, as it suggests that successful public health interventions designed to promote ageing well (see Chapter 7, this volume) and cognitive health (see Chapter 8, this volume) are likely to offer positive flow-on effects for social engagement. There is also, however, a growing interest in the potential benefits of intervention programs designed to directly address social isolation among older adults. In the next section, we provide an overview of such programs, and outline contemporary thinking regarding how interventions for reducing social isolation might be best designed and implemented into the future.

Programs for reducing social isolation among older adults

Numerous intervention programs with diverse characteristics have been employed worldwide in an effort to reduce social isolation in older adults. Evidence to date indicates that the most effective programs are those that have a theoretical basis, those that include an educational component (e.g. health-related education), and those including social support or activities that target specific groups (e.g. women, caregivers, widowed: Cattan et al. 2005; Dickens et al. 2011). For example, a group-based friendship program offered women weekly lessons over 12 weeks to help them clarify their expectations regarding relationships, develop their interpersonal skills (e.g. listening, self-disclosure), evaluate the potential of their existing friendships to fulfil their relationship needs, and develop plans to achieve personal relationship goals. Participants reported increased friendships and reduced loneliness during the following year (Stevens 2001). Evidence supporting the effectiveness of one-to-one interventions, such as home-based visits and telephone support services, is less compelling (Cattan et al. 2005; Dickens et al. 2011; Findlay 2003).

There has been relatively little research on service-oriented and community development approaches to intervention (Cattan et al. 2005). Although researchers have implemented and evaluated a range of interventions for social isolation, limitations in study design have often led to inconclusive findings (Findlay 2003). For example, many studies are characterised by poorly developed interventions, high attrition rates, small or unrepresentative samples, and failure to consider confounding variables (Dickens et al. 2011). Reviews of intervention projects are consistent in emphasising the need for better-designed, more rigorous approaches to evaluation (Cattan et al. 2005; Dickens et al. 2011; Findlay 2003).

A research-to-practice consensus workshop concerned with advancing research on interventions for social isolation among older adults outlined five practice-based priorities (Sabir et al. 2009):

- A first priority was concerned with shedding light on barriers to service utilisation and ways to increase participation among older adults who do not access free services.

- Second, emphasis was placed on the need to develop an easily administered measure for the identification of older adults at risk of social isolation. Positive outcomes of effective interventions may have been obscured in previous studies through a focus on general populations of older adults assumed to be experiencing isolation, rather than targeting those genuinely isolated (Dickens et al. 2011).

- A third priority concerned the implementation of more effective means of evaluating one-to-one direct and indirect contact interventions. This is important for older adults who face barriers to participation in group interventions due to, for example, physical frailty. One-to-one interventions may prove to be more effective than has been previously established when implemented with a more rigorous research design and approach to evaluation.

- Fourth, the importance of designing and evaluating interventions that address multiple possible causes of social isolation was identified. For many older adults, social isolation could arise from the cumulative effects of multiple risk factors (e.g. poor health, limited transport options, and language barriers); however, the effectiveness of multicomponent interventions designed to address manifold challenges is yet to be established.

- A final priority was concerned with research focusing on how provision of services promoting social engagement needs to be effectively balanced with the rights of older adults to make their own decisions regarding the services they access. Part of this focus on 'self-determination' was also concerned with the value of promoting reciprocity in relationships, whereby older adults have the opportunity to make an active contribution to the wellbeing of others, rather than simply being passive recipients of services (Sabir et al. 2009).

Several Australian-based researchers, policymakers, and organisations are at the forefront of efforts aimed at reducing social isolation among older adults. This is perhaps best illustrated by the Queensland Cross-Government Project to Reduce Social Isolation in Older People (CGPRSIOP: Bartlett et al. 2013). Through literature reviews, community consultations, and the evaluation of multiple demonstration projects, the CGPRSIOP developed a set of best-practice guidelines for reducing social isolation (Department of Communities 2009). A number of these guidelines echo key recommendations and priorities from the international perspectives outlined above (Cattan et al. 2005; Sabir et al. 2009), including the need for theoretically based programs with a built-in evaluation component, the value in targeting high-risk groups, the importance of programs offering meaning and purpose to participants, and the benefits of engaging older adults in the design and implementation of programs for reducing social isolation.

Guidelines from the CGPRSIOP study also emphasise the need for a whole-of-community response, involving collaboration and information sharing across government and non-government sectors, to effectively address the wide array of factors that can contribute to social isolation. One such factor that is worth highlighting is access to appropriate, safe, and affordable transport, which is essential for the equitable access of older adults to programs and services. A group who may be at particular risk of isolation are those who have given up driving due to declining health (Marottoli et al. 2000). Finally, the CGPRSIOP argues that the interventions with the greatest potential for long-term success and sustainability are those that build on existing community programs, resources, and organisations.

Pilot programs set up by the CGRSIOP have included physical exercise and education groups, a focus on better service integration and provision with an associated 'buddy system', and a volunteer service providing resources to older adults from culturally and linguistically diverse backgrounds. Initial evaluation of the pilot programs produced mixed findings, and highlighted a number of methodological challenges associated with implementing a rigorous evaluation. These included problems of adequate sample size, sample composition and representativeness, attrition, the difficulty in controlling for changes in social contact outside the scope of the intervention, and problems with the standardisation and administration of evaluation procedures across different programs, community, and service-provider groups (Bartlett et al. 2013).

Taken together the evidence to date suggests that the establishment of effective, rigorous, and robust means of evaluating interventions for social isolation among older adults may be the most pressing challenge facing researchers. It is also a critical challenge to overcome, as despite the credibility and likely value of many such programs, it will be difficult to justify substantial investment in the absence of their demonstrated efficacy. Here, we reiterate Findlay's (2003) point that 'networking between communities, governments, the private sector and researchers is essential to provide target-group input, financial support and technical expertise necessary for thorough evaluations of interventions' (p 655).

Efforts at improving approaches to implementation and evaluation of social isolation interventions may be boosted by a recently funded Australian Research Council Linkage project concerned with analysing the effectiveness of social isolation interventions, and identifying models of social inclusion that have the potential to make the greatest positive impact (see Noone 2011). Although still in its early stages, findings from this research program will have the potential to inform the further development and implementation of new interventions, and/or the expansion of successful existing approaches.

Social engagement and the economic contribution of older Australians

Maximising opportunities for older Australians to remain actively engaged in their communities is not only critical for the continued wellbeing of individuals and societies, it also represents an important economic goal in the context of population ageing. As outlined in the final report compiled by the Advisory Panel on the Economic Potential of Senior Australians (APEPSA 2011), while projections indicate significant economic challenges arising from population ageing, it is also true that population ageing brings significant economic opportunities. The report advocates a whole-of-government approach to maximising the productive potential of older Australians through addressing discriminatory attitudes that restrict opportunities for workforce participation, increasing workplace flexibility, removing barriers to participation that exist in the built environment, and promoting lifestyle choices that enhance population health, and in turn older adults' potential for productive engagement.

Also recognised in the APEPSA report are the substantial social and economic contributions made by older Australians through their participation in volunteering. For example, in South Australia, volunteering was estimated to contribute just under $5 billion annually to the state economy during the early to mid-2000s. In 2010, among those volunteering formally for organisations, an estimated 22 per cent of the total value was contributed by adults aged 55–64, with 25 per cent contributed by those aged 65 and older (Ironmonger 2011). Of additional significance is the well-established finding that volunteering is of benefit not just to society and the economy, but also to those who volunteer. Volunteering provides a formal social role that can replace previous work-based roles post-retirement (Greenfield and Marks 2004), and studies have linked volunteering among older adults to a range of beneficial outcomes including better health, reduced depressive symptoms, increased life satisfaction, and longevity (Morrow-Howell 2010).

The potential for volunteering to offer a salubrious 'double-whammy' means that identifying opportunities to facilitate volunteering for those with the interest and capacity, and removing barriers to volunteering, represent topics of keen interest to researchers and policymakers. Australian research (Warburton et al. 2007) reveals a need for more effective promotion of volunteering among older adults, including opportunities for training, flexibility of hours, and education for the latent volunteer population, which highlights the fact that volunteering opportunities exist for those with a diverse array of circumstances, needs, and skills.

The APEPSA (2011) also point to concerns regarding personal liability as a potential barrier to older adults' volunteering. They go on to recommend a review of legislation, and discussions involving government and industry regarding the availability of appropriate and affordable insurance cover for older volunteers. Facilitating volunteering opportunities for older adults with a diverse array of backgrounds and skills is likely to be at the centre of future efforts to enhance social participation among older adults. To this end, continuing to effectively link older adults with existing volunteer organisations will be a central component. In addition, flexible and creative thinking concerned with harnessing the potential of older Australians to contribute and remain engaged in novel ways represents an exciting future challenge.

Social engagement among the oldest-old

Much of our discussion so far regarding social engagement among older Australians rests on assumptions of older adults ageing well (see Chapter 7, this volume), retaining independence, and remaining relatively free of significant physical and cognitive impairment during the post-retirement years. As outlined above, good health and cognition are key resources for social engagement, and health promotion efforts aimed at compression of morbidity, and delay of cognitive decline and dementia (see Chapter 8, this volume) are likely to provide downstream benefits for social and productive engagement at the population level. However, as individuals progress into oldest-old adulthood (or the 'fourth age'), more significant ageing-related losses become normative (Baltes and Smith 2003). Consequently, a challenge for public policy, service providers, and communities, concerns how to best provide opportunities for older adults to remain socially engaged in the context of more serious biological limitations.

This challenge is touched upon in a review of evidence concerned with loneliness and isolation among older adults in residential care (Grenade and Boldy 2008). The transition to care may result in a disruption to existing networks and a reduced frequency of contact with family and friends. At the same time, some older adults (particularly those previously living alone) may experience an increase in social contact through day-to-day interactions with staff and other residents. Important considerations for fostering positive relationships among those in residential care include appropriate staff training and retention policies, and providing opportunities for older residents to exercise independence, and promote feelings of autonomy and self-esteem. According to Grenade and Boldy, while evaluation evidence is scarce, interventions aimed at promoting contact among residents in family- and pet-friendly aged-care environments are likely to provide benefits for social connectedness.

The issue of social isolation among older adults with more significant health restrictions is also addressed in a recent briefing paper from the Social Policy Research Centre in partnership with the Benevolent Society (2009), which identified practice implications for community aged-care providers. In line with a number of the strategies for reducing social isolation in the community discussed above, the paper identified the importance of strategic approaches that target specific groups, and involve older adults themselves in program planning, delivery and evaluation. Combining social isolation programs with broader multifaceted approaches to health promotion is also recommended. Another important theme concerned the development of programs that enhance the autonomy of older participants by focusing on their strengths and achievements, facilitating the identification of goals, and building self-worth and confidence.

George and Singer (2011) recently described an innovative intervention involving older adults with mild to moderate dementia participating in a volunteer program that involved mentoring kindergarten children in educational activities in a classroom setting. Results of a small, randomised controlled trial indicated that participants in the intervention typically showed better outcomes in stress, cognition, and sense of purpose relative to a control group. Only group differences in stress reached statistical significance; however, moderate effect sizes evident for other quality of life outcomes suggested that this was a result of small sample size (intervention $n = 8$; control group $n = 7$). The role of the intervention in improving outcomes for participants was also supported by qualitative ethnographic methods that suggested perceived benefits for health, purpose and quality of relationships (George 2011). Intergenerational programs of this type hold significant promise as a means of enhancing quality of life for healthy as well as more vulnerable older adults, and for building more cohesive communities by reducing negative aged-based stereotypes. We return to the discussion of intergenerational programs in the concluding section.

Summary and conclusions

Either by choice, or necessity, the nature of our social relationships tends to change with age. In this chapter, we outlined some of the main factors thought to influence such changes, before discussing approaches to interventions designed to reduce social isolation, the relevance to society and the economy of older adults' social participation in the form of work and volunteering, and the challenges of promoting social engagement and inclusion among the oldest-old. Here, we conclude by reiterating several key points, and by introducing some additional issues for researchers and policymakers to consider.

An important theme that should inform future refinement and development of public policy related to older adults' social engagement concerns how different generations can work together to contribute to, and benefit from, broader approaches to social inclusion. As touched on above, older adults themselves represent a heterogeneous group, with the vitality and productive engagement of many older adults in the third age (e.g. ages 65–84) standing in contrast to the relatively greater dependency and health restrictions of many in the fourth age (e.g. ages 85 and older; Baltes and Smith 2003). Population ageing will see an increase in both of these age groups, and creative approaches to social engagement might focus on how volunteering efforts of the young-old can best support the social inclusion and autonomy of the oldest-old.

Recent years have seen an increased focus on the value of social initiatives and aspects of urban design (e.g. Eheart et al. 2009) that bring together children and/or younger adults with older adults. Such intergenerational programs are concerned with promoting interaction and cooperation among different generations in ways that promote attitudinal change and build social capital (Cummings et al. 2002). Research based on intergenerational programs has revealed promising findings including better school behaviour (Cummings et al. 2002) and reduced ageist stereotypes (Cummings et al. 2002; Pinquart et al. 2000) among child participants, and better perceptions of neighbourhood cohesion among older adults (de Souza and Grundy 2007). However, as is the case with interventions for social isolation, the wider application of intergenerational programs has been restricted by a lack of research evidence regarding their effectiveness (Statham 2009).

A notable exception is the US-based Experience Corps® (EC) program, which recruits older adult volunteers to assist in schools, providing support in programs designed to improve student literacy and behaviour. The EC program is founded on a number of specific elements designed to enhance its broad effectiveness in improving outcomes for students, older volunteers, and the community (Glass et al. 2004). For example, volunteers are required to make a substantial time commitment to the program, which is designed to foster continuity of volunteer–student relationships, and maximise opportunities for health and cognitive benefits for older adults arising from their volunteer activity. The program also offers training and infrastructure support for participants, as well as modest reimbursement for participants' expenses, thereby reducing barriers to participation among those on lower incomes. The EC program also targets schools and volunteers from lower socioeconomic areas, contributing to social capital where it is most needed.

An initial evaluation of the pilot EC program was based on a randomised controlled trial, and pointed to beneficial outcomes for volunteers in terms of aspects of cognitive test performance, physical activity, and social support (Rebok et al. 2011). Its well-developed conceptual basis and the rigorous approach to evaluation that underlies the EC program means that it provides a useful model to draw on in the design of future intergenerational programs in Australia.

As we have emphasised, social connections offer wide-ranging benefits for the health and wellbeing of individuals, and societies. However, we would also add a cautionary note that those concerned with efforts to enhance social participation and engagement among older adults should be mindful of the potential for social relationships to result in tension and conflict as well as positive outcomes. A growing body of research now demonstrates that negative social exchanges are a significant source of stress, and can adversely impact health and wellbeing. Moreover, the detrimental effects of negative social exchanges on wellbeing may be stronger than the positive effects resulting from supportive relationships (Newsom et al. 2005; Rook 2015). Thus, the most effective interventions may be those that enhance engagement and support among older adults while also providing a means for participants to readily disengage from relationships that they see as problematic.

To conclude, physical and cognitive health are important resources for social engagement in older adulthood. As a result, public health interventions designed to promote physical and cognitive health over the life-span are likely to have flow-on benefits for the social engagement of older adults. In addition, interventions that directly target social isolation among older adults show substantial promise; however, better approaches to evaluation are needed to identify those interventions most likely to be efficacious for different at-risk groups, both in the community and in residential care settings. Researchers have emphasised that the inclusion of older adult target groups in all stages of program design and evaluation is likely to be essential for the development of successful interventions for social isolation.

The design of interventions should also ensure that the social connections being fostered, wherever possible, allow older adults to maintain and develop a sense of autonomy, purpose, and meaning around their activities; intergenerational programs appear to hold considerable promise as a means of achieving these goals. Older adults represent a heterogeneous group, with great variation in both capacities for, and individual inclinations toward, broader social engagement. As a result, social engagement and inclusion is likely to be best promoted through multifaceted and multidisciplinary efforts. Promoting healthy ageing and addressing issues of social disadvantage are likely to be central to these endeavours.

Ultimately, removing barriers to social engagement among older adults stands to create more cohesive communities, and to maximise the economic and social contribution of older Australians in the context of population ageing.

References

Advisory Panel of the Economic Potential of Senior Australians (APEPSA) (2011). *Realising the economic potential of senior Australians: Turning grey into gold*. Canberra: Commonwealth of Australia.

Antonucci Toni (2001). Social relations: An examination of social networks, social support and sense of control. In James E Birren and Klaus Warner Schaie (Eds) *Handbook of the Psychology of Aging* (5th ed). New York: Academic Press, pp. 427–453.

Ashida Sato and Heaney Catherine (2008). Differential associations of social support and social connectedness with structural features of social networks and the health status of older adults. *Journal of Aging and Health*, 20: 872–893.

Baltes Paul and Smith Jacqui (2003). New frontiers in the future of aging: From successful aging of the young old to the dilemmas of the fourth age. *Gerontology*, 49: 123–135.

Bartlett Helen, Warburton Jeni, Lui Chi-Wai, Peach Linda and Carroll Matthew (2013). Preventing social isolation in later life: Findings and insights from a pilot Queensland intervention study. *Ageing and Society*, 33: 1167–1189.

Berkman Lisa (1995). The role of social relations in health promotion. *Psychosomatic Medicine*, 57: 245–254.

Bowling Ann and Dieppe Paul (2005). What is successful ageing and who should define it? *BMJ*, 331: 1548–1551.

Broese Van Groenou Marjolein and Van Tilburg Theo (2003). Network size and support in old age: Differentials by socio-economic status in childhood and adulthood. *Ageing and Society*, 23: 625–645.

Carstensen Laura and Lockenhoff Corinna (2003). Aging, emotion, and evolution: The bigger picture. *Annals of the New York Academy of Sciences*, 1000: 152–179.

Cattan Mima, White Martin, Bond John and Learmouth Alison (2005). Preventing social isolation and loneliness among older people: A systematic review of health promotion interventions. *Ageing and Society*, 25: 41–67.

Charles Susan and Carstensen Laura (2009). Social and emotional aging. *Annual Review of Psychology*, 61: 383–409.

Chen Edith and Miller Gregory (2013). Socioeconomic status and health: Mediating and moderating factors. *Annual Review of Clinical Psychology*, 9: 723–749.

Cornwell Erin York and Waite Linda (2009). Social disconnectedness, perceived isolation, and health among older adults. *Journal of Health and Social Behavior*, 50: 31–48.

Cummings Sherry, Williams Mona and Ellis Rodney (2002). Impact of an intergenerational program on 4th graders' attitudes toward elders and school behaviors. *Journal of Human Behavior in the Social Environment*, 6: 91–107.

de Souza Elza Maria and Grundy Emily (2007). Intergenerational interaction, social capital and health: Results from a randomised controlled trial in Brazil. *Social Science and Medicine*, 65: 1397–1409.

Department of Communities (2009). *Cross-government project to reduce social isolation of older people: Best practice guidelines.* Brisbane: Department of Communities, Queensland Government.

Dickens Andy, Richards Suzanne, Greaves Colin and Campbell John (2011). Interventions targeting social isolation in older people: A systematic review. *BMC Public Health*, 11: 647–647.

Eheart Brenda Krause, Hopping David, Power Martha, Mitchell Elissa, and Racine David (2009). Generations of hope communities: An intergenerational neighborhood model of support and service. *Children and Youth Services Review*, 31: 47–52.

Findlay Robyn (2003). Interventions to reduce social isolation amongst older people: Where is the evidence? *Ageing and Society*, 23: 647–658.

Fratiglioni Laura, Paillard-Borg Stephanie and Winblad Bengt (2004). An active and socially integrated lifestyle in late life might protect against dementia. *The Lancet Neurology*, 3: 343–353.

Gallo Linda (2009). The reserve capacity model as a framework for understanding psychosocial factors in health disparities. *Applied Psychology: Health and Well-Being*, 1: 62–72.

George Daniel (2011). Intergenerational volunteering and quality of life: Mixed methods evaluation of a randomized control trial involving persons with mild to moderate dementia. *Quality of Life Research*, 20: 987–995.

George Daniel and Singer Mendel (2011). Intergenerational volunteering and quality of life for persons with mild to moderate dementia: Results from a 5-month intervention study in the United States. *The American Journal of Geriatric Psychiatry*, 19: 392–396.

Glass Thomas, Freedman Marc, Carlson Michelle, Hill Joel, Frick Kevin, Ialongo Nick and Fried Linda (2004). Experience Corps: Design of an intergenerational program to boost social capital and promote the health of an aging society. *Journal of Urban Health: Bulletin of the New York Academy of Medicine*, 81: 94–105.

Greenfield Emily and Marks Nadine (2004). Formal volunteering as a protective factor for older adults' psychological well-being. *Journal of Gerontology: Social Sciences*, 59B: S258–S264.

Grenade Linda and Boldy Duncan (2008). Social isolation and loneliness among older people: Issues and future challenges in community and residential settings. *Australian Health Review*, 32: 468–478.

Hertzog Christopher, Kramer Arthur, Wilson Robert and Lindenberger Ulman (2008). Enrichment effects on adults cognitive development: Can the functional capacity of older adults be preserved and enhanced? *Psychological Science in the Public Interest*, 9: 1–65.

Ironmonger Duncan (2011). *The economic value of volunteering in South Australia*. Adelaide: Office for Volunteers, Government of South Australia.

Lang Frieder and Carstensen Laura (1994). Close emotional relationships in late life: Further support for proactive aging in the social domain. *Psychology and Aging*, 9: 315–324.

Laporte Audrey, Nauenberg Eric and Shen Leilei (2008). Aging, social capital, and health care utilization in Canada. *Health Economics, Policy and Law*, 3: 393–411.

Luszcz Mary, Giles Lynne, Anstey Kaarin, Browne-Yung Kathryn, Walker Ruth and Windsor Tim (2014). Cohort Profile: The Australian Longitudinal Study of Ageing (ALSA). *International Journal of Epidemiology*, 1–10. doi:1093/ije/dyu196.

Marottoli Richard, Mendes de Leon Carlos, Glass Thomas, Williams Christianna, Cooney Jnr Leo and Berkman Lisa (2000). Consequences of driving cessation: Decreased out-of-home activity levels. *Journals of Gerontology: Social Sciences*, 55: S334–S340.

Morrow-Howell Nancy (2010). Volunteering in later life: Research frontiers. *Journal of Gerontology: Social Sciences*, 65B: 461–469.

Newsom Jason, Roo, Karen, Nishishiba Masami, Sorkin Dara and Mahan Tyrae (2005). Understanding the relative importance of positive and negative social exchanges: Examining specific domains and appraisals. *Journal of Gerontology: Psychological Sciences*, 60B: P304–P312.

Noone Yasmin (2011). *Solving social isolation—Successfully*. Australian Ageing Agenda. www.australianageingagenda.com.au/2011/06/28/ solving-social-isolation-successfully/.

Pinquart Martin (2003). Loneliness in married, widowed, divorced, and never-married older adults. *Journal of Social and Personal Relationships,* 20: 31–53.

Pinquart Martin, Wenzel Silka and Sö Rensen Silvia (2000). Changes in attitudes among children and elderly adults in intergenerational group work. *Educational Gerontology*, 26: 523–540.

Rebok George, Carlson Michelle, Barron Jeremy, Frick Kevin, McGill Sylvia, Parisi Jeanine and Fried Linda (2011). Experience Corps®: A civic engagement-based public health intervention in the public schools. In Paula E Hartman-Stein and Asenath LaRue (Eds) *Enhancing cognitive fitness in adults: A guide for use and development of community-based programs.* New York: Springer, pp. 469–487.

Rook Karen (2015). Social networks in later life: Weighing positive and negative effects on health and well-being. *Current Directions in Psychological Science*, 24: 45–51.

Rowe John and Kahn Robert (1987). Human aging: usual and successful. *Science*, 237: 143–149. doi:10.1126/science.3299702: 2.

Sabir Myra, Wethington Elaine, Breckman Risa, Meador Rhoda, Reid MC and Pillemer Karl (2009). A community-based participatory critique of social isolation intervention research for community-dwelling older adults. *Journal of Applied Gerontology*, 28: 218–234.

Smith Jacqui and Baltes Margret (1998). The role of gender in very old age: Profiles of functioning and everyday life patterns. *Psychology and Aging*, 13: 676–695.

Social Policy Research Centre and the Benevolent Society (SPRC) (2009). *Promoting social networks for older people in community aged care.* Research to Practice Briefing 2. Sydney: University of New South Wales and the Benevolent Society.

Statham Elaine (2009). Promoting intergenerational programmes: Where is the evidence to inform policy and practice? *Evidence and Policy: A Journal of Research, Debate and Practice*, 5: 471–488.

Stevens Nan (2001). Combating loneliness: A friendship enrichment programme for older women. *Ageing and Society*, 21: 183–202.

Stoykova Ralitsa, Matharan Fanny, Dartigues Jean-François and Amieva Hélène (2011). Impact of social network on cognitive performances and age-related cognitive decline across a 20-year follow-up. *International Psychogeriatrics*, 23: 1405–1412.

Thoits Peggy (2006). Personal agency in the stress process. *Journal of Health and Social Behavior*, 47: 309–323.

Warburton Jeni, Paynter Jessica and Petriwskyj Andrea (2007). Volunteering as a productive ageing activity: Incentives and barriers to volunteering by Australian seniors. *Journal of Applied Gerontology*, 26: 333–354.

Wenger G Clare (1995). A comparison of urban with rural support networks: Liverpool and North Wales. *Ageing and Society*, 15: 59–81.

Windsor Tim, Fiori Katherine and Crisp Dimity (2011). Personal and neighborhood resources, future time perspective, and social relations in middle and older adulthood. *Journals of Gerontology Series B: Psychological Sciences and Social Sciences*, 67: 423–431.

Windsor Tim, Gerstorf Denis, Pearson Elissa, Ryan Lindsay and Anstey Kaarin (2014). Positive and negative social exchanges and cognitive aging in young-old adults: Differential associations across family, friend, and spouse domains. *Psychology and Aging*, 29: 28–43.

10

Wellbeing and its improvability as a national goal

Richard A Burns and Colette Browning

There is nothing either good or bad, but thinking makes it so
— Hamlet

Wellbeing has long been a discussion point for national policy when considering the impact of social and economic policy. Depending on one's professional outlook, however, we may all arrive at quite different connotations of what wellbeing actually reflects. Consequently, quite different interventions to wellbeing improvement may be considered. Traditionally defined in terms of economic growth and wealth accumulation, more recent wellbeing definitions have incorporated other objective and measurable social indicators including, but not limited to, health-care provision, education access, housing affordability and equality, which have been used to provide an objective measure of quality of life. In contrast, for others, questions of wellbeing relate specifically to the burden of disease and disability in a population, including psychiatric illness (e.g. affective disorders, dementias) and chronic disease (e.g. obesity, diabetes). However, as behavioural scientists, the authors of this chapter relate questions of wellbeing to the experiential and existential dimensions from which we interpret meaning from personal experiences. In this way, wellbeing relates to both objective and subjective dimensions of psychological functioning and feeling, often defined in terms of level of cognitive function, affect, motivation and even notions of spirituality.

As definitions and theoretical models of wellbeing determine what is measured, it is important to interrogate how broadly wellbeing is addressed in population surveys. It is important to measure wellbeing beyond economic and social indicators, and to consider the impact of policy on individuals' experiences. But of those measures that have been implemented to date, they have typically focused on clinically relevant dimensions of mental health or individuals' generalised evaluations of their life satisfaction and satisfaction with different life domains (e.g. work, relationships, etc.), ignoring other important psychological indicators of functioning and feeling. One further issue often neglected in population wellbeing is the assumption that all wellbeing dimensions are equally important to all. Whilst one individual prioritises material wealth for their wellbeing, another may prioritise community engagement, and yet another developing a sense of mastery and competence.

Some nations are actively readdressing their approach to measuring population wellbeing. In the United Kingdom (UK) for example, the government is assessing the impact of changes in public policy on changes in personal wellbeing. As part of this process, the government is taking the opportunity to be informed by its citizens; what do they consider important to provide meaning and fulfilment in their own lives? Future national prosperity and wellbeing are outcomes of individuals being enabled to realise their potential (Foresight Report 2008).

In this chapter, we therefore focus specifically on describing the science of wellbeing at the individual level and its importance for population-level policy. First we examine current population-level approaches to personal wellbeing that recognise the importance of including social as well as economic indicators of a nation's 'wealth'. We then discuss wellbeing at the individual level, describing a distinction between hedonic wellbeing, with its focus on satisfaction judgements, and eudemonic wellbeing, highlighting the limitations of existing population methods with a focus on satisfaction measures. Next, we use the European Social Survey as a case study to show how multiple measures of wellbeing can be used to describe the effects of public policy across a number of wellbeing dimensions at the population level. We then describe contributions to understanding wellbeing in Australia based on two large-scale longitudinal studies. Finally, we reflect on the way forward in terms of incorporating wellbeing outcomes in Australian national policy, and the measurement and data collection issues that need to be addressed.

Current population-level approaches to wellbeing

Governments and policy advocates have increasingly recognised that traditional economic indicators are insufficient alone to describe a population's wellbeing and so broader indicators that encompass social and cultural factors are increasingly considered. In line with a social determinants of health model, this suggests that personal wellbeing is strongly driven by social, economic and health-service factors (Dahlgren and Whitehead 1991), and that health outcomes are strongly related to the lifestyles people live and the contexts in which they live (Wilkinson and Marmot 2003). For example, the most recent US Federal Interagency Forum on Aging-Related Statistics (FIF-ARS 2012) report, *Older Americans 2012: Key Indicators of Well-Being,* focused on issues of poverty, sources of income, living arrangements, housing, diet, physical activity, cigarette smoking, air quality, access to health care, etc., as key indicators of older adults' wellbeing. Developed with input from various US federal departments, the forum aimed to:

> stimulate discussions by policymakers and the public ... By examining a broad range of indicators, researchers, policymakers, service providers, and the Federal government can better understand the areas of wellbeing that are improving for older Americans and the areas of wellbeing that require more attention and effort (p iv).

There is no doubting the role of employment, financial security, air quality and service provision, etc., in providing necessary social and economic conditions that enable individuals and community to thrive, but we note the report failed to consider how individuals themselves value their lives and their personal sense of wellbeing. Maslow's (1968) theory of the hierarchy of needs describes well a model of need motivation whereby a series of underlying basic physical needs, including safety, food and care needs, require addressing before individuals can strive for higher-level outcomes, such as individual growth and actualising needs. That is, as the most basic human needs are satisfied, so the organism can begin to focus on more complex, social, emotional and psychological needs that culminate in higher-order psychological functioning. Reports, such as the FIF-ARS, however, fail to consider this level of human functioning.

Similarly, the recent and long-awaited OECD (2014a) report, *How Was Life? Global Wellbeing since 1820,* examined social progress over the past two centuries. Again, extending the focus of traditional national accounts from simple examinations of trends in GDP per capita growth, *How Was Life?* considered development across a number of other social determinants of wellbeing including life expectancy, education, personal security and gender equality. Whilst reflecting an emergence of the appreciation of social indicators of population wellbeing, the report similarly fails to consider dimensions of individual experiences.

There have been a number of attempts to assess individual-level wellbeing in population surveys, however, and a few notable examples will provide some context for our narrative. For instance, the Bhutanese Government, under the auspices of The Centre for Bhutan Studies and Gross National Happiness Research, has undertaken a series of nationally representative wellbeing surveys that eschew economic prosperity for Gross National Happiness (GNH), defined in terms of social and individual wellbeing. The Bhutanese GNH survey measures nine domains of population happiness that encompass measures of ecology, health, community, governance, education, culture and living standards, and, importantly, several indicators of personal wellbeing including life satisfaction, positive and negative affect, and spirituality. Based on the 2010 survey outcomes (Ura et al. 2012), around 90 per cent of the Bhutanese population were identified as happy to some extent with sufficiency across most of the domains for most in the population. However, cross-national comparisons with other objective wellbeing measures reveal troubling patterns: Bhutan ranks poorly for healthy life expectancy, life expectancy, infant mortality, and suicide (WHO 2014). Specifically, healthy life expectancy at birth for males is 58 years (ranked 127th out of 194) and for females 59 years (ranked 138th out of 194) whilst infant mortality for children under one is reported at 30 deaths per 1,000 live births (ranked 69th highest out of 194). And despite Bhutan's focus on 'happiness', age-adjusted suicide rates indicated males reporting 23.1 suicides per 100,000 (ranked 33rd highest out of 172) and females reporting 11.2 suicides per 100,000 (ranked 14th highest out of 172).

Consequently, serious re-examination of the extent to which the GNH survey accurately reflects the wellbeing of its people is needed. Perhaps their findings reflect an expectancy effect? That is, culturally, happiness is seen as a priority and this drives survey responses?

For our current discussion, at least two implications can be drawn from the survey results. First, whilst the Bhutan GNH survey recognises the importance of measuring personal wellbeing, it is clear, in line with Maslow's proposition, that government policy must first address basic social and economic needs as a priority in order for individuals to subsequently flourish and live healthy lives. Second, in the GNH survey, individual wellbeing is perhaps too narrowly defined. This is an issue we will expand on further in this chapter.

Developed nations have also increasingly focused on reconciling notions of economic and social wellbeing with an understanding of individual wellbeing and happiness. Of particular note was the British Government's announcement in late 2010, to supplement its national accounts with measures of other social and individual wellbeing indicators. Speaking on the need for a new measure of wellbeing, British Prime Minister David Cameron (2010) stated:

> let me try and address the suspicion that all this is a bit airy-fairy and a bit impractical. Now, of course, you cannot capture happiness on a spreadsheet any more than you can bottle it. If anyone was trying to reduce the whole spectrum of human happiness into one snapshot statistic I would be the first to roll my eyes and write about it in newspapers. But that's not what this is all about. Just as the GDP figures don't give a full story of our economy's growth, but give us a useful indicator of where we're heading. So, I believe a new measure won't give the full story of our nation's wellbeing, or our happiness or contentment or the rest of it—of course it won't—but it could give us a general picture of whether life is improving, and that does have a really practical purpose. First, it will open up a national debate about what really matters, not just in government but amongst people who influence our lives: in the media; in business; the people who develop the products we use, who build the towns we live in, who shape the culture we enjoy. And second, this information will help government work out, with evidence, the best ways of trying to help to improve people's wellbeing.

In a similar vein, the OECD *Better Life Initiative* (BLI) includes measures of personal wellbeing that tap:

aspects of life that matter to people and that shape the quality of their lives. This allows for a better understanding of what drives the well-being of people and nations, and what needs to be done to achieve greater progress for all (OECD 2014b).

The Commission on the Measurement of Economic Performance and Social Progress (CMEPSP) report also emphasised the need for governments to shift emphasis from measuring economic production to people's wellbeing (Stiglitz et al. 2009). Increasingly, there is a growing consensus for governments and policymakers to realise the complexities that underpin our understanding of wellbeing at both individual and population levels, and to extend the focus from GDP to other social, community and, increasingly, individual factors as an end goal of national public policy (Forgeard et al. 2011). However, from a behavioural science perspective, there remains a level of debate about current population approaches to the measurement of individual wellbeing. Traditionally informed by individuals' psychological and emotional health, encompassing dimensions of clinical mental health outcomes (e.g. depression, cognitive impairment), there is increasing theoretical and empirical basis for the need to focus on psychological dimensions of wellbeing. Such a focus would relate to questions of personal growth, autonomy and mastery, areas of human functioning that are significant drivers of future human behaviour, but that are yet to have much impact in the national policy sphere. There is a considerable need for population-level approaches to be informed by our scientific knowledge about drivers of psychological and subjective wellbeing to ensure relevance in shaping population behaviour and to assess the impact of social and economic policy on individuals' wellbeing.

Psychological and subjective wellbeing

Within the behavioural sciences, wellbeing has received considerable focus in recent decades as the interest in 'positive psychology' has featured more prominently in lay and academic literature. It is not, however, a particularly new area of research; it has been a century since Adler's (1929) *The Science of Living* and over half-a-century since Rogers' (1961) *On Becoming a Person*. There are therefore many psychological theories, findings and reviews that purport to best describe and measure wellbeing. In essence, wellbeing is a multifaceted construct. In an increasingly dated but still excellent introduction to the topic, Ryan and Deci (2001) described research on wellbeing as deriving from two perspectives: 1) the *'hedonic'* or Subjective Wellbeing (SWB) approach, which focuses on happiness and defines wellbeing in terms of pleasure attainment and pain avoidance; and 2) the *'eudaimonic'* or Psychological Wellbeing (PWB) approach, which focuses on meaning and self-realisation, defining wellbeing in terms of the degree to which a person is fully functioning.

SWB emerged during the 1960s/70s as an attempt to measure quality of life and monitor the impact of social policy on change in individuals' wellbeing (Bradburn 1969). The SWB approach focuses on three components: life satisfaction, the presence of positive mood, and the absence of negative mood (Diener and Lucas 1999). With its philosophical roots in the ancient philosophy of Aristippus, SWB is based on the hedonic principles that pleasure and happiness are of primary concern to the individual, an idea echoed later by Bentham's (1789) 'greatest happiness principle'. SWB reflects people's subjective evaluations of their lives, incorporating an assessment of the range of emotions they experience. These evaluations comprise cognitive and affective interpretations of external events, and reflect an individual's personal assessment of their own life. SWB models have perhaps been the most often utilised within the literature, with life satisfaction a frequently used index of individual wellbeing, particularly in larger population studies (Diener et al. 1999). Bhutan's Gross National Happiness approach is an example of this conceptualisation of wellbeing.

In contrast, PWB has its foundations in eudaimonic assumptions that wellbeing is related to whether individuals live their lives according to their true nature or *daimon*. Many eudaimonic approaches are critical of hedonism for its focus on momentary pleasure, and disregard of long-term purposefulness and growth. Carol Ryff's (1989a, 1989b) model of Psychological Wellbeing is one PWB approach to the measurement of wellbeing, from gerontological and life-span research, which led to the formulation of six dimensions of PWB: autonomy, positive relations with others, environmental mastery, personal growth, purpose in life, and self-acceptance. Ryff (1989b) argued that these six key areas were consistently identified as indicative of the good life and wellbeing. However, significant overlap between a number of these domains has been reported and suggests that PWB, as operationalised by Ryff, is not so clearly defined (Burns and Machin 2008; Abbott et al. 2006).

Self-Determination Theory (SDT) (Ryan and Deci 2000) reflects another theoretical approach within the PWB paradigm that clearly delineates three basic psychological needs: autonomy, competence and relatedness. SDT posits that fulfilment of these needs is essential for psychological growth, integrity, life satisfaction, and psychological health, as well as experiences of vitality, vigour or energy and self-congruence (Huppert 2009).

PWB proponents (e.g. Ryff and Singer 1998) have argued that SWB models are limited in describing long-term positive functioning given SWB's focus on affective states and generalised evaluations of satisfaction, which are highly reactive in the short-term but are relatively stable as this affective reaction returns to individuals' set-points that appear to be stable over time (Headey and Wearing 1989, 1992). Also, Waterman (1993) has argued that positive functioning may require a degree of effort and discipline that may at times run contrary to the pursuit of short-term happiness. Becker (1992) provides countless examples of people who have lived unjust, pointless lives who have nonetheless been happy in the long run, whilst Brickman et al. (1978) described well the short-term changes in SWB in paraplegics and lottery winners who appear to have returned to their initial SWB levels. Diener (1994) suggests happiness is less an end in itself than a consequence of other, more noble, pursuits. Regardless of these differences, there is growing support for the thesis that PWB and SWB constitute two related yet different approaches to modelling wellbeing (Burns and Machin 2008; Lucas et al. 1996; Compton et al. 1996) and that wellbeing should be considered as both an outcome of lives being lived well, and a driver of future living well.

Mental health and wellbeing

At this point, it is important to emphasise a distinction between wellbeing and mental health. For some, these terms are synonymous. A leading proponent of positive mental health and wellbeing research, Keyes (2002) described:

> mental health as a syndrome of symptoms of positive feelings and positive function in life ... The presence of mental health is described as flourishing, and the absence of mental health, characterized as languishing.

For Keyes, mental health is operationalised in terms of subjective reports of feelings, not clinically relevant dimensions of mental disorders. Similarly, Huppert and So (2013) emphasise the importance of governments conceptualising wellbeing as positive mental health, which lies 'at the opposite end of a spectrum to the common mental disorders (depression, anxiety)'.

However, the current authors argue that there is a need to clearly discriminate between mental health as the degree to which clinically relevant psychological disturbances are present (e.g. affective disorders), and wellbeing that relates to the presence of non-clinical dimensions of psychological feeling and functioning. Hence wellbeing and mental health reflect two, most probably oblique, factors rather than a single factor. Consequently, those with varying degrees of symptoms of mental illness can be described as possessing mental ill health, with absence of these symptoms reflecting mental health. Those who present with high psychological functioning and positive feelings and low negative feelings can be described as possessing high wellbeing, whilst those low in psychological functioning and low positive feelings and high in negative emotions can be described as possessing low wellbeing.

Surprisingly, support for distinguishing between wellbeing and mental health comes from Keyes (2002) himself, in a paper that examined the concordance of Major Depressive Disorder with flourishing (high emotional 'mental' health) and languishing (low emotional 'mental' health). Keyes (2002) identified 4.7 per cent of the languishers as reporting major depression, while 8.5 per cent (those with moderate mental health) and 0.9 per cent (those flourishing), reported major depression. Hence, major depression was itself not indicative of languishing, nor was possessing moderate mental health or flourishing protective against a major depressive episode. This finding emphasises the additional benefit to extending our notion of mental health to consider issues of psychological wellbeing and the contribution they make to describing how well individuals are living their lives.

Most population-level approaches to the assessment of individual wellbeing have focused on clinically relevant mental disorders, with the subsequent burden of mental ill-health on economic growth, labour force participation and community engagement. For example, in Australia, two nationally representative surveys, The National Surveys of Mental Health and *Wellbeing* (emphasis added) 1997 and 2007, estimated the prevalence of mental disorders in Australia and identified those social factors (e.g. marital status, employment, age and gender) that may indicate which sub-populations were most at risk. But what of *'wellbeing'*? In 1997, the General Health Questionnaire (GHQ-12) (a measure used to screen for mental disorders), measured life satisfaction, neuroticism (a personality measure), and self-rated health (SRH). Of these only SRH was included in 2007. Given the theoretical wellbeing models presented earlier, it leaves us asking: Where is this notion of wellbeing?

Sadly, large longitudinal studies that focus on multidimensional dimensions of wellbeing that emphasise personal growth and self-fulfilment are lacking, even though the Foresight Report (2008) emphasised several years earlier the need for policy to concern itself as much with the enhancement of wellbeing amongst 'normal' members of a population (as there are simply more of them), as with maintaining appropriate and effective services for those with serious mental ill health. Instead, a dominant medical approach has emphasised the promotion of wellbeing by the identification and treatment of disease and subsequent burden.

With advances in medical technology, and with greater understanding of the way disease develops, much of the health industry has focused on identifying, treating and eradicating diseases, with the implicit assumption that by treating the disease wellbeing is promoted. Most government policy has followed suit. But this position does little to promote the notion of health and wellbeing; that individuals live with disease and illness (e.g. cancer, diabetes, asthma) does not prohibit their capacity to lead fulfilling and meaningful lives, and to experience positive feelings and happiness. Indeed, in the preamble to its constitution, the World Health Organization (WHO 1946) described health as 'a state of complete physical, mental and social wellbeing and not merely the absence of disease or infirmity'. Two points need to be emphasised here. First, health is a 'state' of wellbeing and, second, wellbeing is not 'simply the absence' of a particular disease, rather wellbeing means that one possesses something. Hence, a person can experience wellbeing whilst living with disease, but those living without disease are not necessarily living with wellbeing.

The limitation of satisfaction judgements as indicators of lives lived well

Advances in psychology and neuroscience indicate that subjective wellbeing can be measured with a degree of accuracy. The last 20 or so years have seen a concerted effort for economic and policy-related research to utilise subjective indicators of happiness and life satisfaction as indicators of interpersonal wellbeing (Kahneman et al. 1999). However, despite our earlier description of the way in which personal wellbeing can be operationalised, it is surprising that life satisfaction and satisfaction with different life domains, such as with work, relationships, etc., remain the most frequently utilised measure of individual wellbeing in population studies. In Australia for example, The Household and Income Labour Dynamics in Australia (HILDA) survey (Wooden and Watson 2007) uses multiple dimensions of satisfaction with life domains to measure individual wellbeing and has been used to assess the extent to which Australians are happy with their lives (Cassells et al. 2010). However, there have long been questions regarding the utility of satisfaction as a suitable index of wellbeing. The Cassells et al. (2010) report indicated that 88 per cent of the population was satisfied or very satisfied. This may simply correspond with the proportion of the population without psychological distress at a particular moment, but that so many were satisfied leaves little room to examine whether discriminating degrees of satisfaction is really of substantive benefit. Let us consider two further issues in more detail.

First, consider what is known about life satisfaction, happiness and income. Easterlin's paradox (1974) identified that those with high incomes reported higher levels of happiness, but that increases in US income in the 25 years prior to 1970 were not accompanied by long-term changes in happiness—a decline in the 1960s was reported. Similarly, in Japan, self-reported happiness did not increase from 1958 to 1987 despite a five-fold increase in real income. Whilst others (e.g. Hagerty and Veenhoven 2003) have argued that there is evidence for increasing happiness with increasing income, Easterlin (2005) identified issues with the interpretation of these data and subsequently (Easterlin et al. 2010) reaffirmed the paradox in an analysis of 37 countries. Clark et al. (2012) have suggested that other confounding social factors (e.g. marital status, governance, social equality) drive the purported association between level of GDP and wellbeing. They have also highlighted the importance of relative income and wealth compared to level of wealth.

A second example involves a consideration of what is known about life satisfaction and age. Frequently, a curve-linear relationship between age and satisfaction is described, but then in which direction? Are people least satisfied in mid-life when work and family demands are at their highest, or are they most satisfied in mid-life when work and family identities are increasingly cemented and accompanied by job promotion and a growing family network? Clark et al. (2012) have suggested an inverted U-shape is most commonly reported, but Baird et al. (2010) reviewed longitudinal data (>20 years) from the German Socio-Economic Panel and British Household Panel studies and found stable life satisfaction in the German population until age 70, whilst the British population reported increases in mid-life, and substantial declines in late life. In contrast, in Australia, Headey and Warren (2008) did identify life satisfaction as lowest in mid-life, and this corresponds well with what we know about increased suicide rates in mid-life, particularly amongst men. Still, these apparently disparate findings indicate the large differences in life satisfaction across seemingly similar countries.

There are two main reasons for why the existing population wellbeing literature describes such contradictory findings. First, there are issues relating to the validity of global wellbeing indicators. Comparisons of global reports of subjective wellbeing are susceptible to cultural differences in the norms that govern self-descriptions (Diener 2000). Kahneman et al. (2004) have argued that global indicators are typically biased by recency effects and extreme events, and frequently perform poorly in experimental studies as these indicators are susceptible to current mood, context, comparison groups, and survey design.

A second issue relates to differences in survey design and methodology. For example, many population findings relating to age differences in wellbeing are based on single or repeated cross-sectional designs that limit analyses to an examination of between-person differences only. Such designs ignore within-person change and longitudinal designs typically indicate less substantial differences over time. For example, using over 20 years of data from the German Socio-Economic Panel, Headey (2008) identified that for most individuals their SWB does not appear to change over the life-span. Only amongst a small proportion, those high in extraversion and/or neuroticism, were long-term changes in levels of life satisfaction reported. Similarly, when adjusting for within-person changes in physical health, Burns et al. (2014a) reported that terminal decline—sudden and rapid decline in the years preceding death—in wellbeing and mental health was fully attenuated.

Relatedly, many longitudinal designs typically report overall a single population-level trajectory despite significant variance around the population slopes. For example, Jivraj et al. (2014) identified significant and substantial wellbeing declines in their analyses of the English Longitudinal Study of Ageing dataset. However, almost three-quarters of the variance was identified around the slope and this can have serious implications for our understanding of the extent of consistency in SWB changes within the population. For example, Burns et al. (2015) identified overall population decline in wellbeing and mental health in late life in a traditional multi-level/latent growth analysis, but when utilising a growth mixture modelling framework, identified wellbeing and mental health decline in only 10 per cent of the population, suggesting 1) stability of wellbeing and mental health over time for most, and 2) that substantial declines in only 10 per cent of the population was enough to drive an overall population decline. Only with further substantial investment in longitudinal cohort studies that adequately assess both within- and between-person effects on various wellbeing indicators over substantial temporal context can appropriate conclusions about the course of wellbeing over the life-course be made.

The European Social Survey: A new approach for modelling personal wellbeing?

Recognising the limitations of satisfaction judgements, and in the light of the scientific wellbeing literature, a recent collaboration of wellbeing researchers has sought to consolidate the different wellbeing approaches into a coherent measure of national wellbeing that could be used in national and international surveys to:

systematically assesses key wellbeing variables for representative samples, including positive and negative emotions, engagement, purpose and meaning, optimism and trust, and life satisfaction, as well as satisfaction with specific domains of life (Huppert et al. 2009).

The European Social Survey (ESS) Well-being Module (Huppert et al. 2009) reflects one of the first systematic attempts to reconcile both SWB and PWB approaches, which can be conceptualised in terms of psychological feeling and functioning, reflecting dimensions of SWB and PWB respectively (See Table 1). Huppert et al. (2009) argue that the development of such a module provides an:

> opportunity for a richly textured description of how the citizens of Europe experience their lives. It complements more objective data on economic, social and environmental influences on well-being, which can be derived from other items within the ESS and from other data sources. We believe that the Well-being Module will provide invaluable information for behavioural and social scientists, and contribute to the development of policies and practices for enhancing well-being across Europe (p 311).

There is evidence for the utility of using a complex model of wellbeing in population research. For example, using data from the ESS, Clark and Senik (2010) identified that those who emphasised the importance of economic wealth and frequently compared their economic wealth with others were more likely to report lower happiness, optimism, life and job satisfaction, and higher levels of depressive feelings. Also, Hooghe and Vanhoutte (2011) identified that both individual and social factors, such as unemployment, drive wellbeing outcomes, but importantly noted that economic and social factors were more strongly related to wellbeing for those individuals living in communities that were more heterogeneous in nature. That is, wider variability in individuals' economic and social capital resources within a community was associated with lower wellbeing for those with lower capital resources. Plagnol and Huppert (2010) identified significant national differences in volunteering rates between ESS nations, and highlighted the role of government policies that to a large extent may determine levels of volunteering within nations and personal wellbeing.

Table 1. Conceptual framework of the intra-personal feeling
and functioning domains in ESS Well-being Module

Feeling	Functioning
Satisfaction	Autonomy
Positive affect	Competence
Negative affect	Interest in learning
Optimism	Goal orientation
Vitality	Sense of purpose
Self-esteem	Resilience

Source: Adapted from Huppert et al. 2009.

An increasing evidence base in Australia

Unfortunately, a comparable Australian study that examines the impact of social and economic changes on such a range of wellbeing indicators is not available. However, some of our findings, utilising existing longitudinal Australian studies, may provide evidence for the utility of a more complex approach to assessing personal wellbeing, and identifies a future need for governments to incorporate additional measures that tap multiple dimensions of individual wellbeing in future population surveys. For example, using data from The Dynamic Analyses to Optimize Ageing (DYNOPTA) project (Anstey et al. 2010), a harmonisation of several longitudinal studies of ageing, Burns and colleagues have examined the role of vitality, as one indicator of positive feeling, in promoting positive health outcomes in older adults, in comparison to traditional models examining the effects of mental health or psychological distress. Their findings indicate a poor level of wellbeing is a stronger predictor of the likelihood of falls (Burns et al. 2012), poorer self-rated health (Burns et al. 2014b), and mortality (Burns et al. 2015a).

Using data from the PATH study (Anstey et al. 2011), Burns and colleagues (Burns, Anstey and Windsor 2009) have explored both psychological functioning and feeling across the life-span, particularly in relation to mental health outcomes. They explored the temporal associations between measures of SWB or psychological feeling, reflected by positive and negative affect, and PWB or psychological functioning, reflected by mastery/competence and resilience, with measures of depression and anxiety. They identified strong support for a model whereby SWB mediated the effects of PWB on depression and anxiety. That is, perceptions of mastery and resilience drove positive and negative feelings, which in turn predicted depression and anxiety outcomes. More recent evidence indicates psychological functioning and feeling to be more sensitive to external life events and work strain (Burns et al. 2016; Burns 2014).

There is clearly a need for future population studies in Australia to consider implementing measures that tap a greater array of human functioning. This will allow a more detailed examination of the effects of policy change on individuals' lives, reflected by changes in their wellbeing. Relatedly, in the UK, following Cameron's (2010) announcement, the Office of National Statistics' survey of national wellbeing now utilises an array of wellbeing and mental-health indicators that identify levels of depression and anxiety, and also reports on happiness, anxiousness, satisfaction and worthwhileness Matheson (2011).

The way forward: Implications for policy directions

A number of conceptual issues need to be addressed in order to provide robust wellbeing measurement frameworks that can be used to monitor the impact of policy on national wellbeing. First, levels of wellbeing may be of secondary importance to the stability of wellbeing levels over time. Research by Kernis et al. (1998) has demonstrated that wellbeing researchers should perhaps be less focused on levels of wellbeing than the stability of wellbeing over time. Their study investigated the role of self-esteem in the development of depressive symptoms and their findings indicated that level of self-esteem was not a risk for increased depressive symptomology, whilst greater self-esteem variability was a significant risk factor. These findings echo earlier reports (Roberts and Monroe 1992), where even individuals with low self-esteem were likely to report less depressive symptoms than those individuals with high but unstable self-esteem. The importance of this lies in the proposition that the degree of emotional reactivity could be more important as an indicator of health outcomes than level of wellbeing, but this requires longitudinal designs with multiple assessments to capture intra-individual wellbeing variation.

A second related issue is the extent to which different wellbeing dimensions are weighted equally for all individuals. Different wellbeing dimensions may not be of the same importance for all. One person may emphasise the need for positive relationships while, for another, spiritual growth may be more important. And it is likely that the rank importance of these wellbeing dimensions changes over the life-course as a consequence of normative age experiences (e.g. widowhood, unemployment). For example, Ryff (1991) identified significant differences in the importance of different wellbeing dimensions across the life-course. Whilst middle- and older-aged adults prioritised the importance of social connections, middle-aged adults placed greater emphasis than older-aged adults on the need for a future time perspective, assertiveness and self-acceptance.

Given the malleability of personal wellbeing, the role of public policy in promoting policy demands serious consideration. However, as wellbeing is defined here in terms of psychological functioning and feeling, one may well ask whether we would want government intervening at the individual level where wellbeing reflects the individual's lived experience.

Frey and Stutzer (2012) propose that wellbeing research does not offer an approach to public policy:

> Citizens as ultimate decision makers are disregarded, and governments are seen as benevolent maximizers of social welfare … This view neglects that people differ in what judgments they consider to reflect their normative preferences. Moreover, the processes of adaptation and aspiration change require a decision on how to treat them in policy decisions. This decision is not part of the social welfare maximization approach … the social welfare approach neglects the negative incentives for manipulating empirical welfare measures (p 671).

Perhaps more appropriate is a social determinants approach and an examination of the role public policy can make in shaping lives by providing the economic and social foundations upon which citizens live their lives and promote their wellbeing. Such policies could relate to current policy areas such as the provision of safe and healthy workplaces free from harassment, bullying and discrimination; aged-care provision that is driven by the needs of individual consumers; and affordable and accessible health care that prioritises prevention of chronic disease and mental ill health. Frey and Stutzer's (2012) conclusion placed the focus 'thus on rules and institutions rather than on specific policy interventions' (p 671).

Relatedly, the National Economic Foundation's *Five Ways to Wellbeing* report (Aked et al. 2008) is one example of an evidenced-based set of policy directions that has been implemented at varying levels of UK governance, from Westminster to local UK councils, to promote population wellbeing. Commissioned by Foresight to examine evidence and develop public health messages concerned with promoting and maintaining positive mental health, the Five Ways to Wellbeing program focuses on engaging individuals to 1) connect with others, 2) be active life participants, 3) take time to notice people and the world around them, 4) continue to strive for learning and knowledge, and 5) express gratitude through giving to others. Rather than developing wellbeing policies per se, their recommendations emphasised the need for policymakers to consider 1) the capacity of their policies to enable citizens to engage with one or all of these wellbeing pathways, and 2) the need to examine the impact of emerging policies on a range of individual wellbeing dimensions. For example, Frey and Stutzer (2000) identified that in Switzerland, those cantons that afforded citizens with greater rights and opportunities to propose and vote on laws and constitutional amendments reported higher personal wellbeing outcomes.

Marmot (2014) summarises a number of areas whereby national policy can intervene to promote public mental health. These include a focus on 1) psychosocial development and medical health in early childhood, 2) access to education and lifelong learning, 3) fair and equitable working conditions, 4) an income to satisfy conditions for health living, including a social security net, 5) safe communities, and 6) sustainable housing; and a recognition of the importance of social determinants in the prevention of poor health outcomes. In a similar vein, we would argue that such measures will also facilitate improvements in flourishing and feeling. The role of government and advocates is then in promoting policies that build the social and economic foundations upon which citizens can flourish. And, as we have importantly emphasised throughout this chapter, the extent to which we adequately capture a range of functioning and feeling outcomes.

Future population-level approaches to measuring wellbeing need to examine the question of what it is for an individual to feel that they live well, with a sense of vigour, vitality and engagement, in the context of work, families, and communities, both within and between nations. This involves extending our focus on dimensions of mental health and generalised evaluations of life satisfaction to encompass dimensions of psychological function and feeling. However, there are considerable limitations in the existing research base in understanding the way factors enhance or adversely impact on people's wellbeing over the life-course.

There is a need for longitudinal cohort studies to examine how different socioeconomic experiences impact across the life-course and to understand how life experiences shape older adults' capacity to age well, in health, social and economic terms. In addition, future longitudinal cohort studies require multidisciplinary approaches in order to ensure they maintain relevance with the research base. Such capacities in Australia are considerably limited by current funding models and by study designs that are not multidisciplinary. As we have described, much of the capacity to understand individual-level wellbeing in existing population studies is limited. Such limitations can be overcome with appropriate reference to the scientific literature, as it continues to evolve. The Dynamic Analyses to Optimise Ageing project (Anstey et al. 2010) provides one example of how a multidisciplinary approach, with leading experts from the psychological, social, medical and statistical sciences, could examine ageing experiences from a bio-psychosocial perspective using existing longitudinal data. Currently, within CEPAR, there is an emphasis on combining these perspectives with an attempt to understand the economic foundations which underpin successful and healthy ageing. However, new cohort studies that may inform the impact of social and economic policy changes on future wellbeing demands are sorely needed.

References

Abbott Rosemary, Ploubidis George, Huppert Felicia, Kuh Diana, Wadsworth Michael and Croudace Tim (2006). Psychometric evaluation and predictive validity of Ryff's psychological well-being items in a UK birth cohort sample of women. *Health and Quality of Life Outcomes*, 4: 76.

Adler Alfred (1929). *The Science of Living*. New York: Anchor Books.

Aked Jody, Marks Nic, Cordon Corrina and Thompson Sam (2008). *Five ways to wellbeing: The evidence*. A report presented to the Foresight Project on communicating the evidence base for improving people's well-being. London: The New Economics Foundation.

Anstey Kaarin, Byles Julie, Luszcz Mary, Mitchell Paul, Steel David, Booth Heather, Browning Colette, Butterworth Peter, Cumming Robert, Healy Judith, Windsor Tim, Ross Lesley, Bartsch Lauren, Burns Richard, Kiely Kim, Birrell Carole, Broe Tony, Shaw Jonathan, Kendig Hal (2010). Cohort profile: The dynamic analyses to optimize ageing (DYNOPTA) project. *International journal of Epidemiology*, 39: 1, 44–51.

Anstey Kaarin, Christensen Helen, Butterworth Peter, Easteal Simon, Mackinnon Andrew, Jacomb Trish, Maxwell Karen, Rodgers Bryan, Windsor Tim, Cherbuin Nicolas and Jorm Anthony (2011). Cohort Profile: The PATH Through Life Project. *International Journal of Epidemiology*, 41(4), 951–960. doi: 10.1093/ije/dyr025.

Baird Brendan, Lucas Richard and Donnellan Brent (2010). Life Satisfaction Across the Lifespan: Findings from Two Nationally Representative Panel Studies. *Social Indicators Research* 99(2): 183–203.

Becker Gary (1992). Habits, Addictions, and Traditions. *Kyklos*, 45: 327–346.

Bentham Jeremy (1789). *An introduction to the principles of morals and legislation*. Oxford: Clarendon Press.

Bradburn Norman (1969). *The structure of psychological well-being*. Chicago: Aldine.

Brickman Philip, Coates Dan, Janoff-Bulman Ronnie (1978). Lottery Winners and Accident Victims: Is Happiness Relative? *Journal of Personality and Social Psychology*, 36(8): 917–927.

Burns Richard (2014). *Mental Health and Wellbeing Across the Lifespan: Implications for healthy ageing outcomes*. Presentation to the APS Ageing—Special Interest Group. 16 May, Adelaide, Australia.

Burns Richard and Anstey Kaarin (2011). *Positive and Negative Mental Health Dimensions report differential non-linear effects on mortality*. 64th Annual Scientific Meeting of the Gerontological Society of America 18–23 November, Boston, USA.

Burns Richard, Anstey Kaarin and Windsor Tim (2009). Subjective well-being mediates the effects of resilience and mastery on depression and anxiety in a large community sample of young and middle-aged adults. *Australian and New Zealand Journal of Psychiatry*, 45(3): 240–248.

Burns Richard, Butterworth Peter and Anstey Kaarin (2016). An examination of the long-term impact of job strain on mental health and wellbeing over a 12-year period. *Social Psychiatry and Psychiatric Epidemiology*, 51(5): 725–733. doi: 10.1007/s00127-016-1192-9.

Burns Richard, Butterworth Peter, Browning Colette, Byles Julie, Luszcz Mary, Mitchell Paul, Shaw Jonathan and Anstey Kaarin (2015a) Examination of the association between mental health, morbidity and mortality in late life: Findings from longitudinal community surveys. *International Psychogeriatrics*, 27(5): 739–746.

Burns Richard, Byles Julie, Magliano Dianna, Mitchell Paul and Anstey Kaarin (2015b) The utility of estimating population-level trajectories of terminal wellbeing decline within a growth mixture modelling framework. *Social Psychiatry and Psychiatric Epidemiology*, 50(3): 479–487.

Burns Richard, Byles Julie, Mitchell Paul and Anstey Kaarin (2012). Positive components of mental health provide significant protection against likelihood of falling in older females over a 13-year period. *International Psychogeriatrics*, 24(9): 1419–1428.

Burns Richard and Machin Tony (2008). Investigating the Structural Validity of Ryff's Psychological Well-Being Scales Across Two Samples. *Social Indicators Research*, 93(2): 359–375.

Burns Richard, Mitchell Paul, Shaw Jonathan and Anstey Kaarin (2014a). Trajectories of terminal decline in the well-being of older women: The DYNOPTA project. *Psychology and Aging*, 29(1): 44–56.

Burns Richard, Sargent-Cox Kerry, Mitchell Paul and Anstey Kaarin (2014b) An examination of the effects of intra and inter-individual changes in wellbeing and mental health on self-rated health in a population study of middle and older-aged adults, *Social Psychiatry and Psychiatric Epidemiology*, 49(11): 1849–1858.

Cameron The Rt Hon David (2010). PM speech on wellbeing, 25 November 2010. www.gov.uk/government/speeches/pm-speech-on-wellbeing. Accessed 18 October 2014

Cassells Rebecca, Gong Cathy and Keegan Marcia (2010). *The pursuit of happiness: Life satisfaction in Australia*, AMP-NATSEM Income and Wealth Report, Issue 26, Sydney.

Clark Andrew, Layard Richard and Senik Claudia (2012). The causes of happiness and misery. *UN World Happiness Report*, pp. 59–89.

Clark Andrew and Senik Claudia (2010). Who compares to whom? The anatomy of income comparisons in Europe. *The Economic Journal*, 120: 573–594.

Compton William, Smith Maggie, Cornish Kim and Qualls Donald (1996). Factor structure of mental health measures. *Journal of Personality and Social Psychology*, 71: 406–413.

Dahlgren Goren and Whitehead Margaret (1991). *Policies and strategies to promote social equity in health*. Stockholm: Institute for Future Studies.

Diener Ed (1994). Assessing subjective well-being: Progress and opportunities. *Social Indicators Research*, 31: 103–157.

Diener Ed (2000). Subjective Wellbeing: The Science of Happiness and a Proposal for a National Index. *American Psychologist*, 55(1): 34–43.

Diener Ed and Lucas Richard (1999). Personality and subjective well-being. In D Kahneman, E Diener, and N Schwarz (Eds) *Well-being: The foundations of hedonic psychology*. New York: Russell Sage Foundation, pp. 213–229.

Diener Ed, Suh Eunkook, Lucas Richard and Smith Heidi (1999). Subjective Well-Being: Three Decades of Progress. *Psychological Bulletin*, 125(2): 276–302.

Easterlin Richard (1974). Does Economic Growth Improve the Human Lot? Some Empirical Evidence. In Paul A David and Melvin W Reder (Eds) *Nations and Households in Economic Growth: Essays in Honor of Moses Abramovitz*. New York: Academic Press.

Easterlin Richard (2005). Feeding the Illusion of Growth and Happiness: A Reply to Hagerty and Veenhoven. *Social Indicators Research*, 74(3): 429–443.

Easterlin Richard, McVey Laura, Switek Malgerzata, Sawangfa Onnicha, Zweig Jacqueline (2010). The happiness-income paradox revisited. *Proceedings of the National Academy of Sciences*, 107(52): 22463.

Federal Interagency Forum on Aging-Related Statistics (FIF-ARS) (2012). *Older Americans 2012: Key Indicators of Well-Being.* Washington, DC: US Government Printing Office.

Foresight Report (2008). *Mental Capital and Wellbeing: Making the most of ourselves in the 21st century: Final project report.* London: Government Office for Science.

Forgeard Marie, Jayawickreme Eranda, Kern Margaret and Seligman Martin (2011). Doing the right thing: Measuring wellbeing for public policy. *International Journal of Wellbeing* 1(1): 79–106.

Frey Bruno and Stutzer Alois (2000). Happiness, economy and institutions. *Economic Journal* 110(466): 918–938.

Frey Bruno and Stutzer Alois (2012). The use of happiness research for public policy. *Social Choice and Welfare*, 38: 659–674.

Hagerty Michael and Veenhoven Ruuf (2003). Wealth and Happiness Revisited–Growing National Income Does Go with Greater Happiness. *Social Indicators Research* 64: 1–27.

Headey Bruce (2008). The Set-Point Theory of Well-Being: Negative Results and Consequent Revisions. *Social Indicators Research,* 85: 389–403.

Headey Bruce and Wearing Alexander (1989). Personality, life events and subjective well-being: Toward a dynamic equilibrium model. *Journal of Personality and Social Psychology,* 57: 731–739.

Headey Bruce and Wearing Alexander (1992). *Understanding happiness: A theory of subjective well-being.* Melbourne, Australia: Longman Cheshire.

Headey Bruce and Warren Diana (2008). *Families, Incomes and Jobs, Volume 3: A Statistical Report on Waves 1 to 5 of the HILDA Survey.* Melbourne Institute of Applied Economic and Social Research, University of Melbourne.

Hooghe Marc and Vanhoutte Bran (2011). Subjective well-being and social capital in Belgian communities. The impact of community characteristics on subjective well-being indicators in Belgium. *Social Indicators Research*, 100(1): 17–36.

Huppert Felicia (2009). Psychological Well-being: Evidence Regarding its Causes and Consequences. *Applied Psychology: Health and Well-Being*, 1(2): 137–164.

Huppert Felicia and So Timothy (2013). Flourishing Across Europe: Application of a New Conceptual Framework for Defining Well-Being, *Social Indicators Research*, 110(3): 837–861.

Huppert Felicia, Marks Nic, Clark Andrew, Siegrist Johannes, Stutzer Alois, Vitterso Joar and Wahrendorf Morten (2009). Measuring Well-being across Europe: Description of the ESS Well-being Module and Preliminary Findings. *Social Indicators Research*, 91(3): 301–315.

Jivraj Stephen, Nazroo James, Vanhoutte Bran and Chandola Tarani (2014). Aging and Subjective Well-Being in Later Life. *Journals of Gerontology, Series B: Psychological Sciences and Social Sciences*, 69(6). doi: 10.1093/ geronb/gbu00.

Kahneman Daniel, Diener Ed and Schwarz Norbert (Eds) (1999). *Wellbeing: Foundations of hedonic psychology.* New York: Russell Sage Foundation Press.

Kahneman Daniel, Krueger Alan, Schkade David, Schwarz Norbert and Stone Arthur (2004). Toward National Wellbeing Accounts. *American Economic Review* 94: 429.

Kernis Michael, Whisenhunt Connie, Waschull Stephanie, Greenier Keegan, Berry Andrea, Herlocker Caryn and Anderson Craig (1998). Multiple Facets of Self-Esteem and their Relations to Depressive Symptoms. *Personality and Social Psychology Bulletin*, 24(6): 657–668.

Keyes Corey (2002). The mental health continuum: From Languishing to Flourishing in Life. *Journal of Health and Social Research*, 43: 207–222.

Lucas Richard, Diener Ed and Suh Eunkook (1996). Discriminant validity of well-being measures. *Journal of Personality and Social Psychology*, 71: 616–628.

Matheson Jil (2011). Measuring what matters: National statistician's reflections on the National Debate on measuring National Well-being. Office of National Statistics. Newport, South Wales. www.ons.gov.uk.

Marmot Michael (2014). Commentary: Mental health and public health. *International Journal of Epidemiology*, 43(2): 293–296. doi: 10.1093/ije/dyu054.

Maslow Abraham (1968). *Toward a psychology of being* (2nd edition). New York: Van Nostrand.

Organisation for Economic Co-operation and Development (OECD) (2014a). *How Was Life? Global Wellbeing since 1820*. www.oecd.org/statistics/how-was-life-9789264214262-en.htm. Accessed 12 October 2014.

Organisation for Economic Co-operation and Development (OECD) (2014b). *Better Life Index Executive Summary, 2014*. www.oecdbetterlifeindex.org. Accessed 12 October 2014.

Plagnol Anke and Huppert Felicia (2010). Happy to help? Exploring the factors associated with variations in rates of volunteering across Europe. *Social Indicators Research*, 97(2): 157–176.

Roberts John and Monroe Scott (1992). Vulnerable self-esteem and depressive symptoms: Prospective findings comparing three alternative conceptualizations. *Journal of Personality and Social Psychology,* 62(5): 804–12.

Rogers Carl (1961). *On Becoming a Person*. Oxford: Houghton Mifflin.

Ryan Richard and Deci Edward (2000). Self-determination theory and the facilitation of intrinsic motivation, social development, and well-being. *American Psychologist*, 55: 68–78.

Ryan Richard and Deci Edward (2001). On happiness and human potentials: A review of research on hedonic and eudaimonic well-being. *Annual Review of Psychology*, 52: 141–166.

Ryff Carol (1989a). Beyond Ponce de Leon and life satisfaction: New directions in quest of successful aging. *International Journal of Behavioral Development*, 12: 35–55.

Ryff Carol (1989b). Happiness is everything, or is it? Explorations on the meaning of psychological well-being. *Journal of Personality and Social Psychology*, 57: 1069–1081.

Ryff Carol (1991). Possible selves in adulthood and old age: A tale of shifting horizons. *Psychology and Aging*, 6: 286–295.

Ryff Carol and Singer Burton (1998). The contours of positive human health. *Psychological Inquiry*, 9: 1–28.

Stiglitz Joseph, Sen Amartya and Fitoussi Jean-Paul (2009). *Report by the Commission on the Measurement of Economic Performance and Social Progress*. www.stiglitz-sen-fitoussi.fr/documents/rapport_anglais.pdf. Accessed 10 November 2010.

Ura Karma, Alkire Sabina, Zangmo Tshoki and Wangdi Karma (2012). *A Short Guide to Gross National Happiness Index*. Thimphu, Bhutan: The Centre for Bhutan Studies. www.bhutanstudies.org.bt. Accessed 1 November 2014.

Waterman Alan (1993). Two conceptions of happiness: contrasts of personal expressiveness (eudaimonia) and hedonic enjoyment. *Journal of Personality and Social Psychology*, 64: 678–691.

Wilkinson Richard and Marmot Michael (2003). *Social Determinants of Health: The Solid Facts* (2nd edition) Denmark: WHO Regional Office For Europe.

Wooden Mark and Watson Nicole (2007). The HILDA survey and its contribution to economic and social research (so far). *Economic Record*, 83: 208–231.

World Health Organization (WHO) (1946). *Preamble to the Constitution of the World Health Organization as adopted by the International Health Conference, New York, 19–22 June, 1946*. Official Records of the World Health Organization, No. 2: 100.

World Health Organization (WHO) (2014). *Global Health Observatory Data Repository 2012 and 2013*. www.who.int/gho/database/en/.

Part 4. Responses by government and families/individuals

11

Retirement income strategies for an ageing population

Hazel Bateman

The aim of this chapter is to assess the ability of Australia's system of retirement income provision to withstand the implications of population ageing. It is argued that Australia's retirement income arrangements are better placed that those in most other developed countries due to both a slightly slower pace of population ageing and its unique approach to policy design for retirement income provision. However, an implication of the increased fiscal pressures associated with population ageing will be a greater role for the private sector in funding of retirement incomes, health and aged care. The greatest challenge will be to work out how both the government and private sector can best assist individuals and households to deal with increasingly complex financial decisions, particularly as they relate to saving for and spending down in retirement.

The chapter proceeds as follows. In the next section, Australia's current retirement income arrangements and relevant demographic trends are summarised. This is followed by an assessment of the impact of the demographic trends on the ability of the retirement income arrangements to deliver adequate and sustainable retirement incomes. We then evaluate the effectiveness of the current policy framework to assist older Australians in their interactions with the increasingly complex decision environment, and a final section concludes with a menu of possible policy options.

Policy and demographic background

Retirement incomes

Over the past 30 years, Australia's system of retirement income provision has evolved into a multi-pillar arrangement comprising a means-tested Age Pension financed from general tax revenues, a mandatory employer-financed defined contribution (DC) scheme known as the Superannuation Guarantee, and tax incentives to encourage voluntary superannuation contributions and other private savings. The 'first pillar' Age Pension is paid at a rate of around 28 per cent of male average full-time earnings for singles and 41 per cent for couples and is currently indexed to keep up with wages in the rest of the economy. Net replacement rates are higher because no tax is paid on Age Pension payments. The Age Pension is available from age 65 (increasing to 67 between 2017 and 2023)[1] and is paid subject to income and assets (means) tests, which have the effect of excluding the top 30 per cent of the wealth distribution from the Age Pension. Around 60 per cent of retirees (of eligible age) receive the full rate, while the remainder receive a part pension (Department of Social Services 2014). The means tests are comprehensively defined, although the assets test excludes owner-occupier housing.

The 'second pillar' Superannuation Guarantee commenced in 1992 as a derivation of productivity award superannuation introduced in the 1986 National Wage Case. The Superannuation Guarantee requires all employers to make contributions on behalf of their employees into a superannuation fund. The mandatory contribution gradually increased from 4 per cent to 9 per cent between 1992 and 2002 and, following a decision to increase it to 12 per cent, currently stands at 9.5 per cent.[2]

---

1 In its 2014–15 Budget, the government announced plans to further increase the Age Pension eligibility age to 70 by 2035.
2 The mandatory employer contribution is scheduled to rise to 12 per cent by 2026.

These first two pillars are supplemented by 'third pillar' voluntary long-term savings that include voluntary superannuation contributions (currently made by around one-third of super fund members—ABS 2009) and property, shares, managed funds and home ownership.

Benefits from superannuation savings can be taken at the statutory preservation age, currently age 55, but increasing to age 60 by 2024. Individuals are free to choose how they take their retirement benefits from a menu that includes lump sums, account-based pensions and life and term annuities. When the multi-pillar design was first adopted in 1992, differential tax and means tests encouraged purchase of lifetime annuities. However, due to low take-up of these products and strong lobbying from the financial services sector, these targeted provisions were diluted over the following 15 years. The Simpler Super reforms of 2007 (Australian Government 2006) removed all taxes on superannuation benefits taken from age 60 and eliminated the differential treatment and are considered largely responsible for the (temporary) disappearance of the annuity market in the late 2000s (Bateman and Piggott 2011). Today, almost all retirees take their superannuation benefits in a non-annuitised form (lump sums or account-based pensions), although, as discussed later, there has been a recent sharp increase in the number of life annuity policies sold, albeit from a very low base of less than 30 annually in 2009 to over 4,000 in 2014 (Plan for Life 2015).

Around 95 per cent of employees are covered by the mandatory superannuation arrangements, and compliance is high, with only those who are too young (i.e. under 18) or too poor (i.e. earning less than $450 per month) excluded from the arrangements.

For many retirees, mandatory and voluntary superannuation is supplemented by a full or part Age Pension. Including Age Pension eligibility, the Australian Treasury estimates that a fully mature Superannuation Guarantee can be expected to deliver a net replacement rate of around 90 per cent (78 per cent) for a worker on median (average) earnings (Gallagher 2012).

Australia's ageing population

The most recent statement of Australia's demographic position is set out in the *2015 Intergenerational Report* (Commonwealth of Australia 2015). According to this report, Australians will live longer than projected previously and will continue to have one of the longest life expectancies in the world. Currently, Australia ranks equal first along with Iceland in terms of male life expectancy and fifth for female life expectancy after Japan, Spain, France and Italy. Male life expectancy at birth is projected to increase from 91.5 years today to 95.1 years in 2055, and female life expectancy from 93.6 years to 96.6 years. Despite later retirement ages, it is expected that there will be an increase in the number of years spent in retirement, and therefore an increase in the funds required to sustain living standards throughout retirement.

As a consequence of both increased longevity, and a stabilisation of the fall in the fertility rate, the proportion of the population aged 65 and over is expected to increase from 15 per cent today to 22.6 per cent by 2055, and the absolute number of people aged 65 and over will more than double, from 3.6 million today to around 8.9 million by 2055. The obvious implication of these trends is that there will be fewer people of working age to support those in retirement. More specifically, the number of Australians of working age (15–65) available to support each Australian over age 65 will fall from around 4.5 today (which itself has fallen from 7.3 in 1975) to around 2.7 by 2055. While these trends appear severe, they must be considered in the international context where, due to a slightly higher birth-rate and higher immigration, Australia is ageing at a much slower rate than many other developed countries (OECD 2014a).

On the basis of these demographic projections, the *2015 Intergenerational Report* reveals an increasing gap between Commonwealth government expenditure and tax revenue under an unchanged tax system (that is, assuming tax revenue remains at 23.9 per cent of GDP over the projection period).[3] In particular, with no change to current policy settings, Commonwealth government spending on health is projected to increase from 4.5 per cent of GDP today to 5.5 per cent in 2055, on aged care from 0.9 per cent of GDP to

---

3   23.9 per cent is the average of tax revenue to GDP over 2000–08.

1.7 per cent, and on the Age Pension from 2.9 per cent of GDP today to 3.6 per cent in 2055.[4] These figures suggest that there will be continued pressure on successive governments to reduce expenditure on these aged-related budget items.

In sum, the most likely impact of population ageing on retirement incomes and retirees will be an increase in the role of private provision in the funding of retirement incomes, health and aged care for possibly longer retirements. Next we explore the extent to which Australia's retirement income arrangements are designed to withstand this demographic pressure.

What does population ageing mean for retirement income policy?[5]

The design of Australia's multi-pillar approach to retirement income provision has long been considered international best practice (World Bank 1994; OECD 2014b) largely due to the risk diversification provided through a combination of public and private provision (the Age Pension and superannuation), pay-as-you-go (PAYG) and pre-funding (the Age Pension and DC superannuation) and compulsion and individual choice (the mandatory Superannuation Guarantee and tax concessions for voluntary superannuation). Australia is consistently ranked in the top three pensions systems worldwide under the Melbourne Mercer Global Pension Index where scores reward adequacy, sustainability and integrity (Mercer 2014). However, a more careful assessment raises concerns about gaps in overall policy design (particularly as they relate to superannuation taxation and decumulation), and the increasing emphasis on individual responsibility and decision-making, the latter of which is an inevitable consequence of its DC design.

---

4   The 2015 Intergenerational Statement reports that the future cost of the Age Pension would fall to 2.7 per cent of GDP by 2055 had a 2014 Budget proposal to reduce the level of indexation been implemented. The long-term budgetary implications of the subsequent decision (announced in the 2015–16 Budget) to instead alter the assets test taper has not been officially reported, although the impact will be a reduction in future cost of the Age Pension to below 3.6 per cent GDP, the no policy change counterfactual.

5   Parts of this section are drawn from Bateman et al. (2016a).

Retirement income systems are typically assessed from the perspective of their impact on both the broader economy and its citizens as they enter and move through retirement. The individual criteria focus on the ability of the retirement income arrangements to provide insurance against the key economic and financial risks an individual may face over this period (specifically replacement risk, investment risk, longevity risk, inflation risk and contingency risk),[6] while the economy-wide criteria relate to economic efficiency and equity, the standard measures for evaluating public policy, as well as long-term sustainability and administrative efficacy.

Economy-wide assessment

Turning first to sustainability: on the face of it, the projected future population trends reported in the *2015 Intergenerational Report*, which feed into a projected 50 per cent increase in the aged dependency ratio over the next 40 years, could signal severe problems for the future funding of retirement incomes. However, in the case of Australia, the policy framework of a means-tested Age Pension combined with mandatory superannuation participation and contributions (as required under the Superannuation Guarantee), and a relatively slower ageing of the population than much of the developed world, results in some of the lowest current and forecast levels of spending on public pensions in the OECD. The projection that spending on age-related pensions will increase from 2.9 per cent of GDP in 2015 to 3.6 per cent of GDP by 2055 (Commonwealth of Australia 2015)[7] is far more sustainable than corresponding projections for other OECD countries (OECD 2014b). By comparison, over the next 40 years, public pension expenditure is projected to increase to 25 per cent of GDP in Greece, 15 per cent of GDP in Italy, Germany and Norway and 8–10 per cent in the Netherlands and Denmark (or 2.5 times the spending in Australia), who, with Australia, make up the top three in the global pension index rankings (Mercer 2014).

---

6   The individual criteria are drawn from Bodie (1990) as extended by Bateman and Piggott (1997).

7   In the absence of policy change. This does not include spending on public sector pensions, which is projected to fall from 0.4 per cent to 0.2 per cent of GDP over this period.

Australia's retirement income arrangements also fair well in terms of overall economic efficiency and equity. Economic efficiency is enhanced where policy settings facilitate incentives to work and save, and DC systems, such as Australia's Superannuation Guarantee and voluntary superannuation arrangements, implicitly include incentives to work and save because later retirement translates into more contributions over more years and fewer years over which to spread the resulting income, resulting in higher replacement rates. This compares with publicly provided defined benefit (DB) PAYG second pillars operating in many OECD countries, which are generally funded from payroll taxes, and where inbuilt benefit formulas make it costly to deviate from a set retirement age. While the Age Pension means tests will erode the advantages in the Australian arrangements for some levels of earnings and superannuation assets and income, recent changes have been made to the Age Pension means tests to lower the penalty for income from employment. And, although the availability of superannuation benefits up to 10 years prior to the Age Pension eligibility age may encourage early retirement and dissaving, analysis of drawdown behaviour suggests that Australian retirees are not in a hurry to dissipate their superannuation accounts (Wu et al. 2015).

It is widely agreed that the pre-funding associated with Australia's DC superannuation has enhanced private saving. Superannuation assets now total more than $2 trillion, well over 100 per cent of GDP and one of the largest pools of retirement assets in the world (APRA 2015). And, despite initial concerns about saving substitution, most of this represents 'new' saving (Gruen and Soding 2011). Furthermore, being pre-funded, Australia's superannuation arrangements score well on intergenerational equity, with each generation funding its own retirement.

However, concerns about intragenerational equity remain, largely due to the tax regime for superannuation that has resulted in tax concessions skewed towards the higher end of the income/wealth distribution (Henry 2010; Department of Treasury 2012). Super tax has been on and off the reform agenda since the early 1980s, and, in spite of constant tinkering, successive governments have failed to develop an effective tax regime. Australia's approach differs from international practice and departs significantly from the standard approaches that are more consistent with an economically efficient system.[8] In particular, Australia operates a TTE system, where contributions to super funds are taxed (T), super fund earnings are taxed (T) and benefit payments are tax-free (E). Most of the rest of the world operates an EET system, where contributions are free of tax (E), fund income accumulates tax-free (E) but benefits are taxed (T) generally under the personal marginal tax schedule. Since under Australia's TTE regime, employer contributions and super fund earnings are taxed at a flat rate, they are also separated from income tax and its progressivity. Separating superannuation taxes from personal income tax has facilitated tinkering because changes are not obvious to fund members. Moreover, the regressive nature of flat rate taxes has resulted in regular, but piecemeal (and often politically motivated), policy initiatives designed to improve intragenerational equity—such as the excess contributions tax, low-income superannuation contributions, government co-contributions and the extra contributions tax now applying to high-income earners (which income plus employer superannuation contributions in excess of $300,000 pa).

In its final report, the Henry Tax Review recommended that the taxation of superannuation contributions be linked to the progressive personal rate schedule, and that the tax on superannuation fund earnings be reduced to help the power of compound interest generate more accumulations and reduce price distortion between assets and over time (Henry 2010). Unfortunately, governments from both major political parties have ignored these recommendations and instead continued to tinker with the tax treatment of contributions at the top and bottom end of the income distribution.

Finally, while international comparisons of mature-age poverty rates appear to paint a negative picture of Australia's retirement income system, with recent OECD data indicating that older Australians have some of the lowest incomes and highest poverty rates in the OECD (OECD 2013), it is essential to point out that this particular comparison is misleading in the case of Australia. First, as the OECD acknowledges, the Australian figures may be subject to upwards bias, since a large proportion of retirement benefits are taken as lump sums, which are excluded in the OECD analysis. Second, closer analysis

---

8   See Bateman et al. (2001).

of the data reveals that the average difference between the poverty line and the incomes of poor households is one of the lowest among developed countries, and that many Australian retirees have incomes just below the poverty line. Finally, unlike most OECD countries, older Australians have very high levels of owner-occupied housing, and public spending on services for the aged is one of the highest in the OECD. Once housing costs are taken into account, old-age poverty rates are around 15 per cent, which is low compared to many other countries (ACOSS 2014).

Individual assessment

Coverage against the economic and financial risks individuals face as they enter and move through retirement is assessed by the ability of the retirement income system to insure against the risk of running out of retirement savings due to one or a combination of investment risk (the risk of unevenness in income due to volatility of investment returns), longevity risk (the risk of outliving savings), and inflation risk (the risk of erosion of purchasing power), as well as the ability to access funds to address uninsurable risks (often known as contingency risk). Here, Australia's retirement income system performs poorly.

The superannuation system, in common with DC schemes generally, does not guarantee a final benefit (let alone one that is at least CPI-indexed with payment guaranteed irrespective of age and market conditions). While the Superannuation Guarantee mandates participation in the superannuation system and a minimum contribution rate into a superannuation account, there is no requirement that the retirement accumulation be taken in a form that would provide cover against the key retirement risks.

Current take-up of retirement benefits is split evenly between lump sums and income streams, with very little interest in annuitised benefits. Recent trends are illustrated in Figures 1 and 2 below, which show a clear switch from lump sums to income streams since the mid-1990s (Figure 1) and a sharp increase in the take-up of account-based pensions (Figure 2). It is important to point out here that despite being called a 'pension', an account-based pension is in fact a phased (or programmed) withdrawal from a superannuation account, which provides flexibility of payment (subject to the minimum drawdown requirements for tax purposes), but no insurance against investment, inflation or longevity risk. The least popular benefits (term and lifetime annuities) do provide protection against market risk (both) and longevity risk (for the lifetime version) and can be purchased with CPI indexation.

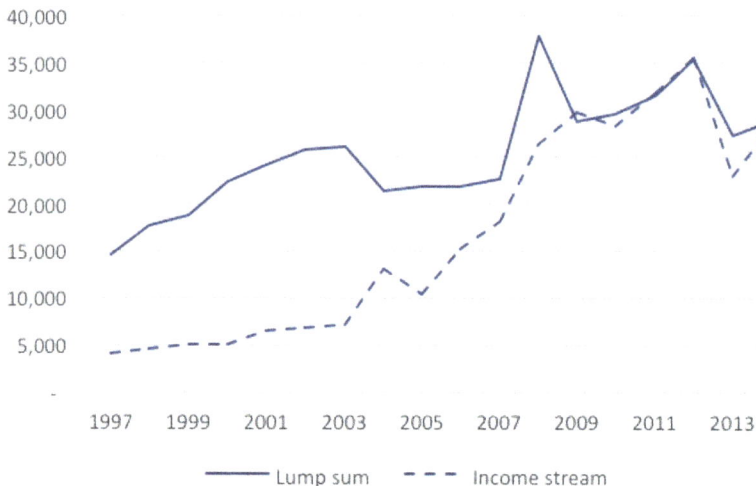

Figure 1: Superannuation benefit payouts, $'000 pa
Source: APRA (2014, 2015).

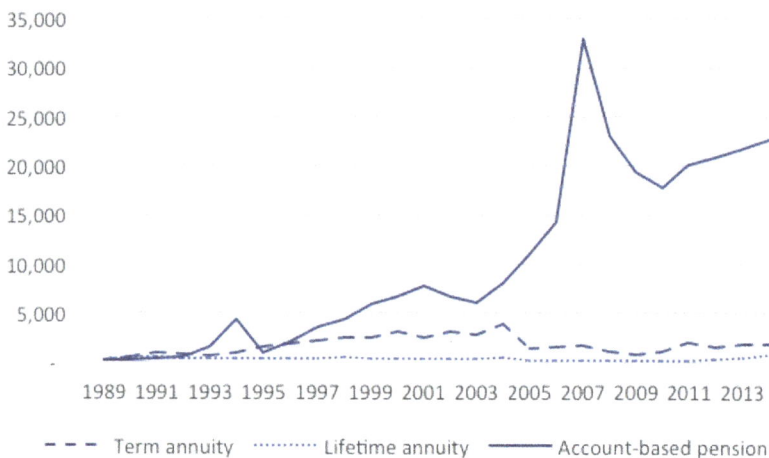

Figure 2: Take-up of retirement income streams, $'000 pa
Source: Plan for Life (2015).

The lack of interest in lifetime annuities is likely due to a complex range of factors relating to the demand for annuities, the supply-side of the annuity market and the regulatory and policy framework. The demand-side is influenced by standard rational factors such as adverse selection, incomplete markets, demand for liquidity, desire to leave a bequest, pre-existing annuitisation (for example, from the Age Pension and/or DB pensions) and intra-family transfers (Brown 2008) as well as behavioural factors due to framing (Brown et al. 2008; Agnew et al. 2008), defaults (Benartzi et al. 2012), loss aversion, myopia and complexity (Brown 2008). The supply-side in Australia has all but disappeared, with only one provider remaining (down from between 12 and 15 in the late 1990s) and is characterised by a short menu of products, and an overall lack of interest by the financial planning community, which increasingly influence decisions at retirement.[9] Finally, the policy framework is also partly to blame with regulatory restrictions on the features of retirement benefit products that receive concessional treatment under the Age Pension means tests and tax rules. Current regulations exclude deferred and variable annuities from the menu of possible products and is partly to blame for the diminished supply-side, as highlighted in the Henry Tax Review Final Report (Henry 2010).[10]

That said, interest in lifetime annuities, which fell to a record low of 29 new policies in 2009, reached a record high in 2014 with over 4,000 new policies. This renewed interest in lifetime annuities can be attributed to product design and marketing, which address key behavioural biases, as well as targeted retirement planning education for financial planners in the relevant distribution networks. The most popular annuities are called 'liquid' life annuities where a 15-year guarantee and a one-off option to withdraw the annuity within this period address loss aversion, regret aversion and concerns about access to liquidity. The marketing strategy uses the 'consumption' frame, highlighting spending and income, rather than the traditional 'investment' frame, with the official product description highlighting

---

9   A recent industry survey indicated that less than one-third of financial advisers were aware of life annuities.

10   At the time of writing the Treasury is undertaking a review of these regulations.

that the product 'provides regular payments for your lifetime'.[11] Nevertheless, take-up of lifetime products is very small relative to the retiring cohort.[12]

In other words, the majority of Australian retirees take benefits that leave them uncovered for longevity risk, investment risk and inflation risk. While the public Age Pension does insure against these retirement risks, it is paid at a low rate (around 28 per cent of male average earnings) and, due to the operation of the income and asset means tests, less than 50 per cent of those of eligible age receive the full rate (Department of Social Services 2014). This partial Age Pension coverage, coupled with the preference for non-annuitised products, could raise concerns about retirement income inadequacy in very old age as non-annuitised benefits run out. However, analysis of a panel of Age Pension beneficiaries suggests the opposite, with households in the bottom two wealth quintiles (of full and part Age Pensioners) actually accumulating wealth through retirement (Wu et al. 2015). This suggests that these low-income/low-wealth households are self-insuring against longevity risk and possibly future aged-care costs, and thereby denying themselves a higher standard of living in retirement.

As discussed further below, retirement income stream products are complex and their insurance characteristics are likely to be little understood. It could be the case that Australians are unintentionally exposing themselves to retirement risks because they are unaware of and/or don't understand the characteristics and insurance features of the available products. This lack of awareness and specific product knowledge is likely to be part of a larger problem relating to an increased interaction with complex financial products across the lifecycle.

---

11   www.challenger.com.au/funds/PDS/GA_Lifetime_PDS.pdf.
12   Less than 7,000 of these liquid lifetime annuities have been sold in the past eight years, yet there are currently 1.1 million retirees aged 60–69.

The challenge of individual decision-making

Australia's DC superannuation system mandates participation and a minimum contribution rate, but then leaves individual retirement savers with the responsibility of making often high stakes and complex saving and spending decisions over their lifetime. Typical decisions for individuals include choosing the super fund in which their superannuation savings are managed and accumulate (including the option of setting up their own self-managed fund), superannuation account management (such as switching funds and account consolidation), choosing the investment option or options (from increasingly long menus of single and multi-manager diversified and single options), whether to make or increase voluntary contributions, and if so whether these contributions should be made before or after tax (that is, whether to salary sacrifice or not, if that is an option), and whether to seek and use financial advice, and from whom. Most super fund members also have choice of life and total and permanent disability (TPD) insurance options. Even more choices confront retirees, who have almost unlimited freedom to manage the decumulation phase, which for many will involve questions around eligibility for the means-tested Age Pension, alternative residential options (including the possibility of monetising the house to provide retirement income) and, later in life, eligibility for means-tested support for aged care.

Current policy design and industry practice does provide some support for these decisions through choice architecture (such as the MySuper default), information provision in the form of financial product disclosure, support for financial advice through the regulation of financial advisers and some initiatives to improve financial literacy. However, it is not clear that this support as currently designed really helps people as intended.

Financial literacy and super system and product knowledge

Every three years since 2002 the ANZ Bank has conducted a national survey of financial literacy, and each subsequent survey has revealed low levels of financial literacy across much of the Australian population (ANZ Bank 2015). These findings are confirmed in

Australia's contribution to the Financial Literacy around The World (FLaT) study (Agnew et al. 2013a).[13] The FLaT study was implemented by fielding a survey to a nationally representative sample in each of the contributing countries where financial literacy was measured by answers to three questions (known as the Big Three) that address the basic concepts required to plan for retirement.[14] The wording of the questions are as follows:

> *Understanding of interest rate*: Suppose you had $100 in a savings account and the interest rate was 2% per year. After 5 years, how much do you think you would have in the account if you left the money to grow? (More than $102, Exactly $102, Less than $102, Do not know, Refuse to answer.)

> *Understanding of inflation*: Imagine that the interest rate on your savings account was 1% per year and inflation was 2% per year. After 1 year, how much would you be able to buy with the money in this account? (More than today, Exactly the same, Less than today, Do not know, Refuse to answer.)

> *Understanding of risk diversification*: Buying shares in a single company usually provides a safer return than buying units in a managed share fund. (True, False, Do not know, Refuse to answer.)

The first two questions address economic topics related to saving for retirement, including calculating interest rates and understanding the effect of inflation on purchasing power. Correct responses to these questions also test numeracy. The third question tests understanding of the concept of diversification.

The Australian survey was administered in 2012 to a representative sample of just over 1,000 people over age 18. The responses of the Australian sample are reported in Table 1, and, comparable with other developed countries, find only modest levels of financial literacy (Lusardi and Mitchell 2011b).

---

13   See Lusardi and Mitchell (2011a, 2011b).
14   The questions were developed by Annamaria Lusardi and Olivia S Mitchell (see Lusardi and Mitchell 2011a).

Table 1: Proportion of correct answers to the Big Three financial literacy questions

Age	% correct answers			
	Interest rates	Inflation	Diversification	Total
< 35	79%	55%	42%	31%
36–50	85%	69%	58%	44%
51–65	80%	86%	62%	52%

Source: Agnew et al. (2013a), Table 2.

While a high proportion of Australians could answer the question about interest rates, the under-35s had trouble with the inflation question, and understanding of diversification was universally poor. It is particularly worrying that less than one-third of younger respondents and only around 50 per cent of 51–65 year olds could answer all three questions. Moreover, in a question asking respondents to self-assess their financial literacy, 86 per cent of the sample considered themselves above average.

Subsequent regression analysis in Agnew et al. (2013a) found an association between financial literacy and retirement planning consistent with international studies reported in Lusardi and Mitchell (2011a), however, other studies suggest that one should be extremely cautious in concluding direct causation between financial education and downstream financial behaviour (Fernandes et al. 2014). In fact, numeracy (tested in the first two of the Big Three questions) has been identified as more important for financial decision-making in a number of experimental studies. In particular, subjects with low numeracy skills have trouble understanding diversification (Bateman et al. 2014), are more likely to be confused by alternative presentations of investment risk (Bateman et al. 2016c), and are insensitive to increasing risk of ruin (Bateman et al. 2016d). Overall, the success of initiatives to improve financial literacy is unclear. Perhaps the 'just in time' alternative, as advocated in Fernandes et al. (2014), should be considered?

At least as important as financial literacy in Australia's DC-world is specific knowledge of the superannuation system to which almost all workers belong. Responses to a subset of superannuation-knowledge questions, included in the 2012 financial literacy survey discussed above, are reported in Table 2 and reveal gaps in key knowledge by a large minority of the sample.

Table 2: Super system knowledge of a representative sample
of super fund members

	% incorrect or 'do not know'
What is the mandatory employer contribution rate under the SG?	34%
For most people, superannuation is taxed at a higher rate than a similar investment outside superannuation	38%
A 'balanced fund' is invested only in safe assets, such as bank accounts and cash management trusts and term deposits.	60%
Do you know the minimum age at which you can access your superannuation account?	48%
If you have any superannuation you will qualify for the Age Pension	29%

Source: Agnew et al. 2013b.

For example, one would expect all super fund members (irrespective of age) to be aware of the mandatory employer contribution rate, and whether or not superannuation is tax-preferred. However, more than one-third of respondents could not correctly answer either question. More worrying was the large proportion of the sample (close to 60 per cent) who were unaware of the asset allocation of a 'balanced fund'—the typical default option at that time, despite the super savings of around 60 per cent of superannuation members being invested in that option.

In a related study focusing on decumulation decisions, a representative sample of over 800 50–64 year olds, with a super fund but not yet retired, revealed extremely poor understanding of retirement income products. In this survey, respondents were asked to identify which products they were familiar with (from a long list of financial products) and for those nominated were asked to identify key product features relating to period of payment, income guarantee, drawdown flexibility, etc. Responses relating to account-based pensions and life annuities are reported in Table 3.

It is clear from these responses that Australian super fund members approaching retirement have very poor knowledge of the most common retirement benefit product (an account-based pension), and little understanding of an alternative (the lifetime annuity) that provides comprehensive insurance against the retirement risks discussed earlier. More specifically, only one-third of respondents reported that they had heard of a life annuity, and few were aware of its insurance characteristics: only 22 per cent of the sample knew that a life annuity paid a 'lifetime' income and only 8 per cent knew that payments are guaranteed. Close perusal of the detailed responses suggested confusion between life annuities and account-based pensions, which may be a further explanation of the trends in take-up of retirement benefits presented earlier.

Table 3: Understanding of retirement benefit products

Life annuity	Yes
Have you heard of this product?	37%
Does a life annuity offer lifetime income?	22%
Does a life annuity provide a guaranteed income level?	8%
Account-based pension	Yes
Have you heard of this product?	48%
Does an account-based pension offer choice of income subject to a regulated minimum?	25%
Is withdrawal of capital possible?	20%

Source: Bateman et al. (2014b).

In a practical sense it is unreasonable to expect all Australian retirement savers (and spenders) to be experts in lifecycle finance and product design. However, the level of understanding and knowledge revealed in these surveys is disappointing and raises questions about the ability of Australian super fund members to make appropriate superannuation and retirement decisions. Policy responses to assist members with these decisions, including information disclosure, choice architecture and financial advice are discussed next.

Information provision through financial product disclosure

Australia's financial product disclosure initiatives were initially framed in the 1990s on the underlying principle that 'consumers are assumed, for the most part, to be the best judges of their own interests' (Commonwealth of Australia 1997: 191) and that 'disclosure rules would aid and improve the quality of decision making' (Gruen and Wong 2010: 3). Possibly as a response to the 'high-level' regulatory approach and coupled with a focus by product providers on compliance and disclosure obligations, the 'first generation' financial product disclosure statements were long, detailed and complex.

More recently a series of second-round reforms have included shorter (eight-page) product disclosure statements and the introduction of a regulated default product, known as MySuper, (with its own mandatory disclosure format via a 'product dashboard'). A feature of both new disclosure formats is a 'standard risk measure', endorsed by the superannuation industry and both regulators (ASIC and APRA), where investment risk is required to be presented as 'the expected frequency of negative returns over a 20-year period'.

However, the extent to which this information provision has helped or hindered retirement saving and spending decisions is unclear. Experimental evidence from the US indicates that shorter financial product disclosure statements do not enhance financial decisions (Beshears et al. 2011) and that even well-informed investors may be influenced by non-salient information (Choi et al. 2010).

In the Australian context, Bateman et al. (2016b) investigated whether Australia's newly mandated short-form product disclosure had assisted superannuation fund members to better use and assess the information relevant to super fund investment options. Here the prescribed information includes a description of the option, an expected return objective, suggested time frame, strategic asset allocation, standard risk measure (as discussed above) and risk level. The format for disclosure is prescriptive for all information items except strategic asset allocation where, in practice, super funds present this information in pie charts or tables. A key goal of the regulators, as indicated in the regulatory impact statement (Department of Treasury 2010), was to prescribe risk and return information in a clear format. However, in a lab experiment where student and super fund member subjects were asked to make a series of (incentivised) investment choices using the prescribed information, neither the return nor the risk information were used as expected, with subjects using return information in the opposite direction than expected and generally ignoring the risk information. Surprisingly, the strategic asset allocation information, whether presented as a pie chart or table (and not the main focus of the information disclosure), had the largest marginal impact of all information provided for most of the subjects. This behaviour is consistent with use of the 1/n decision rule, as found in other asset allocation studies including Benartzi and Thaler (2001) for US 401k investment options and Hedesstrom et al. (2007) for investment choice in the Swedish Premium Pension Scheme. An overall conclusion is that regulators need to take more care with the testing of product disclosures.

An important motivation for the short-form disclosure was to better communicate expected returns and investment risk for the menu of investment options. Communication of investment risk was specifically investigated in the Australian context in Bateman et al. (2016c), who designed and implemented a discrete choice experiment to investigate the impact of alternative formats for investment risk presentation (including Australia's standard risk measure) on the propensity of individuals to violate some implications of expected utility maximisation when making retirement investment choices. Investment risk was presented in nine alternative formats, including textual and graphical ranges, right and left probability tails and right and left frequency tails (i.e. the standard risk measure). Results identified large differences in rates of violation of rational behaviour by risk presentation format—from around 14 per cent (for range presentations) to 37 per cent (for frequency presentations, which included Australia's standard risk measure). In particular, subjects with low scores on the numeracy and financial literacy scales were less able to 'see through' the alternative risk presentations and for many subjects the effect of the risk presentations was far greater than large changes in the underlying risk levels.

These findings support previous experimental studies that identify the impact of information framing on retirement benefit decisions (including Agnew et al. 2008 and Brown et al. 2008)—and suggest that more care be taken by Australian financial services regulators and industry to address behavioural biases when prescribing formats for mandatory disclosure.

In introducing the short-form disclosure format, the intention of ASIC, the regulator, was to reduce complexity, increase comparability and encourage engagement with financial decisions (Department of Treasury 2010). While there was extensive consultation and even some independent consumer testing of the proposed format, the pre-testing focused on simplicity and comparability but not on how people would use the information provided.

In other words, the 'information disclosure' approach needs further development to be of help to Australian retirement savers when making their retirement saving and spending decisions. This issue was in fact raised in the final report of the 2014 Financial System Inquiry (FSI 2014), which recommended to 'remove the regulatory impediments to innovative product disclosure and communication with consumers, and to improve the way risk and fees are communicated to consumers' (Recommendation 23).

Choice architecture

The superannuation system has always made some allowances for members who fail to or just don't want to make decisions. Traditionally, if an employee didn't choose a superannuation fund (if indeed choice was an option), the employer placed contributions in a nominated 'default superannuation fund' and most super fund investment choice menus included a default investment option for members who did not elect one themselves. These arrangements were recently formalised with the introduction of MySuper. Since 2014, new employees who do not choose their super fund have been defaulted into a MySuper product and by 2017 all remaining default fund balances must be transferred into a MySuper product. These products are regulated to have a simple set of product features, irrespective of who provides them, including a single diversified investment option (or a lifecycle strategy where asset allocation is varied with age). Standard fees must be charged to all members, and are generally restricted to administration fees, investment fees, and certain transaction fees on a cost-recovery basis, and standardised reporting on a 'product dashboard' includes information on the 10-year average return, the return target, the standard risk measure, the level of investment, and fees and other costs.

The jury on MySuper is still out, and, while the initiative provides regulated defaults in the accumulation phase, it does not carry over to decumulation—as was the intent of its architect (Cooper 2010). The absent choice architecture at retirement was another issue raised by in the FSI Final Report, in which it was recommended that the superannuation system 'meet the needs of retirees better by requiring superannuation trustees to pre-select a comprehensive income product in retirement for members to receive their benefits, unless members choose to take their benefits in another way' (Recommendation 11).

Overall, it is clear that the current approach to choice architecture is not meeting the needs of Australia's retirement savers and spenders. It is now time for policymakers and industry participants to consider a wider range of choice architecture tools such as use of technology and decision aids, and customised information (Johnson et al. 2012).

Financial advice

The final arm of support for retirement savers and spenders as they navigate Australia's DC retirement income system is financial advice. Unfortunately, while greater system and product complexity has increased the need for financial advice, questions continue to be raised about conflicts of interest and the quality of advice. A review of the financial planning industry by a Joint Parliamentary Committee (the Ripoll Inquiry) was triggered by several episodes of poor outcomes for clients of some planners (JPCCFS 2009), and there are still regular reports of 'bad behaviour' by advisers. However, the Ripoll Inquiry did lead to the Future of Financial Advice (FoFA) reforms, which aim to improve financial advice by (among other measures) banning conflicted advice, restricting trail commissions, and introducing standards for the conduct of advisers.

Nevertheless, there are still many concerns surrounding financial advice and advisers. Importantly, both public policy and academic studies raise questions about the ability of ordinary people to discern advice quality. A clear example here is an ASIC Shadow Shopping Study of retirement financial advice conducted in 2012, which found that while 86 per cent of clients believed that they had received good advice, only 14 per cent of clients had received good advice under the criteria set by ASIC (ASIC 2012). As well, there are ongoing concerns about the licensing, competence and qualifications of financial advisers. Financial advice was also highlighted in recommendations in the FSI final report, which aim to enhance the quality of advice, including addressing some of the issues surrounding the financial advice industry, such as 'rais[ing] the competency of financial advice providers and introduc[ing] an enhanced register of advisers'

(Recommendation 25). However, it is clear that there is still a lot to do to ensure that retirement savers and spenders have access to affordable, high-quality and unbiased advice.

In sum, it is not yet clear that we have found the best way to 'help' or 'guide' people through these complex retirement saving and spending decisions.

Concluding comments

Overall, Australia's retirement income arrangements are well placed to cope with the implications of the ageing population. The multi-pillar framework for retirement income provision represents world best practice and provides risk diversification, the pre-funded DC Superannuation Guarantee facilitates incentives to work and save, pre-funding enhances intergenerational equity, and the means-tested Age Pension promotes fiscal sustainability.

However, the retirement income arrangements perform poorly in a number of areas. Particularly in need of review are the tax arrangements for superannuation, the lack of policy focus on decumulation, and strategies to 'help' people with increasingly complex financial decisions as they enter and proceed through retirement. A key message is that the retirement income system needs to better support fund members and retirees as they navigate the decision points inevitable in a DC system, which are further complicated under the Australian design through interaction with the Age Pension and aged-care means tests.

It is increasingly evident that super fund members are not equipped to make such decisions, and there is increasing evidence that there are deficiencies in the support framework of financial product disclosure, choice architecture and financial advice. To assist with effective decision-making, future policy will require a combination of broad education and 'just-in-time' knowledge delivery, greater sophistication in choice architecture, improved information provision (through innovative product disclosures and super fund and industry communications) and access to good, unbiased and reasonably priced financial advice.

References

Agnew Julie, Anderson Lisa, Gerlach Jeffrey and Szykman Lisa (2008). Who Chooses Annuities? An Experimental Investigation of the Role of Gender, Framing and Defaults. *American Economic Review*, 98(2): 418–422.

Agnew Julie, Bateman Hazel and Thorp Susan (2013a). Financial Literacy and Retirement Planning in Australia. *Numeracy*, 6(2): 1–25.

Agnew Julie, Bateman Hazel and Thorp Susan (2013b). Superannuation Knowledge and Plan Behaviour. *JASSA*, 1: 45–50.

ANZ Bank (2015). ANZ Survey of Adult Financial Literacy in Australia, May 2015, The Social Research Centre, ANZ, Melbourne.

Australian Bureau of Statistics (ABS) (2009). Employment Arrangements, Retirement and Superannuation, Australia, Cat. No. 6361.0. April to July 2007 (Re-issue). Canberra: Australian Bureau of Statistics.

Australian Council of Social Services (ACOSS) (2014). *Poverty in Australia 2014*, Australian Council of Social Service, Australia.

Australian Government (2006). *A Plan to Simplify and Streamline Superannuation*, 9 May, Canberra.

Australian Prudential Regulatory Authority (APRA) (2014). Annual Superannuation Bulletin, June 2013 (Revised 5 February 2014).

Australian Prudential Regulatory Authority (APRA) (2015). Statistics—Quarterly Superannuation Performance, March 2015 (Issued 21 May 2015).

ASIC (2012). Shadow Shopping Study of Retirement Advice, Report 279, Sydney.

Bateman Hazel, Eckert Christine, Geweke John, Louviere Jordan, Satchell Stephen and Thorp Susan (2014). Financial competence, risk presentation and portfolio preferences. *Journal of Pension Economics and Finance*, 13(1): 27–61.

Bateman Hazel, Chomik Rafal and Piggott John (2016a). Australia's Retirement Income Policy. In Kate O'Loughlin, Colette Browning, and Hal Kendig (Eds), *Ageing in Australia: Challenges and Opportunities*. New York: Springer.

Bateman Hazel, Dobrescu Isabella, Newell Ben, Ortmann Andreas and Thorp Susan (2014b). As easy as pie: How retirement savers use prescribed investment disclosures, *Journal of Economic Behavious and Organisation*, 121: 60–76.

Bateman Hazel, Eckert Christine, Geweke John, Satchell Stephen and Thorp Susan (2016c). Risk presentation and retirement portfolio choice. *Review of Finance*, forthcoming. rof.oxfordjournals.org/content/early/2015/03/01/rof.rfv001.full.

Bateman Hazel, Eckert Christine, Iskhakov Fedor, Louviere Jordan, Satchell Stephen and Thorp Susan (2016b). Individual capability and effort in retirement benefit choices, *Journal of Risk Insurance*, forthcoming.

Bateman Hazel, Kingston Geoffrey and Piggott John (2001). *Forced Savings: Mandating Private Retirement Incomes*. Cambridge: Cambridge University Press.

Bateman Hazel and Piggott John (1997). Private Pensions in OECD Countries—Australia, Occasional Papers No. 23, Labour Market and Social Policy, OECD, Paris.

Bateman Hazel and Piggott John (2011). Too Much Risk to Insure? The Australian (non-) Market for Annuities. In OS Mitchell, J Piggott and N Takayama (Eds) *Securing Lifelong Retirement Income: Global Annuity Markets and Policy*. Oxford University Press, pp. 139–176.

Benartzi Shlomo, Previtero Alessandro and Thaler Richard (2012). Annuitisation Puzzles. *Journal of Economic Perspectives*, 25: 143–164.

Benartzi Shlomo and Thaler Richard (2001). Naive diversification strategies in defined contribution plans. *American Economic Review*, 91(1): 79–98.

Beshears John, Choi James, Laibson David and Madrian Brigette (2011). How does simplified disclosure affect individuals' mutual fund choices? In David A Wise (Ed) *Explorations in the Economics of Aging*. Chicago: University of Chicago Press, pp. 75–96.

Bodie Zvi (1990). Pensions as Retirement Income Insurance. *Journal of Economic Literature*, 28: 28–49.

Brown Jeffrey (2008). Understanding the role of annuities in retirement planning. In A Lusardi (Ed) *Overcoming the Saving Slump*. Chicago: University of Chicago Press.

Brown Jeffrey, Kling Jeffrey, Mullainathan Sendhil and Wrobel Marion (2008). Why Don't People Insure Late Life Consumption? A Framing Explanation of the Under-Annuitization Puzzle. *American Economic Review*, 98(2): 304–309.

Choi James, Laibson David, and Madrian Brigette (2010). Why does the law of one price fail? An experiment on index mutual funds. *Review of Financial Studies*, 23(4): 1405–1432.

Commonwealth of Australia (1997). *Financial System Inquiry Final Report*. Canberra: Department of Treasury.

Commonwealth of Australia (2009). *Australia's Future Tax System*, Report to the Treasurer, December 2009, Part One: Overview. Canberra: Department of Treasury.

Commonwealth of Australia (2015). *2015 Intergenerational Report: Australia in 2055*, Canberra: Department of Treasury. www. treasury.gov.au/PublicationsAndMedia/Publications/2015/2015-Intergenerational-Report.

Cooper Jeremy (2010). *Super System Review*, Final Report, Canberra: Commonwealth of Australia.

Department of Social Services (2014). *Annual Report 2013–2014*, Canberra: Department of Social Services. www.dss.gov.au/sites/default/files/documents/10_2014/dss_annualreport2013-14.pdf.

Department of Treasury (2010). Regulation Impact Statement (RIS)—Financial Services Disclosure Reform, May 2010. ris.finance.gov.au/files/2010/07/FSWG_PDS-RIS_20100713.pdf.

Department of Treasury (2012). Distributional analysis of superannuation tax concessions, presented to the Superannuation Roundtable, 23 April 2012.

Fernandes Daniel, Lynch John, and Netemeyer Richard (2014). Financial Literacy and Downstream Financial Behaviors. *Management Science*, 60(8): 1861–1883.

Gallagher Phil (2012). Treasury Measurement of Retirement Income Adequacy, presentation to FEAL Pre-Forum Discussion, 9 February 2012.

Gruen David and Wong Tim (2010). MySuper—Thinking seriously about the default option, presented at the Special Session on Superannuation, Australian Conference of Economists, September 2010, Sydney. archive.treasury.gov.au/documents/1922/PDF/03_MySuper.pdf.

Gruen David and Soding Leigh (2011). Compulsory superannuation and national saving, Economic Roundup, Issue 3, 2011. www.treasury.gov.au/PublicationsAndMedia/Publications/2011/Economic-Roundup-Issue-3/Report/Compulsory-superannuation-and-national-saving.

Hedesstrom Ted, Svedsater Henrik and Garley Tommy (2007). Determinants of the use of heuristic choice rules in the Swedish Premium Pension Scheme: An internet-based study. *Journal of Economic Psychology*, 28(1): 113–126.

Johnson Eric, Shu Suzanne, Dellaert Benedict, Fox Craig, Goldstein Daniel, Haubl Gerald, Larrick Richard, Payne John, Peters Ellen, Schkade David, Wansink Brian and Weber Elke (2012). Beyond Nudges: Tools of Choice Architecture. *Marketing Letters*, 23: 487–504.

Joint Parliamentary Committee on Corporations and Financial Services (JPCCFS) (2009). *Inquiry into financial products and services in Australia*, Commonwealth of Australia, November.

Lusardi Annamaria and Mitchell Olivia (2011a). Financial Literacy around the World. *Journal of Pension Economics and Finance*, 10(4): 497–508.

Lusardi Annamaria and Mitchell Olivia (2011b). *Financial Literacy: Implications for Retirement Security and the Financial Marketplace.* Oxford University Press.

Mercer (2014). *Melbourne Mercer Global Pension Index*. Melbourne: Australian Centre for Financial Studies.

Organisation for Economic Co-operation and Development (OECD) (2013). *Pensions at a Glance*. Paris: OECD.

Organisation for Economic Co-operation and Development (OECD) (2014a). OECD Factbook 2014—Economic, Environmental and Social Statistics, OECD Publishing. dx.doi.org/10.1787/factbook.2014-en.

Organisation for Economic Co-operation and Development (OECD) (2014b). OECD Pensions Outlook 2014, OECD Publishing. dx.doi.org/10.1787/9789264222687-en.

Plan for Life (2015). Detailed annuity statistics, Plan For Life Actuaries and Researchers, Mount Waverley, Victoria, Australia.

World Bank (1994). *Averting the Old Age Crisis: Policies to Protect the Old and Promote Growth.* Washington, DC: Oxford University Press.

Wu Shang, Asher Anthony, Meyricke Ramona and Thorp Susan (2015). Age pensioner profiles: A longitudinal study of income, assets and decumulation, CEPAR Working Paper 2015/17. Sydney: ARC Centre of Excellence in Population Ageing Research.

12

Ageing, entitlement and funding health care

Jane Hall and Kees van Gool

Universal access to health-care services funded under Medicare is one of the universal benefit programs targeted for scrutiny as government moves to end, or at least reduce, the age of entitlement. Successive Intergenerational Reports have demonstrated the extent to which health-care expenditure is predicted to grow more rapidly than Commonwealth government spending on aged care and pensions (Commonwealth of Australia 2010; 2015). While the latter is clearly related to population ageing, the former has also been attributed to the same demographic change (for example, Dutton 2014a, 2014b). The predicted growth in health-care expenditure has been characterised as inevitable and as threatening the viability of the health system as it is currently unless some significant changes are made (Ley 2015; Knott 2015). Thus the rhetoric posits causative links from ageing of the population to poorer population health to health-spending blowout to justification for major changes to current health-care financing.

Our intent is to assess these propositions: first, that ageing will inevitably place undue pressure on Medicare; and second, that a system of tax-funded health care is not economically viable. At first glance, it seems paradoxical that improved levels of health (as reflected by decreasing premature mortality) are accompanied by rising outlays on health service use. Therefore, we explore the relationships between old age and health status, and health status and expenditure. What we observe is that, although average expenditure increases with age and with number of chronic conditions, the decrease in median health status and the increase in median expenditure is substantially less. There is considerable variability in health levels, particularly at older ages, and in health-care expenditure. As a result, we see a concentration of spending in a relatively small proportion of the population.

We then turn to the need for insurance. Insurance comes about as a way to manage exposure to risk. Individuals face the risk of poor health and potentially high costs for treatment. Although this is uncertain for the individual, it is predictable for population groups when risks are pooled. We explore the role of government in managing risk and argue that the provision of health insurance is a rational response. Medicare is not an unjustified entitlement.

We then turn to recent increases in national health expenditures, to address whether current trends support the view that rising health-care expenditure is out of control. We conclude that ageing per se is not a threat to the sustainability of the Australian health-care system, and that current rates of expenditure are not out of control; so that drastic reductions in access to health care are not justified. Nonetheless the provision of universal insurance introduces other forms of risk and these warrant more investigation to improve health system efficiency.

Expectations of survival and health

Dramatic falls in mortality have occurred not just in the younger age groups but also in the age group generally regarded as elderly, the over-70s. The result is rising life expectancy. The prevalence of chronic disease is also increasing, with those at older ages more likely to experience multiple chronic conditions and presenting Australia's biggest health challenge (AIHW 2014). To the extent that improved survival means that people are living with diseases that once were fatal, it is likely their health is relatively poor. An increasing prevalence of people in poor health is actually an improvement in overall health once deaths avoided are considered. There have also been important changes in what it means to have a chronic disease. Earlier diagnosis is not just possible but encouraged, meaning that even if treatment had not changed people would be living longer with a disease and that is reflected in increasing prevalence of chronic conditions. New US guidelines, for example, have greatly expanded the population for whom initiation of drug therapy for cholesterol is recommended (Stone et al. 2013). If fully implemented in clinical practice, around 13 million more US citizens would be treated with the cholesterol-lowering medications called statins, with most of these patients aged between 65 and 75 (Pencina et al. 2014). But for many diseases, if not most, treatment has changed in a way that has dramatically altered quality of life. In diabetes, for example, new technologies have transformed monitoring and treatment (Polonsky 2012), and patients without complications report quality of life scores only slightly lower than similar aged counterparts (Redekop et al. 2002). Today patients expect to manage their condition, not to have to withdraw from normal life. So it is important not to conflate having a chronic condition with a much poorer health state. It is important to know not just how many conditions people have been diagnosed with, but how they feel.

This can be done by looking at surveys where respondents are asked to rate their own health. We use data reported in 2010 from a large panel household survey in Australia, the Household, Income and Labour Dynamics in Australia (HILDA) survey, of 7,700 Australian households (around 20,000 individuals). This survey uses a standardised measure of health, the SF-6D; respondents are asked to rate their health and functioning against six criteria which cover pain, vitality, physical activities, usual activities such as work, social activities and mental health. The distribution of SF-6D scores by age is shown in Figure 1. More than half the elderly population remains in reasonably good health. These results are consistent with other survey evidence. In the Australian Health Surveys around two-thirds of those over the age of 75 rate their health as good or better (AIHW 2014).

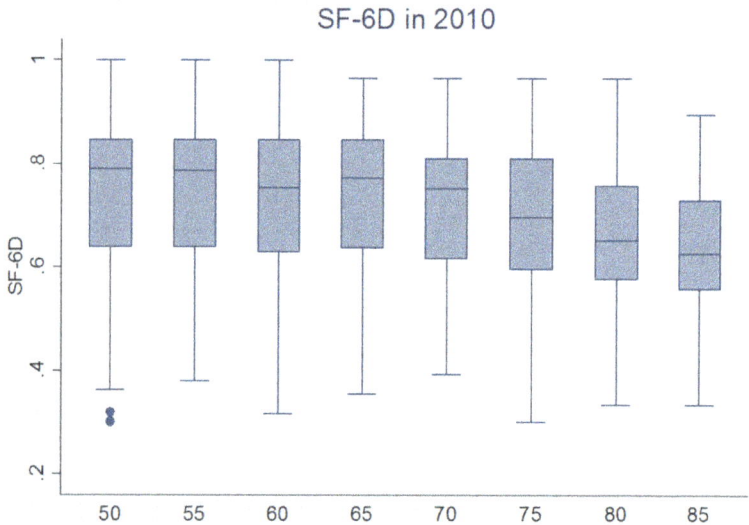

Figure 1. Self-assessed health by age group
Source: van Gool, Mu and Wong's own work based on data provided by HILDA Survey.

Ageing, illness and health-care costs

Health-care expenditure per person varies over the lifecycle with the lowest average spending in childhood (5–14 year olds) and rising rapidly in the over-50s (AIHW 2014). It is now generally accepted that historical growth has been driven by non-demographic factors, particularly advances in technology. For the future, though, it has been argued that increasing numbers of the older-old, with higher levels of chronic disease, and expectations of new treatments and technologies, will interact to push health-care expenditure to much higher levels. We now turn our attention to the extent to which higher levels of health-care spending are uniform across age groups, and explained by the presence of chronic conditions.

Again we use data from HILDA, in this case the number of self-reported GP visits in 2009. We are interested in moving beyond the mean to consider the median and the range. The median number of visits does change with age, as shown in Figure 2, but only slightly. However, we do see greater variability with increasing numbers of high users at older ages.

This can be explored in more detail using another data source, the NSW 45 and Up Study, which surveyed more than 267,000 non-institutionalised people aged 45 and over and can be linked to multiple health administrative data sets covering all out-of-hospital medical services, all subsidised prescription pharmaceuticals, and hospital use. Total average health expenditure by age demonstrates the expected pattern. Median expenditure increases gradually after the age of 65, but with a much greater increase in variability for men and women (see Figure 3). The number of chronic conditions explains some but not all of this increase. Median expenditure increases with the number of chronic conditions but the mean increases more rapidly, reflecting high levels of spending in a small group. Interestingly, the same pattern is evident even at older ages, and Figure 4 shows the results for the older age group. Although health cost increases with the number of chronic conditions, there is much greater variation in cost in this sicker group.

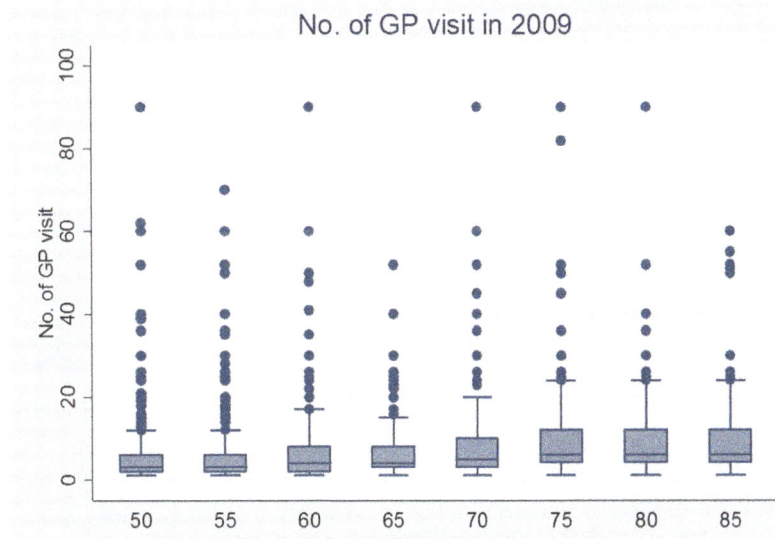

Figure 2. Variation in GP visits by age
Source: van Gool, Mu and Wong's own work based on data provided by HILDA Survey.

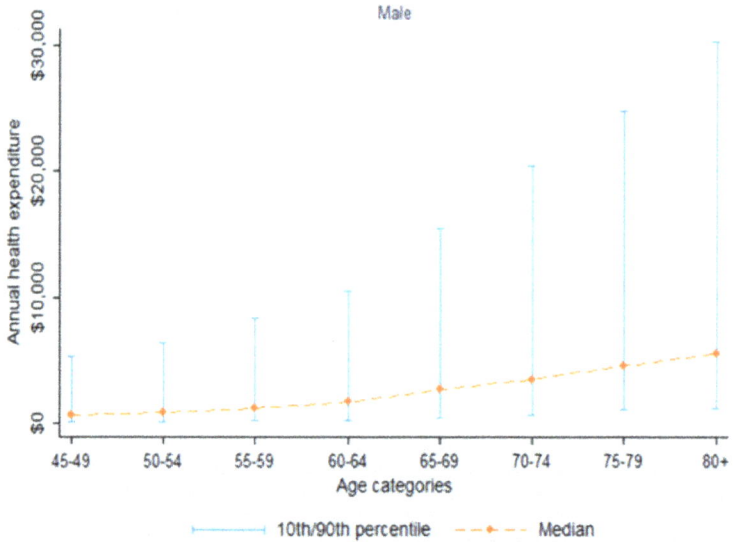

Figure 3A. Health expenditure by age in men 45 and up

Source: van Gool, Mu and Wong's own work based on data provided by the 45 and Up Survey linked to MBS and PBS and hospital, NSW Australia (2010).

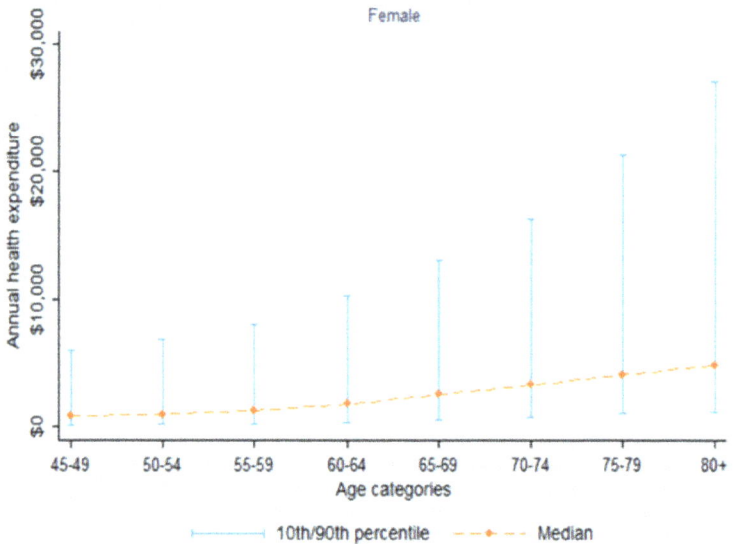

Figure 3B. Health expenditure by age in women 45 and up

Source: van Gool, Mu and Wong's own work based on data provided by the 45 and Up Survey linked to MBS and PBS and hospital, NSW Australia (2010).

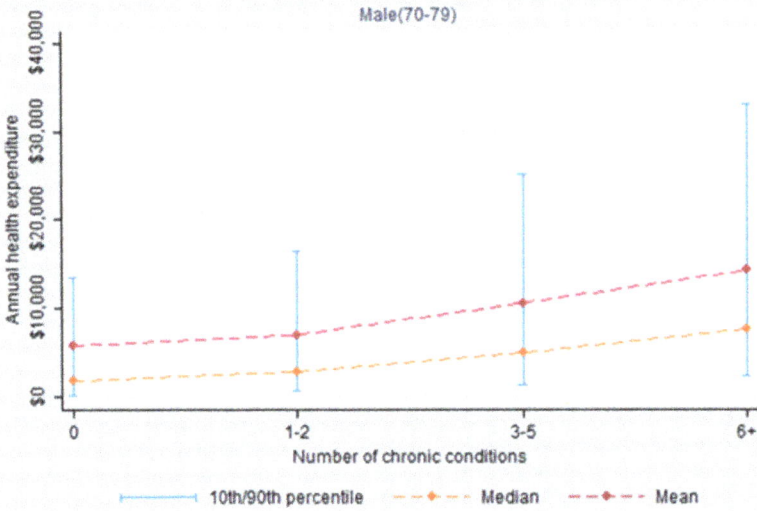

Figure 4A. Health expenditure in men 70–79 years by number of conditions

Source: van Gool, Mu and Wong's own work based on data provided by the 45 and Up Survey linked to MBS and PBS and hospital, NSW Australia (2010).

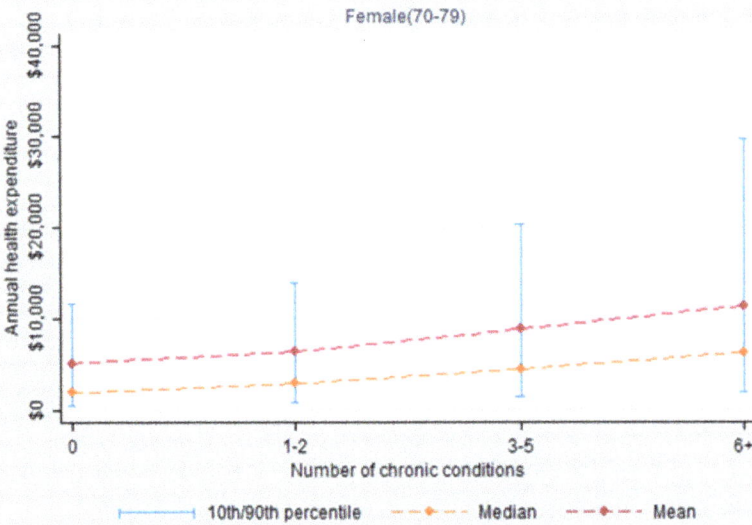

Figure 4B. Health expenditure in women 70–79 years by number of conditions

Source: van Gool, Mu and Wong's own work based on data provided by the 45 and Up Survey linked to MBS and PBS and hospital, NSW Australia (2010).

However, the increasing number of chronic conditions is a measure of multi-morbidity but not necessarily the seriousness of the conditions or the frailty of the patient. Our observation of increased variability with multi-morbidity may reflect that we have not captured severity adequately. Time to death has also been shown to be associated with higher levels of expenditure (Hoover et al. 2002; Moorin and Holman 2008), with a marked increase in the year before death. The linkage of 45 and Up with death registrations allows us to investigate this. Similarly, the increase in spending in the 12 months prior to death is marked (Figure 5). Again, the mean level of expenditure increases more than the median, with much greater variability in spending in the year before death. Further, we find that the largest share of costs is hospital inpatient care, a finding that replicates others (Kardamanidis et al. 2007).

To some extent, this is simply explained: hospitals are expensive places. Over half of Australian deaths occur in hospitals, even at older ages (Broad et al. 2013). Death at younger ages is less expected and less accepted, and so intensive (and expensive) treatment is justified. But this is not the case for older people, most of whom would prefer to die at home (Gomes et al. 2013). A survey of US physicians asked which of various potentially intensive treatments they would want for themselves if they were considered towards the end of their lives (Gallo et al. 2003). Such therapies included chemotherapy, artificial feeding, ventilation, dialysis and invasive testing. Over 80 per cent would definitely want pain relief; but most would not want other frequently used interventions. It is important to ask whether health-care spending is being driven by expensive and invasive therapies that the recipients actively do not want.

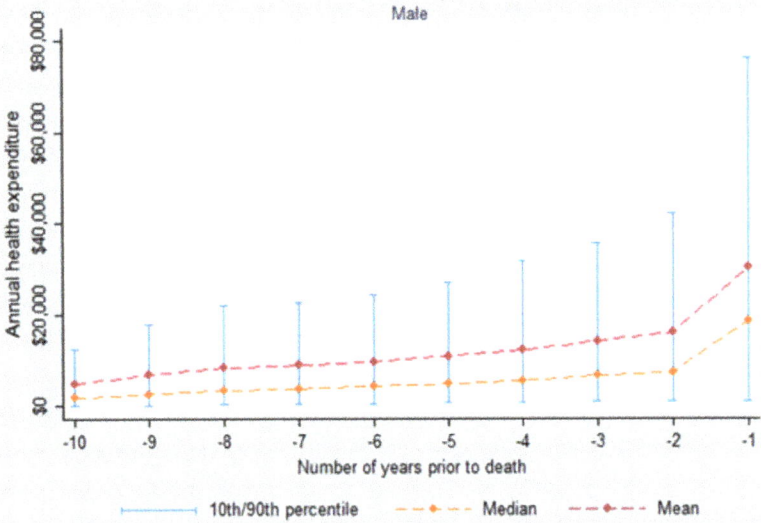

Figure 5A. Expenditure by time to death

Source: van Gool, Mu and Wong's own work based on data provided by the 45 and Up Survey linked to MBS and PBS and hospital, NSW Australia (2010).

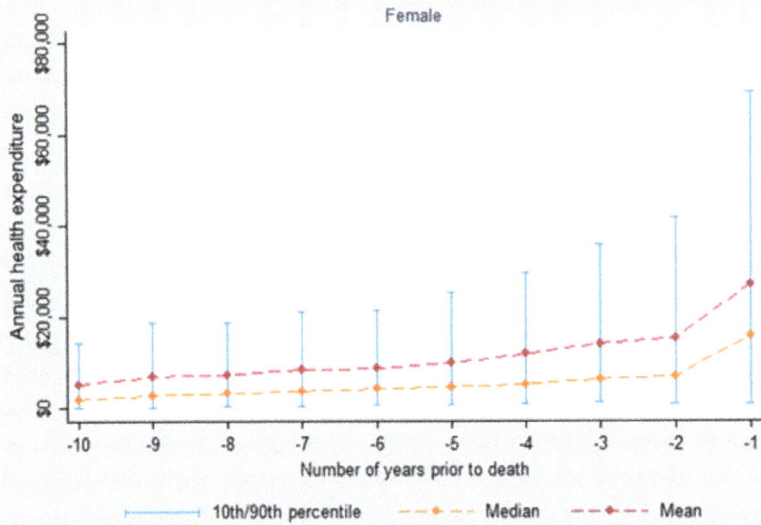

Figure 5B. Expenditure by time to death

Source: van Gool, Mu and Wong's own work based on data provided by the 45 and Up Survey linked to MBS and PBS and hospital, NSW Australia (2010).

The concentration of health-care spending

Australian data show wide variation in health status at every age, and at older ages. Many older people are in good health or better. And a growing number with poorer health could well be a consequence of what was once acute, life-ending illness being transformed into a chronic condition. Improvements in medical technology have allowed for earlier detection of conditions (e.g. diabetes) with the benefits of earlier intervention and better management. This has also created new medical conditions (high cholesterol) and new opportunities for commercialisation; after all, a medical condition is generally something for which there is a viable treatment. As a result, it is not valid to compare 'chronic conditions' measured today with those observed a generation ago. The growing prevalence of chronic conditions does not mean people feel worse. Although there is an increase in health-care expenditure with age and with increasing conditions, what is more striking is that there is such an increase in variability with the number of conditions, and with proximity to death.

The concentration in health-care spending is well summarised by the concentration curves in Figure 6, again using the NSW 45 and Up data. These rank individuals by health-care spending and show how the share of total expenditure corresponds to the proportion of the population. This pattern of high levels of expenditure concentrated in a fairly small proportion of the population has been well established with US data (Cutler and Zeckhauser 2000); but to our knowledge this has not been demonstrated with Australian data. It is not surprising that there is a high degree of concentration with 25 per cent of the population accounting for 80 per cent of total expenditure. Remember this is for an older group, NSW residents aged 45 and over. We would expect an even stronger concentration for all ages. Perhaps more surprisingly, when this is analysed by age group, as shown in Figure 6, the pattern remains, even for the older groups.

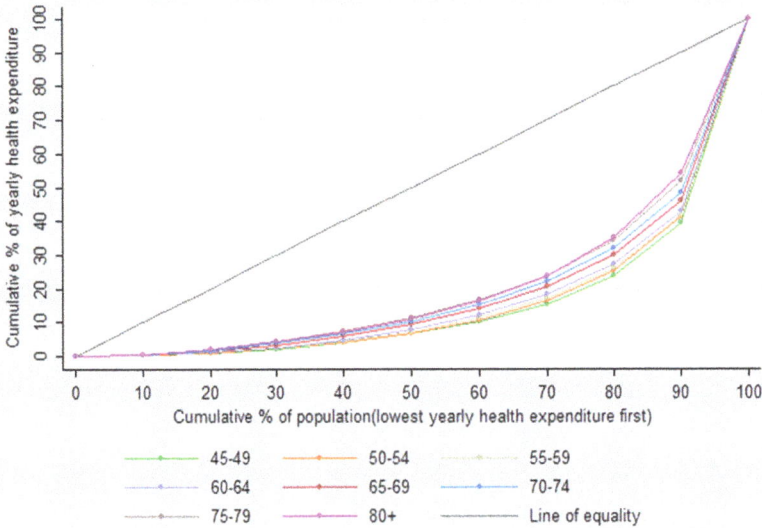

Figure 6. Concentration curves for health care expenditure by age

Source: van Gool, Mu and Wong's own work based on data provided by the 45 and Up Survey linked to MBS and PBS and hospital, NSW Australia (2010).

At this point, it seems clear that ageing is not the problem. We see that many Australians live into old age with good health, and even for those with multiple chronic conditions, many remain low spenders. The challenge is to understand why some people are healthy and why some are big spenders. There are potentially a number of underlying reasons, each of which suggest a different response: unpredictability at the individual level; poor management and high prices; missed opportunities for prevention. The unpredictability of illness for any individual and the potentially high (catastrophic) financial losses provides the case for insurance; better to exchange a certain small loss (the cost of insurance) rather than face the uncertain prospect of very expensive treatment, or no treatment because it is beyond one's means. As we have already shown, the concentration of health-care spending remains after accounting for age and chronic conditions, which suggests that these two factors do not explain much of the observed variation. The observation of higher expenditures and hospital use in the months before death is consistent with a greater severity explanation. There are other uncertainties in addition to severity. Some illnesses are simply more expensive to treat while some individuals do not respond well to one treatment and may require alternative interventions or treatment for complications.

The challenge for health care insurance

A system of health-care financing is needed to prevent people not getting health care when they cannot afford it; and to ensure that people do not face unreasonable financial hardship when sick and needing care. This type of risk is generally addressed by some form of insurance, which allows for the pooling of financial risk. However, insurance brings with it moral hazard; if the results of loss are ameliorated, then individuals may take less care to avoid the loss.

The whole concept of moral hazard needs to be considered carefully in the context of health. Health insurance actually provides protection against the cost of health service use. It cannot guarantee to restore lost health, and even where treatments are completely effective they frequently involve time, pain, discomfort and loss of dignity. So it is unlikely that individuals will intentionally risk their health for the fun of consuming health care. Moral hazard does enter the picture, though. Insurance typically includes some services and excludes others, so providers, simply by selecting what services they fund, will encourage consumers to use those services in preference to others. Historically, this has favoured treatment for an identified disease/ condition and excluded prevention; and Medicare favours services provided by a medial practitioner where the patient is present over allied health providers, or telephone or email consultations. Now it would seem sensible for an insurer to invest in prevention to avoid expensive payouts for treatment; but the time required to reap the returns on prevention is often many years.

Once individuals become patients they rely on medical providers' advice as to what type of health-care consumption they require and who is best placed to provide that. The combination of moral hazard and asymmetry of information results in higher expenditure, as the patient/doctor decision tends towards higher use of services and to be less price sensitive than if they faced the full costs. This is not necessarily over-use in any normative sense; after all the point of insurance is to reduce the costs faced at the point of service so as to encourage people to consume health care. But there is a challenge in distinguishing needed (or more valuable) from unnecessary (or less valuable) care. There is also the opportunity for providers to charge higher prices than they would without insurance.

So however insurance is organised, there is a need to address the various issues raised by moral hazard and information asymmetries. Some strategies involve passing some risk back to the customer, for example co-payments, front-end deductibles, a limit to the amount that the insurer will pay. Others involve passing the risk on to providers, such as through capitation arrangements or encouraging use of government-financed services. Yet another approach is favourable risk selection, that is to encourage good risks and discourage bad risks from buying insurance. Risk is pervasive and the challenge for health financing is how to manage and share it, while still meeting the goal of universal access but not introducing perverse incentives.

The role of government

Government has an essential role to play in regulating markets. This applies no less in health care, where government involvement in health-care markets is a prerequisite for efficient market functioning. Indeed, without government's power to ensure some redistribution, many groups would be priced out of the health-care market. Given that many chronic conditions are associated with low socioeconomic status and age, an important aspect of universal coverage is that it raises the health care purchasing power of the poor and sick, which then affects the type and distribution of health care supplied. Universal coverage is not just vital for financial protection from high health-care costs for these groups but is likely to generate better population health outcomes.

Even without the need for redistribution, government will intervene to regulate competition. The market for health insurance is beset with widespread failure, including risk selection, the potential for individuals to under-insure, and protecting the insured from an insurance firm going out of business. A broader way to see this, rather than just regulation of a market, is as regulation and management of risk. As Moss (2002) explains and chronicles in his book, government, even in the US, plays a major and pervasive role in managing risks through various approaches but is the ultimate risk manager. Once that view is adopted, we can see that there are different ways to meet the insurance function with differing degrees of government involvement. At one extreme is a market of competitive private insurance funds. Even in such a private market, regulation will be required to manage risk, particularly under-insurance and the failure of a particular firm. Government will be required to cover poor risk groups, either directly, such as in the US with Medicare and Medicaid, or though regulation of premiums (such as community rating) or subsidy. The other extreme is a national health service where government is not just the insurer, but the provider of care, for example, owning and operating hospitals and contracting with doctors such as the British National Health Service. In between, government may provide the insurance function financed through general taxation, as is the case in Australia. Whichever approach is chosen, there will be government involvement as the ultimate risk manager.

There are benefits to government as insurer. Universal cover can be assured through the government's power to collect payments. The government can directly address the need for redistribution and provide the disadvantaged, low-income groups and those with multiple diseases with insurance cover. Government can save on the costs of monitoring market functioning, in addition to the savings from the overheads and administrative costs of multiple insurers. Government will benefit from the long-term investment in prevention. In our view, government tax-based insurance is not an entitlement but a rational option for addressing society's need for health insurance.

Can Australia afford to spend more on health care?

Health-care expenditure has increased at a faster rate than national income; this phenomenon has been observed over time and across countries (OECD 2013). The real growth in health-care expenditure for Australia has averaged 5.1 per cent pa over the decade to 2012–13 (AIHW 2014). Even though ageing is not 'the problem', it is reasonable to ask whether this can be maintained in the future. Financial sustainability can be considered from the perspective of the economy and whether future economic growth can continue to support a growing share. Compared to other OECD countries, Australia still is very average in the proportion of GDP spent on health care; countries that spend more include New Zealand and Canada. The most recent health-care expenditure data for Australia has shown some slowdown in growth. While one data point does not establish a trend, international evidence shows a similar slowing of growth in other developed countries. Across the OECD, many countries hit by the global financial crisis (GFC) in 2009 have achieved a significant reduction in the growth in health spending. This is not surprising given the dimensions of the GFC and, in many countries, the imposition of strict austerity. What is interesting, and perhaps less expected, is that across 16 OECD countries, the economic recessions of the 1970s, the 1980s, and 2000s were followed by a downturn in health-expenditure growth, and that lower rate of growth has been sustained even during the following economic booms.

And for the future, even conservative predictions of economic growth will easily cover the expected increases in expenditure (Richardson 2014). Thus it is difficult to argue that health expenditure is out of control. The perspective of the economy as a whole is a more important question than the limited perspective of the Australian Government taken in the successive Intergenerational Reports. Successful constraint of federal government outlays may simply shift cost to other payers in the system; reducing the funding of public hospitals shifts the burden to states and territories, while consumer co-payments shifts financing to patients.

That conclusion does not rule out the question of whether the health system can be made more efficient. We have already pointed to the potential for moral hazard and its effects on health-care spending. We have demonstrated that there is substantial variation in spending patterns. More research is required to disentangle warranted and unwarranted variation and expenditure. Opportunities for improving the performance and efficiency of health services can meet any challenges of rising expenditures; and, as the Productivity Commission pointed out, is a superior way of meeting the challenges ahead (Productivity Commission 2013).

Conclusion

The ageing of the Australian population is not a threat to the continued viability of the Australian health-care system. Many older people remain in good health, and place modest demands on the health services. The high concentration of health-care expenditure at all ages, with a relatively small group of the population accounting for the bulk of expenditure, points to the need for insurance. Insurance can be provided in different ways with tax-financed universal health-care insurance as one option. Medicare with its universality is a reasonable social choice. Indeed, universal coverage and high levels of public insurance must be part of the solution to the healthy ageing policy challenge. The new analyses presented here demonstrate that there is widespread variation in health service use and expenditure, which is not explained by age or health status. More research is needed to disentangle warranted variation that should be addressed by insurance, and unwarranted variation that should be addressed by improving incentives. Meanwhile, policy reforms that are aimed at the average are likely to miss their target and have sub-optimal health and financial consequences.

References

Australian Institute of Health and Welfare (AIHW) (2014). Australia's health 2014. Australia's health series no. 14, Cat. no. AUS 178. Canberra: AIHW.

Broad Joanna, Gott Merryn, Kim Hongsoo, Boyd Michael, Chen He and Connolly Martin J (2013). Where do people die? An international comparison of the percentage of deaths occurring in hospital and residential aged care settings, using published and available statistics. *International Journal of Public Health*, 58(2): 257–267.

Commonwealth of Australia (2010). *Australia to 2050: Future challenges. The 2010 Intergenerational Report*. Canberra: Department of Treasury. archive.treasury.gov.au/igr/igr2010/report/pdf/IGR_2010.pdf. Accessed April 2013.

Commonwealth of Australia (2015). *2015 Intergenerational Report: Australia in 2055*. Canberra: Department of Treasury. March 2015.

Cutler David and Zeckhauser Richard (2000). The anatomy of health insurance. In AJ Culyer and JP Newhouse (Ed) *Handbook of Health Economics*. Elsevier.

Dutton Peter (2014a). Address to Australian Private Hospitals Association, 33rd National Congress, Brisbane, 24 March 2014. www.health.gov.au/internet/ministers/publishing.nsf/Content/6 7B35AD121B08BABCA257CA500700E7D/$File/PDSP130324.pdf. Downloaded September 2014.

Dutton Peter (2014b). Rising Cost of Good Health. Press Release. 24 June 2014. www.health.gov.au/internet/ministers/publishing.nsf/ Content/97704DD4D6734CB8CA257D0200076F22/$File/PD044.pdf. Downloaded September 2014.

Ellis Randall, Fiebig Denzil, Johar Meliyanni, Jones Glenn and Savage Elizabeth (2013). Explaining Health Care Expenditure Variation: Large-Sample Evidence Using Linked Survey And Health Administrative Data. *Health Economics*, 22(9): 1093–1110.

Gallo Joseph, Straton Joseph, Klag Michael, Meoni Lucy, Sulmasy Daniel, Wang Nae Yuh and Ford DE (2003). Life-sustaining treatments: What do physicians want and do they express their wishes to others? *Journal of the American Geriatrics Society*, 51(7): 961–969.

Garner Jessica (2014). GP trial wins more loyalty. *Australian Financial Review*. 17 October 2014.

Gomes Barbara, Calanzani Natalie, Gysels Marjolein, Hall Sue and Higginson Irene J (2013). Heterogeneity and changes in preferences for dying at home: A systematic review. *BMC Palliative Care* 12: 7. doi: 10.1186/1472-684x-12-7.

Gosden Toby, Forland Frode, Kristiansen Ivar, Sutton M, Leese B, Giuffrida A, Sergison M and Pedersen L (2011). *Capitation, salary, fee-for-service and mixed systems of payment: Effects on the behaviour of primary care physicians*. The Cochrane Database of Systematic Reviews, (3): CD002215.

Hoover Donald, Crystal Stephen, Kumar Rizie, Sambamoorthi Usha and Cantor Joel C (2002). Medical Expenditures during the Last Year of Life: Findings from the 1992–1996 Medicare Current Beneficiary Survey. *Health Serv Res*. 37(6): 1625–1642.

Kardamanidis Katina, Lim Kim, Da Cunha Cristalyn, Taylor Lee K and Jorm Louisa R (2007). Hospital costs of older people in New South Wales in the last year of life. *Medical Journal of Australia*, 187(7): 383–386.

Knott Matthew (2015) Joe Hockey raises the prospect of Australians living until 150 to justify budget cuts. *Sydney Morning Herald*, 19 January. www.smh.com.au/federal-politics/political-news/joe-hockey-raises-prospect-of-australians-living-until-150-to-justify-budget-cuts-20150119-12t3m1.html.

Ley Sussan (2015). Government to consult on Medicare reform. Media Release. sussanley.com/government-to-consult-on-medicare-reform/. Accessed 23 January 2015.

Moorin Rachael and Holman D'Arcy (2008). The cost of in-patient care in Western Australia in the last years of life: A population-based data linkage study. *Health Policy*, 85: 380–390.

Moss David (2002). *When All Else Fails: Government as the ultimate Risk Manager*. Cambridge MA: Harvard University Press.

Organisation of Economic Co-operation and Development (OECD) (2013). *Health at a Glance 2013: OECD Indicators*. Paris: OECD Publishing.

Pencina Michael, Navar-Boggan Ann Marie, D'Agostino Ralph, et al. (2014). Application of new cholesterol guidelines to a population-based sample. *New England Journal of Medicine*, 370: 1422–1431. doi: 10.1056/NEJMoa13156.

Polonsky Kenneth (2012). The Past 200 Years in Diabetes. *New England Journal of Medicine*, 367: 1332–40. doi: 10.1056/NEJMra1110560.

Productivity Commission (2013). An Ageing Australia: Preparing for the Future, Productivity Commission Research Paper, Canberra: Productivity Commission.

Redekop Ken, Koopmanschap Marc, Stolk Ronald, Rutten Guy, Wolffenbuttel Bruce and Niessen Louis (2002). Health-Related Quality of Life and Treatment Satisfaction in Dutch Patients with Type 2 Diabetes. *Diabetes Care*, 25(3): 458–463. doi: 10.2337/diacare.25.3.458.

Richardson Jeffrey (2014). Can we sustain health spending? *Medical Journal of Australia*, 200(11): 629–631.

Sax Institute 45 and Up Survey: www.saxinstitute.org.au/ou-work/45-up-study (accessed 23 January 2015).

Stone Neil, Robinson Jennifer, Lichtenstein Alice, et al. (2013). ACC/AHA guideline on the treatment of blood cholesterol to reduce atherosclerotic cardiovascular risk in adults: A report of the American College of Cardiology/American Heart Association Task Force on Practice Guidelines. *Journal of the American College of Cardiology*, 63(25).

Wooden Mark and Nicole Watson (2007). The HILDA Survey and its Contribution to Economic and Social Research (So Far), *The Economic Record*, vol 83, no. 261, pp. 208–231.

13

Financing aged care: The role of housing wealth and intergenerational relationships

Rachel Ong

The financing of aged care is in many ways the new frontier of policy response to population ageing. Over the next 40 years, the group that dominates demand for aged care—the 'old-old'—will increase more than any other. For example, the number of people aged over 85 is expected to quadruple. It is estimated that Australian Government aged-care expenditure will nearly double from 0.9 per cent to 1.7 per cent of GDP over the next 40 years (Commonwealth of Australia 2015).

Given the population and expenditure projections above, there exists an urgent need for establishing a sustainable system that offers adequate funding for aged residential and community care without crippling the fiscal budget. However, conflicting views persist in regard to the kinds of financing strategies that should be deployed. Successful execution of proposed solutions for financing aged care are typically hampered by conflicting ethical and operational issues that afflict co-existing and future generations. A major policy conundrum concerns the question of intergenerational equity, namely preserving the elderly's access to adequate funding for aged-care services without encumbering younger generations in their lifetime economic prospects.

If funding for the needs of the aged are continually financed through government borrowing, and long-term budget deficits are therefore tolerated to support the care (and other) needs of a rapidly expanding group of elderly Australians, servicing and repayment of this fiscal debt will inevitably be borne by current and future generations of taxpayers.

This chapter considers the option of enabling older Australian home owners to draw on their housing assets to make a greater contribution to the funding of their personal aged-care needs. Specifically, the chapter explores the pros and cons of such a financing strategy within an intergenerational context.

The intergenerational housing policy debate

The changes in the demographic landscape introduced by growing longevity, and the fiscal concerns they raise, have been long anticipated in the policy sector. The need for positioning public policy formulation within an intergenerational context has been recognised by government, an obvious indication being the commitment to publication of the five-yearly Intergenerational Reports by both the current federal government and its predecessors.

However, the policy debate has taken on a new overtone in recent years. Traditionally, the elderly have been perceived as a universally resource-poor group in need of access to publicly funded care and support services. This emphasis has changed dramatically in recent years. It is increasingly recognised that many Australian ageing boomers have reaped significant windfall gains from soaring house prices from the mid-1990s to the mid-2000s. Between 1995 and 2005, real house prices in Australia climbed by around 80 per cent, outstripping the growth in real house prices in several other OECD countries that also experienced housing market booms, such as Canada and the United States (Girouard et al. 2006). Home owners also suffered less diminution of their housing wealth during the 2008 global financial crisis (GFC) than many of their counterparts overseas. House price index data from the Australian Bureau of Statistics show that while there was a very slight dip in the weighted average index for all capital cities during 2008 and the first half of 2009, the housing market quickly recovered such that the house price index was higher than pre-GFC levels again by late 2009.

In general, baby boomers have enjoyed favourable conditions during their prime working years, which have provided a significant boost to their capacity to accumulate wealth. These conditions are illustrated in Figure 1 below, where the timing of higher education funding reforms, changes in labour and housing market conditions, and the introduction of the superannuation guarantee are related to the life-course of a median baby boomer. As the Australian Bureau of Statistics (2012) defines baby boomers as individuals born between 1946 and 1966, a median boomer is defined as someone who was born during the median year of this period (i.e. 1956).

As depicted in Figure 1, the Australian Government abolished tuition fees in the higher education sector in 1974 (Jackson 2003). The median boomer would have just turned 18 years old in 1974. S/he would therefore have been commencing higher education when the abolition was implemented. It would be another 15 years before the Higher Education Contribution Scheme (HECS) was introduced in 1989, and yet another eight years before the HECS contribution rate was raised for new students and lower HECS repayment thresholds applied in 1997 (Jackson 2003). Hence, most boomers born around and after 1956 would have enjoyed access to subsidised education that allowed them to build their human capital at a relatively low financial cost.

The years spanning the 80s, 90s and the new millennium also offered favourable labour market conditions for baby boomers during their prime working years. Broadly speaking, stable labour markets prevailed during this period. Unemployment rates generally hovered below 7 per cent, with the exception of the early 1980s and early 1990s when they peaked at above 10 per cent. However, these labour market slumps were short-lived in comparison with otherwise extended periods of high employment coinciding with healthy national economic conditions. Efforts at personal wealth accumulation were of course further boosted by the introduction of the Superannuation Guarantee in 1992, when a 'median' boomer would have been 36 years old. The introduction of the Superannuation Guarantee marked the start of a minimum level of mandated employer contributions to employees' superannuation. When introduced, it covered 80 per cent of employees; by 1999, this coverage had extended to 91 per cent (Australian Taxation Office 2011).

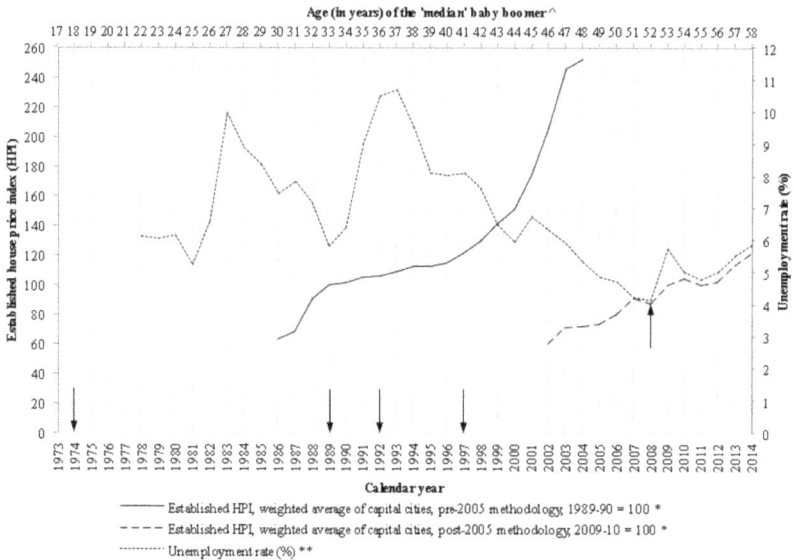

Figure 1. Higher education policies and labour and housing market conditions during the 1970s, 1980s, 1990s and new millennium

Source: Jackson (2003), Australian Bureau of Statistics (2012, 2015b, 2015c).

^ The term baby boomers refers to the cohort born between 1946 and 1966 (Australian Bureau of Statistics 2012). A 'median' baby boomer is defined as an individual born in the median year of this period, that is, 1956.

* Established house price indexes (HPIs) are available from the Australian Bureau of Statistics from 1986. The HPIs reported in this graph are taken from December of each year. In 2005, the Australian Bureau of Statistics changed its HPI methodology. Hence, the pre- and post-2005 trends are not directly comparable. However, they remain insightful with respect to highlighting peaks, troughs and exceptional trends.

** Unemployment rates are available from the Australian Bureau of Statistics from 1978 onwards. The rates reported in this graph are drawn from June of each year.

Housing market conditions played a momentous role in boosting the housing wealth of baby boomers who had owned a home by the mid-1990s. House prices soared exponentially from the mid-1990s to the early 2000s, adding tremendously to the housing asset base of home owners in those years. As shown in Figure 1, the house price index shot up from 112 to 245 between 1995 and 2003, a spike of nearly

120 per cent over an eight-year period. The decline in house prices during the GFC was reflected in just a slight dip in the house price index in 2008, followed by a quick rebound in 2009.

Various studies agree that the favourable economic circumstances that prevailed during baby boomers' wealth accumulation years are unlikely to occur again during the wealth accumulation years of subsequent generations (Olsberg and Winters 2005; Forrest and Izuhara 2009). Housing affordability has been declining over the long-run so that those who were not fortunate enough to have purchased their homes by the time the housing market boom of the mid-1990s ended have found it increasingly difficult to access home ownership. Indeed, the median dwelling price to income multiple rose from approximately four to nearly seven between the mid-1990s and the early 2000s (Fox and Finlay 2012).

Young adults are also currently forging careers within a more precarious labour market environment than baby boomers did. Beer and Faulkner (2009) note that insecure and short-term forms of employment are particularly pronounced among younger people and therefore threaten their chances of attaining first home ownership status. Furthermore, these forms of employment are incompatible with the long-term financial commitment necessary for meeting home loan repayments. Hence, those fortunate enough to break into the home ownership market may find it increasingly difficult to meet mortgage repayments given their income levels after becoming home owners. Indeed, estimates from the Australian Bureau of Statistics' Surveys of Income and Housing (SIH) show that among young home owners aged 25–34 years owing a mortgage debt, the average mortgage debt to income ratio was under 110 per cent back in 1990. However, this ratio had escalated to over 210 per cent for this age group by 2011.

In the post-GFC era, youth unemployment is once again on the rise (Australian Bureau of Statistics 2015b). Furthermore, young people on the verge of entry into higher education are facing a distinct possibility of having to pay unsubsidised tuition fees, should the tertiary sector deregulation reforms proposed in the 2014 Budget (see Hockey 2014) be implemented in some form in the near future. It is therefore conceivable that by virtue of the timing of their birth, younger generations will have fewer opportunities to accumulate economic resources than the average boomer did.

A housing asset-based system for financing aged care

The developments described above have led to a shift in policy perspective that increasingly recognises that some older Australians are in fact well positioned to tap into their personal resources to meet their care and support needs in old age. In particular, many baby boomers currently hold significant levels of housing wealth, so in various countries with high levels of home ownership, the policy direction in relation to funding both residential and community aged care has seen incremental shifts towards encouraging personal responsibility through the use of housing assets.

Government agencies in some countries have explicitly recommended the drawdown of housing equity to help pay for aged-care needs. The Productivity Commission's inquiry into the aged-care sector argues that 'many older Australians with low income have substantial wealth, which gives them the capacity to meet their lifetime accommodation costs and to make a modest contribution to the costs of their care' (Productivity Commission 2011: xxvi). Specifically, the Productivity Commission (2011: 108) has recommended a government-backed Aged Care Equity Release scheme that will allow an older home owner to use 'a maximum amount, say 40 to 60 per cent', of their housing equity to help finance their accommodation and care costs, with no or limited repayments until the ownership of the home is transferred to another individual. A similar shift has been observed in the UK, where the Dilnot Commission Report (2011) has emphasised personal responsibility as the starting point for meeting the costs of care in old age, which can be paid from income, savings, housing assets or financial products that allow equity release. Furthermore, in Australia, recently announced aged-care financing reforms have introduced national means testing and user charges for community and residential care which take into account income and assets including the primary home (Australian Department of Social Services 2014).

In light of these developments, the rest of this chapter examines the pros and cons of positioning housing wealth as an asset base for financing aged care. Specifically, the chapter explores this proposed policy direction vis-à-vis consequences for intergenerational relationships.

Arguments for using housing wealth to finance aged care

Preferential tax treatment of home ownership

The majority of Australia's housing subsidies are provided to encourage home ownership. Housing consumers have traditionally received various forms of direct and indirect subsidies from governments to assist with home purchase and with meeting housing cost burdens once they become owners. Home buyers received non-means-tested direct purchase assistance in the form of the First Home Owners Grant, as well as stamp duty concessions. Existing home owners receive preferential treatment of the family home within both the tax and income support systems. Specifically, home owners have typically enjoyed non-taxation of imputed rent, and the exemption of the family home from a range of taxes include the Goods and Services, capital gains tax and land tax. The family home has also traditionally been exempt from the assets test that determine eligibility for income-support payments such as the age pension.

In comparison to home owners, the range of subsidies available to renters is much narrower and mainly come in the form of Commonwealth Rent Assistance and public housing rebated rents that are tightly targeted at those on low incomes. The amount of housing subsidies received by owners far outweighs the amount received by renters. In their report on housing taxes and transfers commissioned by the *Australia's Future Tax System Review*, Wood et al. (2010) estimated the average housing subsidy received by private renters in 2006 at $901 (1.1 per cent of income), while home owners received an average of $2,201 (2.5 per cent of income).

Successive decades of preferential tax treatments and concessionary assets tests that exclude the primary home from means tests have promoted extensive accumulation of wealth in housing assets by home owners. Some of these favourable tax advantages would no doubt have been capitalised into house prices. Together with historically low interest rate settings, these preferential tax treatments for home owners have pushed house prices to ever higher levels in recent decades, exacerbating barriers to home purchase by the non–home owning part of the population. Furthermore, tax expenditures and means test concessions that apply to home owners only are in fact subsidised by non–home owners. Hence, concerns of inequitable treatment of owners versus renters within the current tax-transfer system could be mitigated if some of the housing wealth accumulated by home owners with the support of preferential policy parameters were diverted to fund their care needs in old age.

A growing intergenerational housing wealth gap

An important society-wide consequence of the developments described thus far is the growing gap between generations with respect to housing wealth. Table 1 compares the housing wealth of two age cohorts. Ironically, what appear to have been large economic gains for baby boomer owner-occupiers have placed the 'great Australian dream' of attaining home ownership increasingly out of the reach of younger generations, now commonly dubbed 'Generation Rent' (McKee 2012).

This growing intergenerational housing wealth gap is documented in Table 1, which compares the housing wealth of those aged 45–64 and 25–44. Households aged 45–64 in 2011 broadly comprise baby boomers, while those aged 25–44 in 2011 are drawn from Generations X and Y (Australian Bureau of Statistics 2012). Table 1 shows that in 2011, the mean housing wealth of those aged 45–64 years was 2.5 times the mean housing wealth of those aged 25–44. In absolute gap terms, the mean housing wealth of those aged 45–64 years in 2011 was over $230,000 higher than those aged 25–34 years. As such, in 2011 the average baby boomer held almost half the population's share of housing wealth, while the 25–44 age group held a comparatively smaller share of 18 per cent. This resulted in an intergenerational gap of 31 percentage points between the two age cohorts in 2011.

Table 1 further explores the housing wealth levels of the two age groups about 20 years prior. Back in 1990, the gap in mean housing wealth between the two age groups was much narrower at $92,000 (compared to $230,000 in 2011). In terms of shares, those aged 45–64 years in 1990 owned around 42 per cent of the population's housing wealth compared to a 34 per cent ownership by those aged 25–44 years. Once again, the gap between the two age groups was much smaller in 1990, at eight percentage points (compared to 31 percentage points in 2011).

Table 1: Gaps in housing wealth between those aged 45–64
and 25–44 years old, 1990 and 2011*

	1990	2011
Mean housing wealth		
25–44 years	$138,302	$149,451
45–64 years	$229,849	$379,739
Gap between age groups	$91,547	$230,288
Share of population's housing wealth		
25–44 years	34%	18%
45–64 years	42%	49%
Gap between age groups	8% points	31% points

Source: Australian Bureau of Statistics Survey of Income and Housing 1990 and 2011.

* Dollar values are reported in 2011 price levels. According to the Australian Bureau of Statistics (2015a), the Consumer Price Index (CPI) was 57.5 in 1990 and 99.3 in 2011. Hence, all 1990 values have been inflated by an inflator of 1.729 (or 99.3/57.5).

Given the estimates reported in Table 1, it is arguably reasonable on equity grounds to expect home-owning boomers to draw on some of their dividends gained (at least partially) from preferential policy treatment of the family home and the housing market boom of the late 1990s to early 2000s to finance their care needs in old age, thus relieving some of the fiscal burden that segments of the population with comparatively lower levels of housing equity would otherwise have to carry.

Intragenerational concerns within older cohorts

While intergenerational housing wealth inequities are a cause for concern, another equally worrying phenomenon is that of intragenerational housing wealth gaps within older cohorts. Thus far, the discussion has revolved around the 'average' or 'median' baby boomer, who is depicted as a home-owning individual who has made significant gains from the favourable economic conditions illustrated in Figure 1 and long-standing preferential tax treatment of owner occupation. However, in reality, significant intra-cohort variations exist among the older segment of the population. Specifically, there are some older persons who cannot benefit from the housing wealth possessed by the typical boomer owner occupier. These are the minority of older persons who do not own housing assets and therefore have comparatively much lower levels of wealth than their home-owning peers.

Estimates from the SIH show that in 2011, approximately one-quarter of persons aged 45–64 years did not own the dwelling they lived in. Over the long-run, the non-home-owning population in this age group has grown in proportionate terms. In 1990, non–home owners made up a comparatively lower one-fifth of the population aged 45–64 years.

These older non–home owners principally comprise lifetime renters who have not had opportunities to accumulate housing wealth or those unfortunate enough to lose home ownership through adverse life events such as divorce or ill-health. Ong et al. (2014) find that among persons aged 45 years and over during the decade 2001–10, around 742,000 spells of home ownership ended with a move out of owner occupation during the decade. The study also found that those who lose home ownership as a result of some unfavourable biographical event such as marital breakdown, bereavement or long-term health conditions are at increased risk of needing publicly funded rental housing assistance in older age.

Older Australian renters who do not own housing assets will be particularly adversely affected if governments are forced to cut spending on housing assistance, income support or care and support services to address long-term budget deficits. Colic-Peisker et al. (2014) highlighted the detrimental effect that asset poverty has on older Australians' ontological security and found that some older renters have had to severely restrict non–housing consumption in order to cope with meeting housing costs post-retirement. Hence, fiscal savings derived from home owners' use of personal assets to finance their aged care would ease the burden on taxpayer funding of care and support for the elderly who do not have access to housing wealth.

Mitigating intergenerational transmission of advantage

Bequest motives are often cited as an argument against the drawdown of equity. However, intergenerational transfers of assets through bequests or inter-vivos transfers may entrench and in some cases exacerbate existing wealth inequality (Angel and Mudrazija 2011; Searle and McCollum 2014). There is a consensus in the international literature that those who come from affluent socioeconomic backgrounds are most likely to receive substantial intergenerational transfers (Kohli 1999; Rowlingson and McKay 2005). Indeed, estimates from the nationally representative Household, Income and Labour

Dynamics in Australia (HILDA) Survey confirm exactly this pattern. The data shows that 26 per cent of bequest recipients in 2011 already resided in an advantaged area[1] in the year prior to receiving the bequest as compared to 20 per cent of those who did not receive bequests in 2011. Furthermore, 72 per cent of bequest recipients were individuals who could themselves easily raise emergency funds compared to 60 per cent of non-recipients. Bequest recipients also possess more well-developed human capital than non-recipients; 77 per cent of bequest recipients in 2011 were already employed in the year prior to receiving the bequest compared to 69 per cent of non-recipients, and 36 per cent of bequest recipients in 2011 had a university qualification compared to 24 per cent of non-recipients. Hence, encouraging equity release by those who can afford it to provide for their own care needs might in fact go some way towards combating the entrenchment of wealth inequality associated with intergenerational transmission of advantage.

In addition, bequests are typically received later in the life-course due to longer life expectancies among aged parents. Thus, the timing of intergenerational wealth transfers through bequests is often not early enough in the life-course to assist young adults at a time when they are purchasing their first home. The 2011 HILDA Survey data shows that the median age at which Australians receive intergenerational transfers through bequests is 49 years old, by which time over three-quarters of bequest recipients have already bought their own homes.

At a macro level, the rationale for encouraging a shift to the use of personal housing assets to finance aged care is therefore obvious. Such a policy reform has the potential to promote intergenerational equity by reducing the fiscal burden on younger cohorts who presently have lower chances of attaining home ownership than similarly aged cohorts did in past decades and (at least partially) addressing the perpetuation of wealth inequality associated with intergenerational transmission of advantage to young cohorts from affluent backgrounds. The reform would also weaken the prospect of government-funding cuts to support systems in core areas such as housing, income and care that would have more acute consequences for older Australians with low asset levels than those who possess housing wealth.

---

1   This is defined as the top two deciles of the Australian Bureau of Statistics' index of relative socioeconomic advantage/disadvantage.

Arguments against using housing wealth to finance aged care

Threats to intergenerational reciprocity

Despite some obvious benefits in adopting a housing asset-based aged-care financing strategy, decisions about asset use and economic provisioning in old age are often complex, and plagued with difficulties. First and foremost is the emotional attachment that owner occupiers and their children have towards the family home. The housing assets of elderly parents are often viewed not just as their personal resources, but as the future inheritance of their children. Equity release by elderly parents might understandably be unpopular if they have the potential to fracture family relationships where adult children had expected to inherit their parents' assets. Indeed, Ong et al. (2013) found that children who are expecting to benefit from inheriting their elderly parents' homes often express concerns about the use of debt finance (e.g. reverse mortgages) by their parents to draw down on the wealth stored in the family home and may get actively involved in decisions by elderly parents with regards to the use of their housing assets. Hence, under a housing asset-based aged-care financing system, some elderly persons will likely face a dilemma at the family level in relation to balancing their desire to transfer as much of their housing assets as possible to their adult children against meeting their personal need for adequate care in old age.

The intra-familial scenario described above is but one example of the complexities that govern the links between intergenerational wealth transfers and intergenerational reciprocity in care. Previous studies have cautioned that a lack of intergenerational asset accumulation may weaken traditional ties between the old and the young, resulting in resentment and growing unwillingness among working-age adults to care for the elderly (see, for example, Hudson 1999). Angel and Mudrazija (2011: 170) note that:

> it would be naïve to think that human motivations are solely altruistic or that we possess an unlimited capacity for self-sacrifice ... a system in which the accumulation of assets ties one generation to the next is one in which bonds of generational reciprocity and affection are maximised. Conversely, a system in which the material ties between children and parents are weak faces the risk of turning the young and the old into strangers.

Even if adult children are supportive of their parents releasing some housing equity for funding personal aged-care needs, financial risks and impediments exist. These financial risks and impediments, as described below, can act to significantly reduce housing assets below levels that are intended for bequest purposes unless adequate safeguards are put in place to counter their impacts on equity levels in old age.

Financial risks and barriers

Any financing strategy that is housing asset–based is predicated on the assumption that investment in 'bricks and mortar' will yield significant returns as house prices continue to rise over the long-term. To date, the Australian housing market has proven to be remarkably resilient even throughout the GFC. However, recent economic events worldwide have undeniably highlighted some risks of relying on housing as a vehicle for supporting retirement needs. Housing asset values are also thought to be more vulnerable to changing consumer sentiments because of greater difficulty in determining true asset values (Shiller 2005; Baker and Wurgler 2007). Furthermore, housing assets are a unique financial investment in that the risks associated with future house price movements cannot be hedged (Shiller 2003). House price volatility can expose home owners who engage in equity release to undesirable levels of house price risks. These risks in turn have the potential to significantly reduce the value of housing assets unless government policy establishes a floor in retained levels of equity.

Another financial concern exists in the form of repayment risk, for those who use equity release products to withdraw housing equity. Baby boomers currently aged 45–64 years are now exhibiting higher degrees of mortgage indebtedness compared to similarly aged cohorts in the past. Long-run trends from the SIH show that the proportion of home owners with a mortgage debt has increased in every age group between 1990 and 2011, but this rise in indebtedness has been the steepest (around 30 percentage points) amongst home owners aged 45–64 years. The incidence of mortgage indebtedness jumped from 38 per cent to 70 per cent among those aged 45–54 years, and from 15 per cent to 44 per cent among those aged 55–64 years between 1990 and 2011. These statistics are complemented by evidence from the 2001 and 2010 HILDA Survey showing that the proportion of boomer owners, who engaged in equity release by increasing debt against their primary home, rose over the decade from 18 per cent to 24 per cent among those aged 45–54 years and 8 per cent to 16 per cent among those aged 55–64 years. These higher levels of mortgage debt can leave baby boomers more precariously positioned financially, with only a limited number of years left in the workforce to pay off their mortgage debt. These risks are augmented should adverse life events such as divorce, unemployment or ill health befall boomers who have not yet paid off their mortgage debt.

% of owners with a mortgage debt

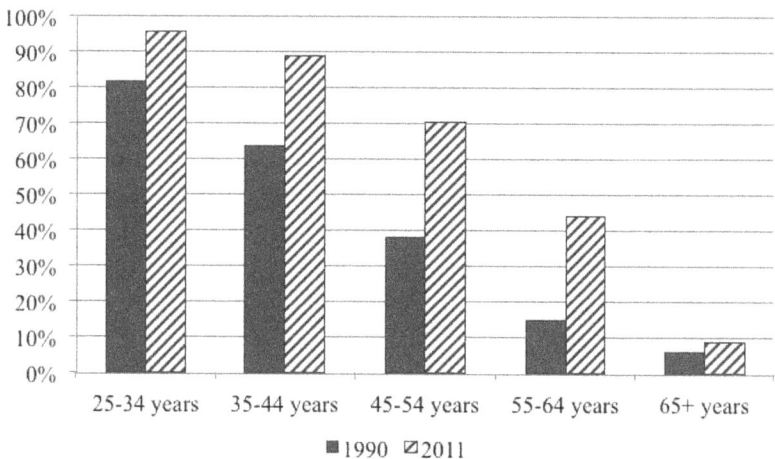

1990   2011

Figure 2. Incidence of mortgage indebtedness amongst home owners, 1990 and 2011

Source: Authors own calculations from the confidentialised unit record files of the Australian Bureau of Statistics Survey of Income and Housing 1990 and 2011.

Government could play an effective role in promoting the acceptance of equity release products for financing aged-care needs, by providing insurance against its downside risks. Indeed, there are several international developments that provide evidence on the merits of such government involvement, such as in the case of the Home Equity Conversion Mortgage (HECM) product in the United States. The HECM is federally insured and therefore the risk is transferred to the Federal Housing Administration, allowing eligible older home owners to release the equity stored in their home in a secure manner (Federal Housing Administration 2010). The HECM is typically considered a safe option for equity release in the United States, where it accounts for a dominant share of the equity release market (Alai et al. 2013). At the same time, Beal (2001) has pointed out that the development of an equity-release market that caters for the elderly is unlikely to be smooth where its development is not facilitated by the government. More recently, the Productivity Commission (2011: 106) makes a similar observation by noting that a 'government-backed … equity release scheme may be more acceptable to some older people. The higher uptake of government-sponsored schemes, relative to private provider schemes, in the US suggests that the added security from government backing can help dispel nervousness about using the products.'

Releasing housing equity via the traditional sale method can mitigate some of the repayment risk concerns associated with the use of equity release products. However, transaction costs may deter home owners considering downsizing because they represent a significant upfront cost on their next purchase. Economists have long opposed the stamp duty because it is an inefficient tax that deters residential mobility and has adverse impacts on home purchase affordability. Indeed, Ong et al. (2013) found that during the period 2001–10, stamp duties ate into 8 to 10 per cent of the housing equity that home owners aged 45+ released via downsizing.

In addition, Judd et al. (2014) identified some major housing market difficulties associated with downsizing in later life. These include a lack of suitable housing types and locations, as well as concerns over the affordability of housing. There seems to be a general consensus that older Australians increasingly wish to age in place for as long as possible. This often involves emotional attachment not just to one's home, to one's neighbourhood. Hence, those who are willing to downsize often express a strong desire to do so within the same area so as to maintain links with their community in old age (Ong et al. 2013; Judd et al. 2014). However, home owners often face difficulties with finding an affordable property within the same neighbourhood to downsize into. Tackling inefficient taxes such as the stamp duty through policy reform would go some way towards alleviating the emotional impact and practical difficulties that often accompany downsizing. For instance, Wood et al. (2012a, 2012b) has provided empirical evidence that the abolition of stamp duty and its replacement by a broad-based land tax would promote residential mobility by reducing upfront cost barriers and mitigate affordability concerns because a broad-based land tax burden will be capitalised into lower land prices. Such a reform has the potential to tackle both mobility and affordability concerns that are impediments to downsizing.

Concluding comments

It is unsurprising that governments are increasingly looking towards those with sufficient assets in old age to contribute to their cost of being supported and cared for in old age. The pressure on individuals to assume greater responsibility for their aged-care needs will only intensify in the coming years, as governments strive to manage the fiscal challenges of accelerated rates of population ageing, especially among the oldest-old.

There are some strong intergenerational equity arguments for instituting housing wealth as a pillar of aged-care policy. If older home owners were enabled to draw on some of their housing wealth to contribute to the funding of their aged-care needs, it would no doubt relieve intergenerational equity concerns at a macro level. However, more research needs to be done to unearth and disentangle the potentially complex links between intergenerational asset accumulation and intergenerational reciprocity to avert the undesirable consequence of alienating the young from the old. Furthermore, much more work needs to done to devise equity release products that allow elderly home owners to draw down on their housing wealth in a secure manner that will leave them with an appropriate minimum level of equity. An in-depth assessment would be required of the multitude of risks (and associated solutions) at each stage of product development, including product design, regulatory framework, pricing, etc.

Policy support for family models of caring for aged parents may alleviate the need for releasing equity to access formal aged-care services and thus avoid some of the more intricate difficulties associated with equity and equality discussed in this chapter. Informal housing and care arrangements often provide opportunities for two-way intergenerational support. For instance, elderly grandparents who provided childcare for grandchildren in earlier years may benefit from family reciprocity in the form of aged care from their adult children when frailty sets in. The leakage of housing wealth outside the family, which typically occurs through the use of equity to pay for formal care services, is averted when family members enter into informal housing and care arrangements within a multigenerational household context. However, informal care solutions are not without its challenges, and will have to be crafted thoughtfully with sufficient safeguards for the wellbeing of all family members.

At a macro level, there also exists a long-standing conflict between the provision of informal care to family members and participation in the paid labour market. For instance, international studies have consistently found that working-age carers who provide informal care for ill, frail or disabled family members typically have depressed levels of labour force participation compared to those who do not carry these care responsibilities (see for instance, Austen and Ong 2010; Carmichael et al. 2008). The issue is particularly pronounced among women, who are over-represented among informal carers. Here, policies will need to carefully navigate the tension between encouraging household production of aged care services and lifting economic productivity vis-à-vis greater labour force participation, both of which are necessary policy ambitions to address fiscal challenges in an era of population ageing.

Acknowledgements

This chapter uses unit record data from the Household, Income and Labour Dynamics in Australia (HILDA) Survey. The HILDA Project was initiated and funded by the Australian Government Department of Social Services and is managed by the Melbourne Institute of Applied Economic and Social Research. The author would like to thank Mike Woods for offering helpful suggestions and comments on the chapter. The findings and views reported in this chapter, however, are those of the author and should not be attributed to any other individual or organisation.

References

Alai Daniel, Chen Hua, Cho Daniel, Hanewald Katja and Sherris Michael (2013). *Developing Equity Release Markets: Risk Analysis for Reverse Mortgages and Home Reversions*, Working Paper No. 2013/01, ARC Centre for Excellence in Population Ageing Research.

Angel Jacqueline and Mudrazija Stipica (2011). Aging, inheritance, and gift-giving. In RH Binstock and LK George (Eds) *Handbook of Aging and the Social Sciences* (7th edition). San Diego: Academic Press, pp. 163–173.

Austen S and Ong R (2010). The employment transitions of mid-life women: Health and care effects. *Ageing and Society*, 30(2): 207–227.

Australian Bureau of Statistics (2012). *Reflecting a Nation: Stories from the 2011 Census,* Canberra: Australian Bureau of Statistics.

Australian Bureau of Statistics (2015a). *Consumer Price Index, Australia, Time Series Workbook*, Cat. No. 6401.0, Canberra: Australian Bureau of Statistics.

Australian Bureau of Statistics (2015b). *Labour Force, Australia, Time Series Workbook*, Cat. No. 6202.0, Canberra: Australian Bureau of Statistics.

Australian Bureau of Statistics (2015c). *Residential Property Price Indexes: Eight Capital Cities, Time Series Workbook*, Cat. No. 6416.0, Canberra: Australian Bureau of Statistics.

Australian Department of Social Services (2014). Aged Care Means Test Assessments. www.humanservices.gov.au/customer/services/aged-care-means-test-assessments.

Australian Taxation Office (2011). *20 Years of Superannuation Guarantee*, www.ato.gov.au/Media-centre/Commissioners-online-updates/20-years-of-super-guarantee/.

Baker Malcolm and Wurgler Jeffrey (2007). Investor sentiment in the stock market. *Journal of Economic Perspectives*, 21(2): 129–151.

Beal Diana (2001). Home equity conversion in Australia—issues, impediments and Possible solutions, *Economic Papers*, 20(4): 55–68.

Beer Andrew and Faulkner Deborah (2009). *21st Century Housing Careers and Australia's Housing Future*, Final Report No. 128, Melbourne: Australian Housing and Urban Research Institute.

Carmichael Fiona, Hulme Claire, Sheppard Sally and Connell Gemma (2008). Work-life imbalance: Informal care and paid employment in the UK. *Feminist Economics*, 14(2): 3–35.

Colic-Peisker Val, Ong Rachel and Wood Gavin (2014, published online). Asset poverty, precarious housing and ontological security in older age: An Australian case study. *International Journal of Housing Policy*. doi: 10.1080/14616718.2014.984827.

Commonwealth of Australia (2015). *2015 Intergenerational Report: Australia in 2055*. Canberra: Department of Treasury. www.treasury.gov.au/PublicationsAndMedia/Publications/2015/2015-Intergenerational-Report

Daley John and Wood Danielle (2014). *The Wealth of Generations*, Melbourne: GRATTAN Institute. grattan.edu.au/report/thewealth-of-generations/.

Dilnot Andrew, Warner Norman and Williams Jo (2011). *Fairer Care Funding: The Report of the Commission on Funding of Care and Support*. London: UK Commission on Funding of Care and Support, Final Report. www.thirdsectorsolutions.net/index.php?id=75.

Federal Housing Administration (2010). *Consumer Fact Sheet for Home Equity Conversion Mortgages (HECM)*, 1 November. portal.hud.gov/hudportal/documents/huddoc?id=DOC13006.pdf.

Forrest Ray and Izuhara Misa (2009). Exploring the demographic location of housing wealth in East Asia. *Journal of Asian Public Policy*, 2(2): 209–221.

Fox Ryan and Finlay Richard (2012). Dwelling prices and household income. *Bulletin*, December quarter: 13–22.

Girouard Nathalie, Kennedy Mike, van den Noord Paul and André Christophe (2006). *Recent House Price Developments: The Role of Fundamentals*, OECD Economics Department Working Papers, No. 475, OECD Publishing. dx.doi.org/10.1787/864035447847.

Hockey Joe (2014). *Budget Speech 2014–15*, 13 May, www.budget.gov. au/2014-15/content/speech/html/speech.htm.

Hudson Robert (1999). Conflict in today's aging politics: new population encounters old ideology. *Social Service Review*, 73: 358–379.

Jackson K (2003). *Higher Education Funding Policy*, Parliament of Australia, www.aph.gov.au/About_Parliament/Parliamentary_ Departments/Parliamentary_Library/Publications_Archive/ archive/hefunding.

Judd Bruce, Liu Edgar, Easthope Hazel, Davy Laura and Bridge Catherine (2014). Downsizing Amongst Older Australians, Final Report No. 214, Australian Housing and Urban Research Institute, Melbourne.

Kohli Martin (1999). Private and public transfers between generations: linking the family and the state. *European Societies*, 1(1): 81–104.

McKee Kim (2012). Young people, homeownership and future welfare. *Housing Studies*, 27(6): 853–862.

Olsberg Diana and Winters Mark (2005). *Ageing in Place: Intergenerational and Intrafamilial Housing Transfers and Shifts in Later Life*, Final Report No. 88, Melbourne: Australian Housing and Urban Research Institute.

Ong Rachel, Jefferson Therese, Wood Gavin, Haffner Marietta and Austen Siobhan (2013). *Housing Equity Withdrawal: Uses, Risks, and Barriers to Alternative Mechanisms in Later Life*, Final Report No. 217, Melbourne: Australian Housing and Urban Research Institute.

Ong Rachel, Wood Gavin and Colic-Peisker Val (2014). Housing older Australians: Loss of homeownership and pathways into housing assistance. *Urban Studies*, published online. doi: 10.1177/0042098014550955.

Productivity Commission (2011). *Caring for older Australians*, Report No. 53, Final Inquiry Report, Canberra: Productivity Commission.

Rowlingson Karen and McKay Stephen (2005). *Attitudes to Inheritance in Britain*. York: Joseph Rowntree Foundation.

Searle Beverley and McCollum David (2014). Property-based welfare and the search for generational equality. *International Journal of Housing Policy*, 14(4) 325–343. doi: 10.1080/14616718.2014.955334.

Shiller Robert (2003). *The New Financial Order: Risk in the 21st Century*. Princeton, New Jersey: Princeton University Press.

Shiller Robert (2005). *Irrational Exuberance*. Princeton, New Jersey: Princeton University Press.

Wood Gavin, Stewart Miranda and Ong Rachel (2010). *Housing Taxation and Transfers*, Final Report, Research Study for the Review of Australia's Future Tax System, taxreview.treasury.gov.au/content/html/commissioned_work/downloads/wood_stewart_and_ong.pdf.

Wood Gavin, Ong Rachel and Winter Ian (2012a). Stamp duties, land tax and housing affordability: The case for reform. *Australian Tax Forum*, 27(2): 331–349.

Wood Gavin, Ong Rachel, Cigdem Melek and Taylor Elizabeth (2012b). *The Spatial and Distributional Impacts of the Henry Review Recommendations on Stamp Duty and Land Tax*, Final Report No. 182, Melbourne: Australian Housing and Urban Research Institute.

14

Conclusions: An historic triumph that presents big challenges for public policy

Andrew Podger

The first conclusion from all the material presented in this book concerns the scale of the changes underway, both nationally and internationally. They are perhaps the most significant demographic changes in human history, building on the dramatic reductions in infant mortality over the last century or so and the fall in fertility rates over the last half-century (the precise timing varying significantly amongst different countries), leading to substantial increases in life expectancy at older ages as well as more people reaching old age. These changes will be permanent, requiring fundamental and ongoing re-conceptions of the life-span of individuals and the age profile of societies, affecting family and community relationships as well as individuals' planning for lifetime wellbeing. As a result, we need perhaps to consider the idea of 'multiple beings' over the life-span with individuals choosing more and different roles at different ages.

A second idea that comes through is the need to cease thinking of the changes as representing a crisis, and to see them as a triumph as per the evidence in Gong and Kendig. They are the result of a series of indisputably positive developments—lower child and other mortality at young and middle ages, more choice and control over fertility, and now more years of healthy living in old age. The conversation needs to shift to how we can take full advantage of the changes.

The policy implications relate to the goals of both individuals and society as a whole, and the capacity of governments to facilitate their achievement. For individuals, the goals include maintaining good physical and mental health, preserving independence and ability to control their lives and exercise choice, being socially connected and being treated with dignity and respect, and having personal security. These goals require access to personally appropriate services, whether provided by government or the market or through social organisations.

Achieving broader social wellbeing requires the optimal use of human resources and social capital. Pakulski suggests that Australia's '3Ps' (population, productivity and participation) strategy has been relatively successful in this regard, a strategy to which he adds a fourth 'P' (provisions) to meet the financial impact of demographic change on pensions, health services and aged care. One advantage of this approach is that it addresses both sides of the ledger: factors that may facilitate continued economic growth and opportunities for improved wellbeing, and cost factors associated with population ageing. Similarly, it combines mitigation and adaptation. Importantly, however, social wellbeing also concerns social cohesion and inclusion, and stability.

In supporting the achievement of individual and social goals, governments need to distinguish between the exogenous factors society (and government) must adjust to, and the things governments can influence. The exogenous factors are not just the demographic changes underway (immigration may continue to moderate the impact, as McDonald notes), but also the structure of the Australian economy and our broad social values and relationships and associated expectations, and any economic turbulence, particularly global turbulence. Governments may be able to influence labour markets, insurance and superannuation and to provide social protection, to smooth transition to new demographic or economic circumstances, to facilitate effective and efficient health- and aged-care services, and to support social engagement through appropriate infrastructure, urban design and access to information. These form a broad menu of possible policy responses.

Social and economic participation

Central to future labour market and social policies is that the concept of 'retirement' needs reconsideration. Rather than being a point-in-time transition, retirement is increasingly a process taking place over a lengthy period. Various contributors highlight how varied that process is amongst individuals (for example, McDonald, Kendig and Browning, Hall and van Gool). They also suggest the likelihood of the process lengthening in future and the variations widening.

Accordingly, the idea of a fixed 'retirement age' needs to be rejected, though for superannuation and social security purposes ages do need to be identified for eligibility for government support. The challenge is to set such eligibility rules in a way that recognises the process of retirement and offers people reasonable choice about the process that best suits them (and best protects those with limited means and ability to work) while not imposing undue costs on the community.

A focus on people choosing how they transition into retirement, rather than facing a fixed retirement age, requires that they have the necessary information and advice, and personal competence, to make their decisions wisely. There is a need to simplify Australia's complicated superannuation and social security system (as Bateman emphasises). It also assumes there is a wide range of options open from which people can choose.

While workforce participation has increased in recent years amongst those over 55, there remains considerable room for improvement in the range of employment options offered by employers. Some shift can be expected as the age profile of labour supply changes (with total numbers aged under 55 slowing significantly) but, as Ryan highlights, more effort could be made to ensure flexible hours, part-time work, suitable contract arrangements, appropriate insurance and compensation arrangements, and so on. Some serious cultural change needs to occur and governments could facilitate this by the sort of structural adjustment programs used over the years for industry restructuring.

Retraining and continued education in old age should be part of such structural adjustment, and is likely to continue as an element of the cultural change required. For some, however, employment opportunities are constrained from a much earlier age—from leaving school—casting a shadow over their capacity to participate when reaching their 50s and 60s. Efforts to improve opportunities in old age must therefore include improving participation in school education and ensuring post-school training offers opportunities for continued up-skilling and new skills development.

While more opportunities for continued participation in the paid workforce are needed, given the increasing numbers of people in this older but active age group, the idea of continued contribution is not limited to paid work. Already many are involved in family caring responsibilities (as grandparents, or as children or spouses of frail-aged people) and in volunteering work. There may be room to widen opportunities in these areas and to make the contributions more productive by suitable training or other support. Such contributions can, however, be burdens rather than 'opportunities' pursued by choice; and those concerned may need support while providing care, and may also need opportunities to participate actively but differently as and when their caring responsibilities cease.

Governments should facilitate choice, ensuring opportunities for continued participation and contribution to society, but also ensure that those bearing the risks involved are able to manage them. Governments need to recognise that their policies may influence the choices being made, being careful not to encourage decisions that are not in people's best interests.

The emphasis on choice extends to the choice between 'work' and 'leisure', and the mix of the two as people transition to retirement. One of the most beneficial aspects of economic growth is to reduce the drudgery of work, making work more pleasant and satisfying and allowing more time for leisure. Today's policymakers and advisers might do well to revisit John Stuart Mills' 'gospel of leisure' as opposed to the 'gospel of work' propounded by some of the moralists of his time:

> In opposition to the 'gospel of work', I would assert the gospel of leisure, and maintain that human beings cannot rise to the finer attributes of their nature compatibly with a life filled with labour. I do not include under the name labour such work ... as is done by writers and afforders of 'guidance', an occupation which, let alone the vanity of the thing, cannot be called by the same name with the real

labour, the exhausting, stiffening, stupefying toil of … agricultural and manufacturing labourers. To reduce very greatly the quantity of work required to carry on existence is as needful as to distribute it more equally; and the progress of science, and the increasing ascendancy of justice and good sense, tend to the result. (John Stuart Mill (1850), quoted in Castles 2014)

Society and governments should not press for increased workforce participation as a goal in itself: better opportunities and better use of available human resources will almost certainly involve increased workforce participation amongst the able-aged, but people should also be free to choose the mix of work and leisure in their lifetimes, subject to their being able to manage the risks associated with their choices, and those choices not being unduly influenced by government (including by too ready availability of taxpayer support).

Health and wellbeing

Health and wellbeing implications of our ageing population are explored by various contributors in this volume, including in respect of income security, physical and mental health, social engagement and housing. A number of public policy concerns arise either explicitly or implicitly.

Several contributors (particularly Bateman and Piggott) highlight the complexity of the current retirement income system and the problems in the 'de-accumulation phase' in particular, notwithstanding the many strengths of Australia's arrangements. The strengths relate in large part to the extent to which the system involves the spreading of individuals' lifetime earnings rather than relying on public and private transfers, by mandating and encouraging superannuation savings, as well as the way it protects the poor and those with limited savings. Indeed, the World Bank and some other international observers see this defined contribution and funded approach, (with the safety net of the means-tested age pension) as a benchmark for good practice. It is seen as providing guidance for how other countries might design contributions and eligibility for benefits in their defined benefits schemes (World Bank 1994, 2008; Podger et al. 2014). On the other hand, it would be better if the Australian system had, as a more prominent benchmark in its de-accumulation phase, the sort of standards that 'defined benefit' schemes use, particularly in terms of income replacement rates and continuing secure lifetime income streams. A specific problem to be addressed is the extent to which people pass on their tax-supported superannuation to the next generation (and the extent to which the next generation feels entitled to estates enhanced by tax-supported savings), or run out of savings and rely too heavily on the age pension.

The age pension remains an important 'pillar' in Australia's retirement income system, ensuring an adequate safety net for those with limited superannuation savings. But 'adequacy' will not be maintained simply by maintaining real rates of pension as was originally proposed in the 2014–15 Budget. Over time, social security payments need to be adjusted to maintain relativities with incomes across the community.

The complexity of the Australian system, and the degree to which individuals bear the risks, suggests the need to consider wider use of default mechanisms to guide individuals, as well as better support for managing the risk of longevity. The Murray Report on the Financial System recommends some modest moves in this direction (Murray 2014) but more effort may be required. Regular 'check-ups' at different stages in the life-span would help people review their investment, accumulation and de-accumulation arrangements during the period from age 50 to age 70 (or more) so they can be confident of achieving their planned retirement incomes; such check-ups might also offer people default options that guide them towards suitable retirement income outcomes.

While there is some uncertainty about whether Australia's high rate of home ownership will continue amongst future cohorts of older people, the possibility of drawing on those assets more efficiently and effectively could help older people to live more comfortably. As Ong suggests, this could also help to fund the increasing costs of aged care particularly in the context of older Australians seeking more choice over their care and accommodation when very old. The Productivity Commission's proposals, which include a form of social insurance (by capping individuals' care costs), offer one possible approach promoting more choice and greater efficiency by relaxing supply-side controls and relying more heavily on user pays and competition (Productivity Commission 2011).

The increasing numbers of older Australians will also have an impact on politics. A key question will be whether they exercise their greater voting power to promote self-interest or to contribute more wisdom and experience into public policy deliberations. The latter may be more likely if older Australians not only increase their increased social and economic participation, but also their participation in political processes such as through political parties, think tanks and other forums for informed dialogue and debate, and by standing for parliament. Such participation could be encouraged if parties, public service organisations, think tanks, universities and parliaments put more effort into networks of expertise and experience amongst people no longer holding full-time positions utilising their skills.

Increasing social and economic participation amongst older people is reliant upon their continued good health and capacity even as it in turn will contribute to wellbeing. While years of good health are increasing, there is more that can be done to enhance health at older ages (recognising that 'good health' needs some calibration as people get older).

Public health and health promotion, and early diagnosis and treatment, are often cost-effective ways to enhance health and independent living, and ability to participate, as Hall and van Gool suggest. They include community effort to support exercise and good dietary practice, and systematic screening and other diagnoses based on evidence of risks. Governments may be able to help by 'making the healthy choice the easy choice' such as through promotional activity and appropriate rewards and penalties for service providers and/or consumers; civil society organisations can also play an important role both in offering information and in facilitating voluntary activities.

Cognitive capacity is particularly important and the evidence Anstey presents of ways in which such capacity can be sustained more effectively offers the potential for significant improvement in the future. It seems that, as with other aspects of healthy living, cognitive capacity at older ages is also related to prolonged mental engagement and healthy living at younger ages. Having some 'cognitive reserve' is highly relevant to the theme of choice and informed decision-making that permeates this book; it is also critical to continued capacity to adjust to new technology and new information.

The evidence of wide variations in the health pathway through older years of life identified by Hall and van Gool also suggests the need for the health and care system to be much more responsive to individual circumstances. A shift from a service-oriented system to a person-oriented one might help to 'normalise old age', by treating older people as individuals with individual needs and preferences just as younger people expect to be treated in their day-to-day lives as workers and consumers and family members. This shift will take time as it will require considerable adjustment by suppliers of goods and services as well as changes in government programs and in consumer behaviour.

In promoting such a shift, governments need to recognise that the supports available to individuals vary significantly, including as a result of changes in marriage and divorce at younger ages (as McDonald notes). There is also a group experiencing deep and persistent poverty whose access to health services as well as social and economic support remains limited. A particular example, which Hall and van Gool mention, is lack of access to dental health services: poor dental health is now a critical indicator of deep disadvantage, reinforcing social isolation.

Suggestions about promoting health, distinguishing between age and age-related disability, and redesigning health and aged-care systems to be person-oriented rather than service-oriented, raises the challenge of applying a wider definition of wellbeing. Such wellbeing is linked to individual factors such as contentedness and independence (the ability to exercise control), feelings and spirituality, and also to societal factors such as the respect society has for older people, how much they value them and their views and experience, and how well younger people want to connect with them, as Windsor, Curtis and Luszcz, and Burns and Browning identify. Burns and Browning also refer to a UK initiative to promote wellbeing based on five actions— connect, be active, take notice (and give time), keep learning and give (contribute)—that may be worth monitoring to see the extent to which it is possible for government and civil society to influence social attitudes and improve wellbeing (Foresight Report 2008).

Specific approaches to building and sustaining active participation include measures to strengthen family, social and community engagement through communications technology and improved transport arrangements. Recognising the current and potential contributions of older people is a pre-condition for their more active participation, and warrants investment, such as in training to be members of NGO boards or to be more effective volunteers in a wide range of community services, or training in child health or elderly care.

In addition to the wide variations in pathways through older ages, there is a wide diversity amongst older population groups including on the basis of ethnicity, Aboriginality, and geographic location (particularly urban versus regional and rural). A more personally responsive approach to promoting health and wellbeing will address this diversity in part, but there also needs to be recognition of for example, the language needs of different population groups and each one's shared interests and values. Variations in the 'density' of older populations in different geographic areas will also impact upon the capacity to engage, the nature of the engagement and the supports required and able to be provided.

Conclusion

The ageing of our population, both in Australia and internationally, represents a profound historic development. A triumph, not a crisis; an enhancement of our overall wellbeing.

Taking advantage of the opportunities involved will, however, require serious societal reflection about the emerging demographic profile and about life-courses over longer life-spans, and also some deft public policy responses. These should facilitate informed choices by individuals looking to maximise their own lifetime wellbeing and that of their families, while recognising a wider diversity of circumstances and the need to protect the vulnerable and to ensure risks are allocated according to who (individually or collectively) is best able to manage them.

References

Foresight Report (2008). *Making the most of ourselves in the 21st century: Final project report*. London: Government Office for Science Mental Capital and Wellbeing.

Castles Ian (2014). Economics and Anti-Economics. In Andrew Podger and Dennis Trewin (Eds) *Measuring and Promoting Wellbeing: How Important is Economic Growth*. Canberra: ANU Press, pp. 92–93.

Commonwealth of Australia (2014). Financial System Inquiry Final Report. A Final Report, Canberra: Financial System Inquiry.

Podger Andrew, Stanton David, Whiteford Peter (2014). Designing Social Security Systems: Learning from Australia and Other Countries. *Public Administration and Development*, 34(4), 231–250.

Productivity Commission (2011). *Caring for Older Australians*, Productivity Commission Inquiry Report No. 53, Canberra: Productivity Commission.

World Bank (1994). *Averting the old age crisis: Policies to protect the old and promote growth*. Washington DC: Oxford University Press.

World Bank (2008). *The World Bank Pension Conceptual Framework*, World Bank Pension Primer Series. Washington DC: World Bank Group.

Appendix 1: International perspectives and global benchmarking

Hal Kendig and Lisa Cannon

New ways of thinking about ageing are emerging in international directions on ageing:

The United Nations, while long preoccupied with children's and women's issues in developing countries, is developing more of a balanced life-span perspective. In *Transforming our World: The 2030 Agenda for Sustainable Development*, Goal 3 is to 'Ensure healthy lives and promote well-being for all at all ages' (UN 2015). It also is leading action to establish a Convention on the Human Rights of Older People.

The World Health Organization, which pioneered the Active Ageing and Age Friendly Cities initiatives, released a comprehensive *World Report on Ageing and Health* (WHO 2015), setting further initiatives in healthy ageing and wellbeing along with references to a substantial evidence base. WHO defines 'active ageing' as 'the process of optimising opportunities for health, participation, and security in order to enhance quality of life as people age' (WHO 2002: 12).

The World Bank, which a generation ago launched its pessimistic and influential report *Averting the Old Age Crisis* (1994), has more recently viewed health as an important investment (not just expenditure) for national investment. Its European office has commented that pension reform in Europe is moving towards sustainability in most nations.

Non-government organisations—notably HelpAge International, the International Longevity Centre, and the International Association of Gerontology—are providing advocacy and leadership in progressing positive approaches to ageing including important initiatives in the Asia-Pacific region (e.g. Kendig and Lucas 2014).

Another important contribution by international organisations is to 'benchmark' progress being made by member countries and to support evidence-based reforms. The United Nations and the International Labour Organization, for example, provide ongoing, robust, and comparable data on population and employment respectively. To complement these contributions HelpAge International with the support of Manchester University, has produced the annual Global AgeWatch (2015) report of country rankings on older people for wellbeing outcomes. These include income security, health status, capability (including employment and education), and enabling environments (including social connections, safety, and perceived freedom).

Table A.1 provides the AgeWatch population dimensions and wellbeing outcomes for Australia and comparator countries of the UK, USA, and New Zealand as well as China and Japan in our Asian region (Chapter 4). Poland is also included as a European comparator country (Chapter 6), which has a history of strong migration links with Australia. Before interpreting the tables, it is important to caution that anomalies of definition nonetheless remain and the results should be interpreted cautiously. The ranking of countries are shown because this is arguable more useful than trying to make sense of absolute measures and their technical definitions. The rankings are shown out of 96 countries for which data is available.

These findings can be summarised as follows:

- Japan has a much older population, while the other countries are broadly comparable, and China is slightly younger. However, by mid-century, China and Poland are projected to approach Japan's level of population ageing, while Australia and the other Western countries are projected to have a slower pace of ageing.

- Life expectancy and healthy life expectancy at age 60 are comparably high across the developed countries, with China six years behind the leaders.

- On the global measure of health status, Australia and New Zealand approach Japan as the world leader, while the UK and USA lag appreciably, and China and Poland are near the middle of the world rankings.

- In terms of income security, Australia surprisingly rates barely better than China, towards the middle of the world rankings, far below the other developed countries. These measures of economic standings relative to others in the population reflect a pension system based on poverty alleviation rather than replacement of pre-retirement earnings. Another factor is that these measures do not take account of the low housing outlays in Australia attributable to the high rates of home ownership. Australia's GNI per capita was second only to the USA (at least in terms of the exchange rates at the time of measurement).

- Australia rates highly in terms of 'capability' at the time as indicated by workforce participation rates in late-middle age and by the proportions of older people having at least a high school education.

- Finally, in terms of the overall global rankings Australian rates highly at 17 out of the 96 countries but this level is slightly below that of the other developed Western countries.

Data on other countries is easily obtained directly from the Global AgeWatch website.

Table A.1 Global AgeWatch Rankings (2015) for Australia and selected countries

	Australia	China	Japan	Poland	NZ	UK	USA
Overall global rank	17	52	8	32	12	10	9
Population							
Number of People over 60 (year 2015)	4.9 million	209.2 million	41.9 million	8.8 million	0.9 million	14.9 million	66.5 million
% of the population over 60 (year 2015)	20%	15%	33%	23%	20%	23%	21%
% of the population over 60 (year 2050)	28%	37%	43%	39%	29%	31%	28%
Health status							
Global rank	5	58	1	48	9	27	25
Life expectancy at age 60	25	19	26	21	25	24	23
Healthy life expectancy at age 60	19	17	20	16	18	18	18
Income security							
Global rank	62	75	33	26	23	14	29
Pension income coverage (65+)	83	74	98	97	98	100	93
Poverty rate (age 60+)	33	24	19	9	9	9	19
Relative welfare (age 60+)	65	50	88	89	86	91	92
GNI per capita ($US)	$41,242	$10,727	$36,093	$21,294	$30,886	$37,053	$51,484
Capability							
Global rank	8	39	7	52	14	20	4
Employment rate (55–64 year olds)	62	60	67	41	74	60	61
Educational attainment (aged 60+)	85	30	74	60	53	66	96

Source: Global AgeWatch (2015).

[1] *Global rank*: Countries are ranked from 1 to 96, with 1 being the highest mark; [2] *Pension income coverage (65+)*: This indicator measures the existence and coverage of the pension system in a country and is what is commonly known as 'beneficiaries coverage rate'; [3] *Poverty rate (age 60+)*: This indicator measures the poverty of older people, using the relative poverty definition. It reports the proportion of people aged 60-plus living in households where the equivalised income/consumption is below the poverty line threshold of 50 per cent of the national equivalised median income/consumption (equivalising factor is the square root of household size); [4] *Relative welfare (age 60+)*: This indicator measures the income/consumption situation of older (60+) people in relation to the rest of the population; [5] *GNI per capita ($US)*: Gross National Income (GNI) expresses the income accrued to residents of a country, including international flows such as remittances and aid, and excluding income generated in the country but retained abroad; [6] *Employment Rate (55–64 year olds)*: The labour market engagement of older people. This indicator measures older people's access to the labour market (both formal and informal) and therefore their ability to supplement pension income with wages, and their access to work-related support networks; [7] *Educational attainment (aged 60+)*: Proportion of the population aged 60+ with secondary or higher education.

References

Global AgeWatch (2015). *Global Age Watch Index 2015*. Help Age International. www.helpage.org/global-agewatch/.

Kendig H and Lucas N (2014). Individuals, Families and the State: Changing Responsibilities in an Aging Australia. In A Torres and L Samson (Eds) *Aging in Asia-Pacific: Balancing the State and the Family*. Quezon City: Philippine Social Science Center, pp. 211–224.

United Nations (UN) (2015). *Transforming our World: The 2030 Agenda for Sustainable Development*, A/RES/70/1. United Nations. sustainabledevelopment.un.org.

World Bank (1994). *Averting the Old Age Crisis: Policies to protect the old and promote growth*. Washington, DC: Oxford University Press.

World Health Organization (WHO) (2002). *Active Ageing: A policy framework*. WHO/ NMH/NPH/02.8. Geneva: WHO.

World Health Organization (WHO) (2015). *World Report on Ageing and Health*. WHO. www.who.int/ageing/publications/world-report-2015/en/.

www.ingramcontent.com/pod-product-compliance
Lightning Source LLC
Chambersburg PA
CBHW050807270326
41926CB00026B/4588